your BUSINESS HANDBOOK

Your Guide to Starting and Running a Business

ALAN & DEBORAH FOWLER

Sphere
Reference

Sphere Books Limited, 27 Wrights Lane, London W8 5TZ
First published by Sphere Books Ltd 1987
Copyright © 1987 by Shepherd's Keep Studio Ltd

TRADE
MARK

Designed and produced by
The Pen and Ink Book Company Ltd

Illustrations by Chris Etheridge

Cartoons by Nigel Paige

Photography by Chris Ridgers and
Chris Perrett

Printed and bound in Great Britain by
Scotprint Ltd, Musselburgh, Scotland

The authors and publishers with to
acknowledge, with thanks, the following
companies for their cooperation:

BUPA; 3i, Investors in Industry plc;
Sasco

Every effort has been made to contact the
copyright holders of material used in this
book. The authors are sorry if they have
been unable to contact any individuals or
organisations quoted in the work.

To: Aunty Vi –
This one's for you!
With grateful thanks, as always.
A. & D.

Contents

Are You the Right Candidate?

Well, are you? Don't turn the page to the next subject, stop here for a moment . . . and think. This is probably the most important question that you will ever ask yourself, in connection with the running of your own business. Forget, for a moment, whether your idea is viable, whether you have the necessary skills, capital, premises – before tackling the validity of your business ideas, we should first be looking at YOU. Self-knowledge is vital for the running of your own business – not only in the early stages, but also as your business grows. You need to be acutely aware of your strengths and weaknesses, so that you can capitalize on your strengths and make sure that there are others around to compensate for your weaknesses. It is often said that there is no room for sentiment in business. This is largely true and never more relevant than in the case of self-analysis.

Don't bother to read on unless you have scored 100 per cent – anything less means you should not be running your own business.

At the moment, in this country, more encouragement is being given to the would-be entrepreneur than at any time in our industrial history. This in itself, of course, is helpful – schemes abound offering capital, subsidized staff hire, rent-free premises and grants for equipment. All these are positive advantages, but they do perhaps tend to make the setting up of a business appear too easy. Without all these incentives, only the strongest and the most innovative of people would ever have attempted to embark on a business of their own in the past, and one is tempted to say that perhaps that was not such a bad thing. It made for fewer successes, but fewer failures, too.

Ask yourself these questions

- Have you confidence in yourself and your abilities – confidence that will enable you to withstand major setbacks, confidence that can rise above criticism and rejection?
- Are you an innovator as well as an administrator? Can you claim to have the power of original thought, or to work effectively, do you need to be a part of an existing operation?
- Are you a workaholic? Are you prepared to work until three in the morning night after night, if necessary, to see your idea off the ground?
- Are you dedicated – not just playing at it? In other words, are you prepared to put your 'all' into the establishment of your business, with the firm conviction that failure is impossible?
- Are you fit, mentally and physically? If you have a tendency to ill-health, the stress of running a business will aggravate it and there can be no days off sick from now on.

Don't start your own business

◆ If, by inclination or ill-health, you are not prepared, or cannot work, all hours of the day and night to fulfil your ambition.

◆ If you cannot cope with taking the ultimate responsibility for your future, nor the resultant stress this will cause.

◆ If you do not feel *positively* vocational about your project – you have to want to do it so badly that you are quite prepared to put it before everything and everyone else.

◆ If you feel daunted by the prospect – if you have your doubts before you even start, then three weeks into running your own business you will be suicidal.

◆ If you do not have a flexible and agile mind. You need to be able to compromise, you need to be inventive and you have to be able to move fast to grasp opportunities and avoid pitfalls.

◆ If you do not have the commitment to succeed, however long the struggle, however hard the fight.

It is necessary, in this process of self-analysis, to consider your motives for wishing to start a business of your own. After all, you are unlikely to be undertaking such a major step purely for fun – you want to achieve something, you have an end product, a goal, in mind, and what you need to ensure is that your own business is the best method by which you can achieve that goal.

Example Everyone, from time to time, fantasizes about, say, owning a villa in the sun. One way to achieve this would be to start your own business, make a lot of money, then sell the business for a vast sum and retire to the West Indies – by which time you will probably be worn out and on the wrong side of sixty. Alternatively you could dispose of your assets now, embark on your lifestyle of sun, sea and cheap plonk, and keep a roof over your head by teaching the tourists to water ski in the summer. Yet a third alternative is to continue working within your existing job, save hard and buy a holiday home. An extreme example, perhaps, but there is more than one way of achieving your ultimate ambition.

What do you want to achieve?

◆ Do you want to be rich?
◆ Do you want to be famous?
◆ Do you want to be more fulfilled in your work?
◆ Do you want to change the world?
◆ Do you want to be your own boss?
◆ Do you want to be more altruistic – do something for someone other than yourself, for a change?
◆ Do you simply feel you are in a rut?

A variety of circumstances may contribute to your ultimate decision to run your own show. Perhaps the knowledge that if your boss criticizes your work just once more, you will smash his teeth down his throat, could provide the incentive! Perhaps that opportunity/order/enquiry that your existing employer continually ignores is building a gap in the market that you can fulfil? One hears, with surprising frequency, of ambitious young people who set about becoming millionaires by a given age and do actually achieve it. Are you one of them?

Analyse yourself, analyse your motives, check and double check. The easiest person in the world to dupe is yourself. Don't let that happen – there's too much at stake.

What Are Your Personal Circumstances?

Whenever you are making a major decision, it is vitally important first to understand exactly **where you are**. Only then can you decide where you should be going. Pedantic it may appear, but what you must do, before putting into operation any sort of business plan, is to fill out the form shown opposite. You may think that you are only too aware of your assets and liabilities, but it is surprising how different the picture can look when committed to paper. You are, in effect, conducting a personal audit, and it is essential to establish the financial base from which you are planning to start a business of your own.

What this form will tell you

◆ Your fixed expenditure.
◆ Your fixed liabilities.
◆ Your current income.
◆ Your current assets.

These pointers will highlight what you actually need to earn to put yourself in the same position as you are in currently. They will also tell you what income and assets you have available to pledge against the raising of money to finance your business. Most important of all, they will tell you the very minimum income you have to achieve to meet your current commitments.

A personal audit is a vital exercise, but of course, it only highlights the financial aspects of your life, which, although important, are by no means the only consideration. Do you actually have the time to run a business? Do you spend four nights of the week working as a youth club leader, or are you dedicated to three rounds of golf at the weekend? Is your spare time spent at the race track, doing embroidery, singing in the church choir, or with your head in a book? And if so, **are you prepared to give up these activities** – at any rate for several years – while you concentrate wholly and single-mindedly on the establishment of a business? Money is **not** everything, though it does feel like it

when you have none! Generally speaking, though, we are becoming increasingly aware that the relentless pursuit of wealth is not necessarily the way to a happy and fulfilled life. If your hobbies and interests absorb the major part of your free time, and you enjoy doing them, you might well be advised not to start your own business.

Why do you want the hassle?

You are sitting comfortably at home, with your feet up, reading this book, and yet you are thinking of embarking on a new phase in your life which will give you very little time for looking at any book **but this one!** Are your personal circumstances dictating the way you are thinking, or is the dog truly wagging the tail? Have you been made redundant and are finding it difficult to get another job? Have you been retired early and feel it is wrong not to be working when other people your age are still in harness? Is it a factor such as this which is making you feel you must create your own employment? There is nothing wrong with these feelings provided that the idea of running a business has always appealed to you. What you must analyse is whether desperation has driven you to considering this step, or whether you would have set up on your own anyway, sooner or later. Do your current circumstances represent the opportunity for which you have always been looking, or are they forcing you into taking a step you would never otherwise have considered?

So . . . you have retired a few years early – why not settle for drawing your pension and finding an interesting hobby? Just because you cannot find a job, it does not necessarily mean you should be creating your own. Be wary of how your personal circumstances are influencing your decision.

PERSONAL AUDIT

NAME _____

AGE _____

STATUS Married ☐   Single ☐   Divorced ☐   Widowed ☐

DEPENDENT CHILDREN No: Ages:

OCCUPATION
Employed ☐   Unemployed ☐   Self-employed ☐   Retired ☐

	Yourself	Spouse
ANNUAL INCOME – EARNED		
SALARY/UNEMPLOYMENT BENEFIT	£	£
BUSINESS/PROFIT SHARE	£	£
PRIVATE PENSION	£	£
STATE PENSION/CHILD ALLOWANCE	£	£
CASUAL WORK	£	£
– UNEARNED		
BANK INTEREST	£	£
BUILDING SOCIETY INTEREST	£	£
INVESTMENT INCOME	£	£
ANNUAL EXPENDITURE		
MORTGAGE PAYMENTS/RENT	£	£
BANK INTEREST ON LOAN/S	£	£
DAY-TO-DAY LIVING COSTS	£	£
HOLIDAYS	£	£
INSURANCE PREMIUMS	£	£
OTHER COMMITMENTS	£	£
ASSETS		
HOUSE (FULL VALUE)	£	£
ADDITIONAL PROPERTIES	£	£
PERSONAL POSSESSIONS	£	£
BANK DEPOSITS	£	£
BUILDING SOCIETY DEPOSITS	£	£
ANTICIPATED LEGACIES	£	£
OTHER INVESTMENTS	£	£
LIABILITIES		
MORTGAGES	£	£
BANK OVERDRAFT/LOANS	£	£
OTHER LOANS	£	£
OTHER BORROWINGS	£	£

Is Your Family Behind You?

Self-inflicted pain is one thing. Visiting it on other people – particularly your nearest and dearest – is quite another. Most advice linked to the starting of a new business tends to concentrate on the importance of family backing. Frankly, backing is not enough. Members of your family need to recognize that, if you are intending to start and run your own business, for the first few years, at any rate, they will take second place – along with everything else in your life. Roles will blur and change. Wives will find themselves standing on the touch-line, cheering on their sons in a game they may have never played. Husbands will be cooking family supper and helping with homework they may well not understand. The ordered traditional roles of the family will be turned upside down. Not only do you have to decide whether this is possible, but also if it is desirable. Your family may well enthuse about the concept of your starting a business of your own, without really having any understanding of the implications involved. It is up to you to ensure that they fully realize what is going to happen, so that there is no room for resentment later on.

The Mediterranean countries specialize in this – it is known as the *Momma and Poppa business*. The whole family becomes involved in the running of a shop, a café, a taverna or a bar. Family participation may be rather extreme in these countries, but the philosophy behind the concept is correct. Resentment develops very largely as a result of misunderstanding. Communicate with your family at all times – that is the key.

Circumstances to avoid

◆ Do not start a business of your own if you have children under two years of age. A terrible generalization, yes, but you cannot cope with sleepless nights and the stress of a business start-up.
◆ Similarly, responsibility for an aged dependant is again stacking the odds too highly against success. You cannot be stretched in too many directions.
◆ Do not put your family home in jeopardy if you have children. However tempting it is to pledge your house and raise a second mortgage to generate extra business capital – **do not take the risk**. Avoid personal guarantees and concentrate on building your business slowly and carefully, if you

A very personal case history

We, the authors, were involved in the start-up of a mail order business ten years ago. From the very first, it was a family affair. The children inserted letters and brochures into envelopes and stuck on stamps. Our daughter, Lucy, modelled the children's clothes we were selling, and even Granny became involved, ironing garments for modelling sessions. It was such a part of our lives that it never occurred to anybody to question the hours of commitment. The business was central to all our lives – we lived and breathed it, and our other activities were fitted in around it.

have a young family relying upon you.

◆ Recognize that if the members of your family are going to have to cope with seeing you on a part-time basis only, you cannot expect them to accept a dramatic reduction in their standard of living as well. In fact quite the contrary. If you are all under pressure and working exceptionally hard, you need to be able to splurge a little extra on a meal out or a holiday in compensation. Budget for this.

◆ Allow at least six months' money to support your family while you are establishing the business. A year's financial back-up would be a more realistic figure, but this is not always possible. Never, for one moment, imagine you can live off the business from Day 1, and you have enough problems to consider, without wondering how you are going to be able to pay the mortgage and feed the children.

The good news

Dire warnings about the need to consider and cater for your family are more than compensated for by the other side of the coin. In moments of black despair and weariness, your family can provide tremendous security and comfort. They are your *raison d'être*. You have to succeed because they are relying on you, and this responsibility will be an additional fillip to help you build a successful business. Certainly, in the past, many a business has been built on the back of one person's ambition to provide a better life for the children. Indeed, many of today's big industrial empires have grown and prospered for the benefit of one family, and there is nothing wrong with that. One of the many advantages of owning one's business has to be that there is something to pass on to children and grandchildren. A family business has a special kind of attraction all its own – the feeling of tradition, of an established proven product or service – and perhaps this is the kind of business you have in mind. Either way, whether you are planning to build a multi-million pound conglomerate or to form a partnership with your child, involve the family from the first, and if they will not give you their full support and backing, forget the whole idea.

The story of Vaselli

Vaselli is a Cretan boy and he is fourteen years old. His father runs a taverna in Ayios Nikólaos. When Vaselli was born, the little town was a sleepy fishing port – now it is the major tourist attraction in Crete. When Vaselli was four, he began working in the kitchen, doing a little washing up and peeling vegetables. When he was six, he learnt Greek dancing and entertained the customers with a commendable cabaret each evening. When he was twelve, a gangling youth, less attractive than the bright-eyed little boy, he gave up dancing and began waiting at table. We asked his father about Vaselli's future. 'When he is eighteen, he will go back to the dancing. All the young girl tourists will want to dance with him. He will be handsome, like his father.' 'And then?' we asked. 'When he is twenty-five, I will retire. I have worked for Vaselli all these years. I will be fifty then – it is his turn to work for me.'
This is a true family business and there are lessons to be learnt from it.

What is Your Business Experience?

What are you? Are you an administrator, salesperson or an operative? It is vital to establish which of these skills is yours in particular, for you need to recognize that no one can do everything within a business. Having recognized which is your special skill, you should stick to your last and gather around you compatible talent, to fulfil those tasks of which you have no experience.

Profile of an administrator

An administrator knows how to turn a potentially viable concept into an up-and-running business. An administrator can mastermind the operatives and salesforce into doing their jobs of producing and selling, pulling the strands together into a cohesive whole, which will run smoothly and efficiently. To use their special skill effectively, administrators are likely to be looking at a comparatively larger business than those who are in the other two categories. Administrators are reliant on other people for product knowledge and production technique and, if they are sensible, will tend to 'poach' the skilled staff who are needed, from former business

contacts, recognizing that employing the right people is everything. Experienced administrators can establish a very succcessful own business, provided they recognize the need to buy in the very best in terms of sales and production personnel.

Profile of a salesman

For an experienced salesman to start a business of his own, it goes without saying, he has to have a product or service to sell – a product or service about which he feels enthusiastic and committed. Salesmen are the lifeblood of any business, and a man with selling experience, going it alone, does have some enormous advantages. Not only is he able to establish a market for the product or service he is offering, but selling skills will help considerably in the development of the business. This applies whether he is selling the viability of the business to the bank manager in order to obtain an overdraft, selling his integrity to a potential supplier to gain credit, or selling to a future landlord the concept that he will make an excellent tenant.

The salesman needs to work with good operatives, whom he both trusts and respects to produce what he has to sell. Few salesmen are good administrators, and they need to recognize that fact, employing the right staff to make sure the office runs smoothly. Traditionally, managing directors tend to be administrators or accountants, rather than salesmen. There is no reason why this should be so. If your particular skill is selling, there is every reason to suppose you would make an excellent managing director. Indeed, it tends to help the selling effort enormously if the customers feel they are dealing with the top man.

There are precious few really good salesmen about. If you are one of them, do not dilute your skill – build your business around it.

Profile of an operative

In many ways it is easier for an operative to establish a business than for either of the other two categories, for the operative holds all the cards. It is he who is producing the product or service, without which there is no business at all. An operative, working within a company, may realize that the product he is producing for someone else is either not quite right, or not being produced in sufficient quantity to meet the demand. This situation may provide the opportunity to set up a business of his own. Often, if he does this in the light of experience within a particular industry, the operative needs very little back-up support in terms of administration or sales, because he or she is working in an existing and known market. However, if that operative should decide to broaden his base in any way, then he should recognize the need for specialist help.

An operative can usually learn the skills of selling and administration more easily than those in the other two categories can learn to be operatives. Therefore he has more choice as to how the business is run, for as an alternative to bringing in specialist skills, he can acquire those skills. Certainly, in some industries, the customers infinitely prefer to talk to the man who has the skill to produce the product they want, rather than deal through a seller who only has third-party knowledge. While the business is small, operatives are the one category who can successfully go it alone – but as the business increases they, too, will need specialist help.

Golden rule

The message here is simple. Do not diversify from your special skills. You know what you do best – **stick to it and subcontract the rest.**

Study Your Product Knowledge

Speak to any banker or financial institution on the subject of new business failure and you will find that invariably they will hold the same view – a view borne out by statistical fact.

Most of the new businesses that fail are those where the principals have had no previous knowledge of their trade.

It is a curious phenomenon that people are so often attracted to a trade in which they have had no previous experience. Manufacturers of ball bearings want to grow tomatoes in Devon, accountants want to run pubs . . . there is this feeling that if you are going to run your own business, you should do it in a field that appeals to you rather than one in which you have direct experience. Pipedreams are all right in their place, but putting them into practice is not to be recommended.

A sound product knowledge is vital for success and you would be very foolish to attempt to go into business in an area in which you know nothing. Having said that, of course, you can learn. Exploit an existing skill or acquire a new one – but either way, **be prepared**.

It may be that you have worked in a sector of industry for some years and have seen that there is a gap in the market, into which you believe you can introduce a new type of product or service. Alternatively, you may feel that the market is large enough for you to produce the same product or service in parallel. This kind of direct involvement is ideal, but make sure that your experience is rounded enough and that you are not purely looking at one aspect, i.e. the role you play currently. A product might be cheap to produce – you know it is because that is the job you do – but it may be very expensive to package, to distribute and to sell. In other words, you may think your product knowledge is extensive, but is it really? You must not leave a stone unturned in your search for relevant detail, for product knowledge is not restricted to the actual goods or service

you are supplying. You need to acquire a background understanding of suppliers, costings, pricing structures, staffing requirements and repair and maintenance implications. If you start a business with these details at your fingertips, you have to stand a better chance than most of making a success of your venture.

Case history

A well-documented story of success proves the need for product knowledge. No doubt you will have heard of the retired American engineer who was upset at watching his daughter lugging a heavy pushchair up and down a flight of steps, while she attempted to keep control of his newly acquired grandson under one arm. The result of his anxiety and his engineering experience? The world famous Maclaren Baby Buggy, which has revolutionized the lives of mothers with toddlers the world over. Many a caring grandparent must have felt as he did, but it took an *engineer* to solve the problem.

One of the pitfalls, into which would-be entrepreneurs regularly fall, is not understanding the difference between the amateur and the professional. Your ceramics/your quiches lorraines/your hand-made furniture may be much admired by your friends – to the point where you feel that their praise justifies trying to make a business out of what, until now, has been a hobby. But your friends are no judges at all, for nobody is asking them to *buy* your creative efforts. Producing something attractive, which receives considerable praise, is light years away from producing something commercial. Not only may there be no market for your hand-painted silk lampshades, you may be unable to produce them at anything like a realistic price, or they may fade after three months, causing enormous customer dissatisfaction. There are so many aspects to be considered in perfecting a product or service before you can offer it commercially, and there are no short cuts to the amount of original research you must undertake.

A little knowledge is never more dangerous than when it forms the foundation for starting a business of your own. DO YOUR RESEARCH THOROUGHLY.

If you do not have the skill to run a business in the area of your choice then that skill can be acquired by training. You can train at night school while you are still in full-time employment; you can re-train full-time with the aid of a Government grant; you can train by practical experience – taking a job in the industry of your choice and learning how to run the business at first hand.

Training as a formalized programme

Universities and technical colleges are not just for school leavers. Increasingly, places are being found for mature students, and most universities now have a hall of residence for students with families. Day release programmes and night schools are alternative ways of training. If you are working and want to obtain a new skill, which ultimately you intend to use to start your own business, there is no need to put your job in jeopardy. There is almost nothing that is not covered by night school classes – make enquiries locally.

Manpower Services Commission/Job Centre programmes

Visit your local Job Centre and the Manpower Services Commission (MSC) training division area office – both of which run extensive courses in sales, marketing, technical skills, new technology and business management, promoted by various commercial companies, professional bodies and trade organizations. There is the YTS scheme for young people and the Job Training Scheme which is the successor to TOPS courses. There is also a specific training programme called Training for Enterprise, aimed at providing training for both the new and existing business owner or manager. There is a training programme called Access to Information Technology, which can bring you up to date with the latest technology by providing courses in the evenings and at weekends. There is a Wider Opportunities Programme which deals with the specialist needs of people who, perhaps, have been out of work for a long time, or for whom English is a second language, or whose skills are outdated – such as women who are wanting to return to work after raising a family.

All these training programmes in time may well be eligible for a career development loan. There is a pilot scheme being set up by the Department of Employment, with the co-operation of Barclays Bank, the Clydesdale Bank and the Co-operative Bank. The idea is that you can apply to these banks for interest-free loans to support your training course. Contact your local Job Centre or MSC training division area office to see if the pilot scheme is operating in your area.

Practical learning experience

For a thorough knowledge of some types of business, a formalized training programme is not necessarily desirable, or even available. In these circumstances, what you need instead is practical experience of the trade. A retail shop falls into this category, as does, say, a travel agency, or a courier service. Because no specialist skill is needed for these types of business, it is very tempting to assume that you can embark upon them without any form of training at all. If you do, you are courting disaster – practical experience is essential, and this means going to work for someone for a few months, or years, to learn the trade. It is training at its best. It is not only free, it is actually paid for – the uncharitable might call it industrial espionage!

The world does not stand still, especially the commercial world. The skills you have today may be out of date, or totally superfluous, tomorrow. **Updating, improving, re-training** – emotive words to keep you out in front, which is where you will need to be if you are going to run your own business. Look at the skills you have, match them with the business of your choice and then see which areas of expertise you lack but none the less need, in order to run the business efficiently. Having identified these, go out and get the training you require to give you fully rounded background experience of your chosen business.

Case history

Ann and George Roper run a delightful pub in North Oxfordshire. It has a cosy bar where farm labourers rub shoulders, amicably, with the local gentry, and a simple restaurant offering good, wholesome food at sensible prices. Ann and George had no experience of the catering trade when they decided that George should throw up his unsatisfactory job in civil engineering, to run a pub instead. While George continued working at his engineering job during the day and looked for a suitable public house to buy, Ann took a job as a live-in barmaid at a large, highly successful pub nearby. She was there six months and it was hard on their marriage, but she thoroughly learnt the trade – what prices she should be charging, where her supplies should come from, how to handle awkward customers . . . At the end of six months, there was very little Ann did not know about running a pub, and ten years later, this knowledge is still standing them in good stead.

The Need for Market Research

If someone said to you – 'Why not buy this fantastic car of mine, it's an absolute bargain' – what would your reaction be? You would say you wanted to know more about the vehicle first. You would test-drive it, you would look under the bonnet, check the bodywork for rust and study the miles on the clock. In all probability, you would take the car to your local garage for a second opinion. Then, and only then, would you make an offer.

This is the sort of attitude you normally would adopt when making any large purchase, where you were committing a considerable sum of money. If you are intending to start a business, you will be committing not only money, but that most valuable commodity of all, TIME. Yet many first-timers in business undertake very little detailed analysis of their chances of success, before taking the plunge – in many cases far less than they would if they were buying a car.

Good ideas are two a penny, putting them into action is quite another matter. You may be able to offer an excellent product or service, you may have sufficient capital to launch it, premises from which to operate it, a trustworthy partner and/or staff to help you, but the million dollar question is – **Does anybody actually want what you have to offer?**

Market research checklist

1   Does your product or service genuinely compare favourably with the competition? This is not just a comparison of the commodity itself, but also its reliability, price, presentation and delivery performance.

2   What is the size of your market? Are there really sufficient people out there who want what you intend to offer?

3   What is the long-term future of your business? Is your idea a seven-day wonder? Has it got staying power?

4   Are you conscious that the buyer and the customer can be two different people? The buyer may have different requirements from what you imagine the customer needs. Are you taking the buyer's views into account, for that is who places the orders?

5   Pricing – can you compete with your rivals on price, and, conversely, are you charging enough? If YOU undervalue your product, so will your customers.

6   The practicalities – are you in the right location, the right premises? Do you have the right staff, machinery, stock levels and production capacity? Your business has to run smoothly in order to appeal to your customer in the long term.

7   Presentation – can you present what you have to offer in the right way? Does your business as a whole have the right image?

8   Accessibility – how accessible are your customers? They may be there alright, but can you get at them without large cash resources?

Identifying your *precise* market is vital. The more you can fine-tune your market approach, the more profitable you are likely to be. Begin by taking the country as a whole – there are fifty-odd million people out there, who could be interested in what you have to offer. Now start striking off those who quite clearly are not applicable. Break it down, step by step, eliminating each section of society until you have located your prime market – in other words, the one in which what you have to offer is going to be most effectively sold. Of course, if you are running a small retail business, you are not looking at the country's population, but at the few hundred square yards immediately around your shop – in which case, location is everything. If, by contrast, you are running a mail order business, it frankly does not matter where you are. Your market research will be geared to a *type* of person you want to reach, whether they are living in Caithness or Clapham.

Market research is the first step towards the establishment of a business. No business should be formed, or even seriously contemplated, until the market research has been done. **But, market research does not stop once a gap in the market has been established.**

Monitoring as well as marketing

Just because you have found a market for your product or service, it does not mean that you and your business *have arrived.* Your thinking needs to be constantly updated in all aspects of your field of operation. You need to be alert to new market trends and be aware of how apparently unconnected factors around the world may alter, quite considerably, your particular marketplace. In every successful business, market research is an ongoing requirement. In today's competitive world, you can never be complacent. **Today's successes are tomorrow's failures, unless they are prepared to move with the times.** Recognize the changing requirements of your customers, and act accordingly. You have to be one step ahead, and the only way to achieve this is through constant and thorough market research.

The Competition

Learning from other people's mistakes is free. Learning from your own COSTS – possibly even your livelihood.

The value of carefully assessing the competition is twofold. On the one hand, it is a question of assessing your competitors' grip on the market, to see whether there is room for you, and your business, as well as theirs. On the other hand, there is a great deal to be learned from your competitors' successes and failures. You need to study the areas where it is advantageous to emulate them, and give a wide berth to those areas where clearly they have gone wrong.

Can you compete?

In assessing the strength of the competition, the factors worthy of consideration will vary enormously from business to business. Your research into their strengths and weaknesses, though, must be very thorough, for it is very easy to be misled. For example, if you see a competitor is displaying, or giving enormous prominence to a particular item, you might be tempted to think that this is a big seller. The reverse could be true. It could be a poor seller and your competitor is trying to shift stock. By contrast, do not assume that because no one is manufacturing, shall we say, sky-blue widgets, the market is wide open for them. There may be a very good reason why no one manufactures such a product, and it is very dangerous to assume that the market is automatically available to you because the competition have not covered it.

It is very easy to be critical of the competition and assume that you can do a better job. Retail outlets are a prime example of this. In your local town, you will have seen certain sites where shop after shop has opened, only to close a few months later. Presumably, each new retailer thinks he knows where the previous trader went wrong, and feels it can be done better. In all probability, it is not the retail operation itself which is at fault. There is far more likely to be something wrong with the premises or its location. However, many a would-be retailer is not prepared to accept this – far from learning from the predecessors' mistakes, the newcomer is blinded by self-confidence, and blunders forward on an ego trip to prove that he or she can do better.

Industrial espionage

All right, so we have recognized the need to research the competition, but how do you go about it? The answer is – by various underhand tactics. People love talking about their businesses. Apply for jobs with your major competitors, even if you have no intention of taking them. Pose as a potential supplier, or better still, a customer. If you have the time, do try and work for a competitor for a few weeks even in a very humble capacity – you will be amazed what you can learn.

If you are going to be operating a parallel product or service to your competitor, you can make a straightforward approach. Simply call to see them, tell them what you are going to do, and ask for some advice. People are extremely generous with advice on the whole, because they are always flattered at having their opinions sought. For the investment of a jolly lunch and a bottle of wine, you can have a lot of your questions answered.

ENTRANCE
SCHOOL
FOR INDUSTRIAL
ESPIONAGE

Case history

Three years ago, John Edgeley, then aged twenty-six, decided that he would like to start his own car hire business, aimed specifically at providing prestige limousines for weddings and other such functions. At the time he was unmarried, but he persuaded his girlfriend to pose as his fiancée. Together they visited all the car hire firms in his area, to obtain quotations for supplying cars on the occasion of his fictitious nuptials. His findings taught him a lot. First, where to pitch his prices – not too low, not too high. Second – and this was a particularly important factor – the other car hire firms in his area were all affiliated to large motor distributors and, as a result, were extremely impersonal. On the establishment of his business, therefore,

John slanted all his advertising and sales material towards a very personal approach, which made him stand out in sharp contrast to his competitors. Third, living in a tourist area, he established that none of his competitors offered their cars for tourist trips, so he immediately contacted the Tourist Board and promoted his services in that market. This meant that his limousines were soon being used in off-peak times – i.e. weekdays – driving Americans round the Cotswolds.

John now has a highly successful business – oh, and a wife. By the time they had finished researching the competition, John's girlfriend decided she rather enjoyed her fictitious role and suggested she should stick with it!

Look carefully at your competitors' strengths and weaknesses and learn from both. A detailed analysis of their operation could prove an invaluable help to you. Take nothing at face value. **Do not assume your competitors are fools – though if they are, so much the better!**

Your Customer Profile

Who are they . . . where are they . . . why are they . . . and what do they want? These questions have to be answered carefully and in detail, in order to find your customers, and keep them. In establishing your customer profile you need to identify their precise specification for the product or service you intend offering, and also how they want it presented – this means pricing, quantity, packaging and delivery.

When confronting a customer, listen carefully to what they have to say. You need flexibility of mind. Your job is to tailor-make your product to your customer, not the other way round. Buyers, on the whole, are very professional people, with a wealth of knowledge at their fingertips. If, for example, the buyer at Selfridges knows that he simply cannot sell an electric toaster over £14.99 – however good it is – there is little point in your trying to sell him some wildly sophisticated model which he will have to retail at £30. He knows his market and you must be guided by that knowledge.

Timing

Most buyers, whether wholesale, retail or buying for mail order, plan their buying at least nine months ahead and you should

bear this in mind. In theory, the best time to sell your revolutionary new snorkel is in the spring but if you go charging into Lillywhites in the first week of March, you are most likely to excite the response that if you were selling ski boots they might be interested. Their snorkel requirements will have been settled back in September.

Is your buyer your customer?

In many businesses, the person to whom you sell is in fact the consumer, but this is not always the case. If you are intending to sell a consumer product to a large retail outlet, you have two people to consider – the buyer and the ultimate consumer. If that product happens to be for a child – an item of clothing or a toy – then there are three people to consider – the child, the store's customer (probably a parent) and the buyer. Producing a toy which appeals to a child is easy, but is it cheap enough for the parent to buy, and does it meet the health and safety standards the buyer will require? The lesson here is that we have a tendency to concentrate solely on the end user, whereas it is the people in between who hold the real power.

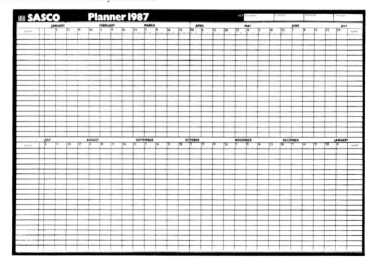

Keeping your customer

Acquiring a customer is one thing, keeping that customer happy is quite another. Most of us prefer to deal with people we like, and finding personal common ground with your customer is important. Very few professional buyers today expect to be bribed with holidays abroad and expensive presents, but such people do exist and, frankly, should be avoided. Good, efficient buyers will enjoy the odd lunch with you and will appreciate it if you remember the name of their children, and their favourite brand of wine. However, all this lip-service is worth nothing if you cannot produce the goods required, of an acceptable quality, in the right quantity and when they are needed. Efficient, reliable service is everything. It will make or break your business.

Can you create the customer?

The story has it that Terence Conran, back in the sixties, had the idea that furniture was crying out for a complete facelift. It needed to be stylish, practical and cheap, with clear, simple lines and fresh, bright colours. Could he sell the concept to furniture stores? He could not – no one wanted to know. The obvious answer was to give up, but he took the ultimate gamble and opened his own shop. The result, of course, was Habitat. He took an enormous risk and in his case it certainly paid off.

Of course, professional buyers do not have all the answers, but they do have their finger on the pulse when it comes to assessing the market's requirements. As in everything, exceptions prove the rule!

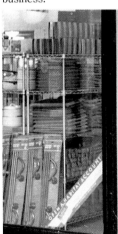

A warning note

A customer is only a customer when he has paid for the goods or service you have provided. Whilst your customer will be constantly checking on you and your performance, **you** must check on **him** – not only initially for a credit rating, but constantly, throughout your relationship. Circumstances change, as do the fortunes of many a business, big and small. Watch for trends. If payments fall behind, however big the customer, however apparently prestigious and important to you, cease supplying them until they pay up. Customers can be replaced, but the money you may lose, if your customer goes into liquidation, very often cannot. Do not let your customer losing his business cause *you* to lose you *yours*.

MARKET POTENTIAL

Product Life

Commerce is not easy and nor does it stand still. Things change so fast – today's bright idea can be old hat tomorrow. Does your business idea have a long-term future, and if not, are you aware of its lifespan? There is nothing wrong with taking advantage of a fashionable trend, so long as you recognize it for what it is. People have made fortunes from a quick in-out deal, by jumping on the bandwagon and then off again at just the right moment, but to succeed at this, you certainly have to know what you are at.

Skating on thin ice

Perhaps one of the best examples of a seven-day wonder is the skateboard craze of the seventies. Children in this country had a momentary obsession with the sport, and everyone took it far too seriously, instead of recognizing it was purely a passing fad. Manufacturing units were set up, skateboard parks were built, newspapers and magazines started. Within months, it was all over and those companies involved in the sport fell by the wayside.

Market trends

Just as deadly as the fad, or fashionable craze, is the declining market. A declining market can eat into your business insidiously, initially without you even realizing what is happening. You need to establish whether your particular industry is in a state of growth or decline, because even a drop in the market of 1 per cent could easily put you out of business. Study your trade magazines, talk to competitors, advertising and media people, and find out precisely where your industry is going.
Pay special attention to local trends. The market, nationwide, may be in a decline, but perhaps, for some reason, your particular area is in a boom period, or vice versa. **Beware of temporary trends**. A temporary boom can be very dangerous. It can cause you to commit yourself to extra machinery, staff and bigger premises, only to find that the bubble

bursts. Similarly, do not panic in the face of a sudden decline – it may only be temporary.

Government legislation

Monopolies, wage restraints, embargoes, environmental changes, Factory Acts . . . all these factors can have a devastating effect on your business. You must keep abreast of political thinking. Conversely, of course, the introduction of new legislation can open up business opportunities for you. A tightening of the Factory Acts may be hard on most businesses, but if you were in the fire extinguisher business, you would welcome it with open arms!

Practical problems

Demand is not the only factor which will affect your product life – it can be quite the contrary. The mere fact that people go on wanting you to produce a particular product may mean it is doomed, because, in the long term, there is only a limited supply of the raw materials available at an economic price. Here again, though, availability of material can be turned to a positive advantage. Developments in technology speak for themselves. Plastic, in many cases, has replaced wood and metal, loop nylon has taken the place of hessian, velour is used instead of velvet . . . the list is endless. If you recognize that your raw materials will run out one day, now is the moment to experiment with a replacement.

Services

It is as easy for a service industry to become obsolete as any product, and the only way to combat this is to make sure that you are absolutely up to date with the latest technology. Take a facile example. If you were starting a bureau today supplying secretarial services, it would be crazy to buy a typewriter and a duplicating machine, even if you were offered them for next to nothing. You need a word processor, the

24

Case history

Christopher Jefferies is a baker. He has run his own business for fifteen years, in a thriving Wiltshire town, but he is in a declining market. With increasing pressure to be more sylph-like, the nation, as a whole, is cutting back on bread, cakes and sticky buns! Christopher has felt the cold wind of change, How has he coped? He has diversified . . . half his shop is now given over to health foods, to wholegrain rice, pasta, dried fruit, nuts, recipe books, local honey and preserves. He has also changed the emphasis of his baking. He uses more wholemeal flour, never touches synthetic cream and bakes quiches and pasties in larger quantities than he does doughnuts and Chelsea buns. At this moment, in a declining market, Christopher's business has never been more successful.

best money can buy, and then you will be able to offer your customers a service they are less likely to have themselves. This applies to all service industries. If you are going to mow lawns, buy yourself the best possible mower. If you are going to clean windows, the best chamois leather. If you are going to repair cars, the best workshop and tools money can buy. To do anything else is a false economy.

Internal protection for your product

Protect your product or service where you can from the competition, by patenting it or registering a trademark (see page 45). It is vital to cover yourself, as far as possible, from the chances of your good idea being poached. However, do also bear in mind that your product, or service, is being made available by people – specialist people – whom you have trained to produce precisely what your customers require. As your business develops, these people will become more valuable, and as they become more valuable, they become more dangerous. Your competitors may seduce them away with the promise of a higher salary, or they themselves may recognize opportunities that you have not, and set up in business on their own. To protect your product, therefore, consider your key staff and where possible, offer them incentives, such as a share of the profits or a stake in the business – any device to keep them loyal.

A word of warning

Never be complacent about what you have to offer. The market will not stand still, so neither should your product or service – it needs adaptation and development. Businesses are never stationary – they either improve or decline. Which they do will largely depend on the life of your product.

Supply

You have a product and you believe you have a market. Now you have to find a way of introducing the former to the latter. The following diagram illustrates the possible links in the chain for the distribution of your product.

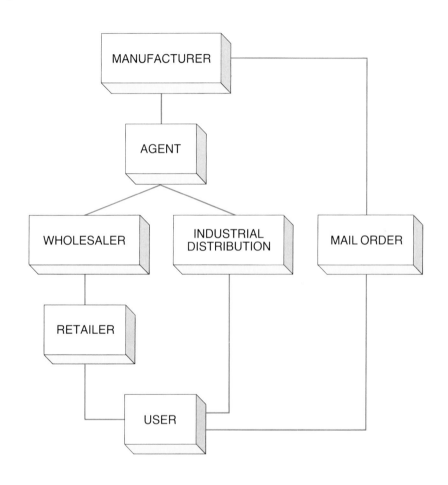

These links, of course, are not all necessary – they simply represent the possible options. For example, the manufacturer can deal direct with the user. This happens most frequently in mail order, but it could equally well be a craftsman selling merchandise to the general public direct from the workshop. You can jump on and off the chain at any point. For example, you might be setting up your own wholesale warehouse and then selling direct to the user, cutting out the retailer completely.

As a general rule, the further removed you are from the user, the bigger profit margin you will need. Middlemen cost money. Let us look at the diagram again, this time showing the average gross profit/commission which is likely to be required by each of the links in the chain.

In theory, the diagram suggests that it would be sensible to cut out as many links in the chain as you possibly can and deal direct with the user. This is not so, for the following reasons:

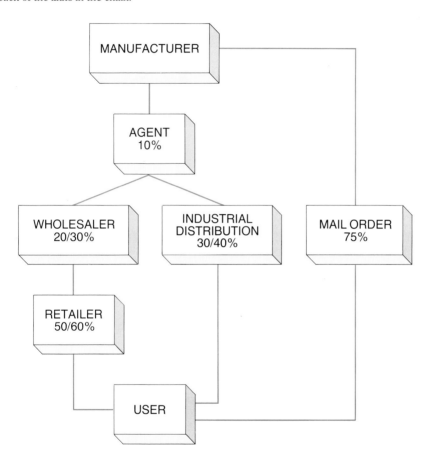

1 The cost of dealing through middlemen may seem high, but it can pale into insignificance compared with the cost of setting up your own marketing and selling operation.

2 Middlemen are professional salesmen

and, on the whole, they are good at their job. They have the contacts, a specialist knowledge of the trade and probably can sell far more effectively than you can do yourself.

Let us take a closer look at the middlemen:

Agents

Having an agent is much like employing a sales representative, except that it is considerably cheaper. Agents are self-employed and work purely on commission. They supply their own car, their own office and telephone and they specialize in a particular field of industry. They normally represent several businesses, selling their merchandise to various contacts, and it is these contacts that you are really buying when you appoint an agent. Most agents work on a commission of up to 10 per cent, that is 10 per cent of your selling price, exclusive of V A T.

Factors

Factors are much like agents, with one notable difference. Factors actually buy your merchandise and then sell it on to their contacts. Again, the commission they take is approximately 10 per cent. Factors are not normally found in any form of consumer industry – their field is in the traditional industries such as engineering.

Wholesalers

The wholesaler stands between the manufacturer and the retailer. There are many different types of wholesaling operation, and they vary enormously from trade to trade. In some industries, wholesalers do not handle the goods at all. The transactions are all done on paper, and they simply arrange for the manufacturers' goods to be delivered to the retailer. In other industries, the reverse is true, and the wholesaler carries vast stocks. A builder's merchant is a wholesaling operation. It acts as a collecting house for the building trade, thus enabling the builder to come to one location, to find various requirements. Wholesalers usually require a gross profit of between 20 and 30 per cent on selling price, excluding V A T.

Industrial distributors

The difference between industrial distributors and wholesalers is that where industrial distributors are concerned, there is no retailing involved. Like factors, industrial distributors tend to be found more often in heavy industry, as their name suggests, and the end user, in this case, is never the consumer. An industrial distributor is very often the link in a chain of manufacturers – all of whom are involved in the making of various component parts for a particular industry. Industrial distributors, on the whole, look for a slightly higher gross profit than the wholesaler – between 30 and 40 per cent on selling price, excluding V A T.

Retailing

Retailing is the shop operation. Whether you are looking at a massive chain of department stores, or the local corner shop, both are retailers – as is the market stall. Anywhere goods are on display for sale to the general public qualifies as a retailing operation. Retailers normally require a minimum gross profit of between 50 and 60 per cent, excluding V A T. In some high streets in major towns and cities, where rents and rates are particularly high, retailers will need considerably more than this.

Mail order

Mail order companies normally buy from the manufacturer and sell to the consumer, and since they cut out all stages in between, expecting a 75 per cent gross profit may seem greedy. However, one needs to bear in mind that the promotional and administrative costs of mail order are enormous. Brochures have to be produced and mailed. Orders, when received, have to be dispatched. Even in the best mail order operations, it is usually necessary to send out fifty brochures to obtain one order, and

it is not unusual for 25 per cent of the orders dispatched to be returned for refund or replacement. To sell to a mail order business, you need to work nine months ahead. You will also need to demonstrate your ability to respond very quickly to demand.

In order to sell your merchandise successfully, you have to find the right mix of price, quality and quantity set against method of distribution. It may be that you simply cannot operate through a wholesaler, because you do not have the necessary profit margin to do so. Alternatively, you may have the profit margin but you cannot produce the goods in the necessary quantity.

As a general rule, in order to break into a market which is new to you, you do need help – professional help. If you are handling or manufacturing a high-cost specialist item, which will appeal to relatively few outlets, then probably you will be best advised to go direct to a retailer. If you are manufacturing, or handling, a low-cost item with appeal to a mass market, operate through a wholesaler and possibly even an agent. Small businesses, selling a low cost item, cannot afford to mount their own selling operation – neither can many large businesses. You need a big, hefty profit margin to sell and promote your own goods direct to the user. It is a question of balance.

How you choose to distribute your product will greatly affect the success, or otherwise, of your business. Get the mix wrong and not only will your operation be unprofitable, but it may be a complete non-starter. Get it right and the sky's the limit. Carefully explore all possible methods of distribution for your goods, and do not finalize either presentation, price or indeed final specifications of your product, until you have decided on its best method of distribution.

Pricing Policy

It is tempting to believe that the quick way to break into any market is to undercut the existing prices of the competition. Everyone is selling, let us say toothbrushes for 19p or 20p each, so all you have to do is sell your toothbrush for 18p. It sounds easy, but in reality it is the most dangerous way to approach a market. Let us look at the disadvantages. One is that if you are successful in obtaining substantial orders for your 18p toothbrush, you are going to have a serious impact on your competitors' business. They are not just going to sit back and let you walk off with their sales. They will drop their price to 18p as well, and suddenly you are in the middle of a price war. What are you going to do then, drop the price to 17p? Bear in mind that in any price war, your competitors are far more likely to win than you are. They have been in the market longer and probably have past profits to live off, while they sell unprofitable toothbrushes in order to put you out of business.

Price cutting, for its own sake, does not impress a buyer. In most instances, buyers are looking for far more than simply the cheapest commodity around. They want regular supply, reliable delivery and consistent good quality. They will be deeply suspicious of your offering a cheaper product, believing – rightly – that either you will not be able to maintain this cheaper price, or you will go out of business – or both.

You need to ask yourself why everyone else is selling toothbrushes at 19p or 20p. The answer is simple. It is because, at that price, they are making a profit, and profit is the reason you are in business. An order for 20,000 toothbrushes at 20p each is far more valuable than an order for 150,000 at 10p. Your competitors will have pitched their prices as a result of a careful costing exercise. It *is* possible that, with clever buying or manufacturing, you are able to produce yours cheaper than the competition, but does this justify a price cutting exercise? Why not simply charge the same price and pocket the extra profit?

What applies to manufacturing toothbrushes, applies to every trade. If you open a fast-food restaurant and sell your hamburgers for 35p when everywhere else is selling them for 55p, you will not attract more trade. People will just think you have used horsemeat – and they will probably be right. The public at large are increasingly aware of value for money and the cheapest item on the shelf will not be necessarily the highest seller. It is *clever* pricing, not *under* pricing which will help you to compete in the marketplace.

Here are some golden rules:

◆ Offer your goods or services at the same price as your competitors, but convince your customer that you are offering better quality.

◆ Offer your goods or services at the same price as your competitors, but offer your customer something extra – faster delivery, a wider choice of colours or sizes, much better presentation . . .

◆ Ask a higher price than your competitors, for a better quality product, and convince your customer that they should be thinking more upmarket.

◆ Offer goods or services to your customer at a lower price than your competitors, by offering a modified version of what is currently on the market. In other words your customer pays less and gets less.

◆ When pricing, do not undervalue what you have to offer. Newcomers to business, particularly, have a tendency to under-rate their product. Remember your product is probably at least as good as everyone else's – think positive.

Pricing, like everything else, is subject to trends. The more an item is in demand, the more you can charge for it. Learn to judge your market fluctuations and react accordingly. Above all, do not be hidebound by what the item you have to sell cost you originally, Sell whatever you have to offer **at the highest possible price**, irrespective of what it cost you to produce or buy. You are in business, trying to earn a living in difficult times. Never feel embarrassed, or guilty, about making excessive profits. You will have your lean times too, so if there are rich pickings to be had, **take them**.

Having advised you not to look at pruning your price as a way of conquering a market, we should say that it is equally unrealistic not to recognize that pricing can very often be a deciding factor as to whether you do, or do not, make a sale. What you must not do, though, is use price as your only weapon.

Case history

John Cameron, a marketing consultant from Bristol, was asked a few years ago if there was anything he could do to save an ailing office display systems business. He had a week in which to do something. If no solution could be found, a receiver was to be appointed. He looked at the company, its products, its competitors, the market and its pricing structure. He then doubled the prices overnight and wrote to all regular customers telling them so. Orders flooded in, the company was saved and today, without doubt, it is the leading name in the field of office display, both at home and abroad.

The moral of the tale is that it is as easy to undervalue your goods, as it is to overprice them. The results can be equally disastrous.

Urgent message

The most important point about pricing is that you cannot look at it in isolation. Whilst you cannot expect to simply undercut a market and get away with it, equally you cannot offer the same goods as everyone else and charge more for them. Vary the quality, the presentation, the delivery, the colour, the size, the design and the material. Then apply the appropriate price, charging more, or less, than your competitors according to what is appropriate. Suddenly you will find you are in business.

Solicitors

Just because you are in business, it does not automatically mean that you need a solicitor. You only need a solicitor if you have something quite specific to do – form a limited company, acquire a property, sue a customer for a bad debt . . .

If you require legal advice and intervention, make sure that you select a solicitor who specializes in the field in which you need advice. Do not be afraid to shop around for your particular requirements. As a general rule, for business matters, it is sensible to have a solicitor with specialist commercial experience. However, this is probably not the person you will use when it comes to the acquisition of a property or collecting debts. In the latter case, you might well be advised to use the services of a debt collecting agency in preference to a solicitor.

Of course, solicitors prefer to handle all your affairs within the one practice, but in the long term you will save time and money by using specialists. In some instances, certain firms of solicitors do specialize in particular work. For example, if you intend opening a pub or a restaurant, you will find that there is a local firm of solicitors who specialize in licensing. Quite apart from the fact that they will handle your case with a greater degree of expertise than a non-specialist firm, they will also be able to advise you as to your likely chances of success – perhaps, therefore, saving you a great deal of wasted time and money. If you are planning the flotation of your company then you should employ the services of a city firm of solicitors. If you are seeking to register business patents, again some firms specialize in this, and so on . . .

Here are a few golden rules for appointing a firm of solicitors to deal with your general business requirements:

1   Choose a firm which has been personally recommended to you, by someone who has seen the firm's work first hand in the commercial field – perhaps your bank manager or accountant could help you here.

2   You must instinctively like and trust the partner with whom you will be dealing on a regular basis. You are not going to confide your troubles to someone who does not appeal to you personally.

3   Choose a firm which is conveniently located close to your place of work. Heaven knows why it should be so, but most legal transactions involve absolutely nothing happening for weeks, and then a mad panic right at the last minute, which can involve couriers and express letters, if your solicitor is not close by.

4   Choose a firm which is compatible in size to your own business. In other words, if you are a solo operation, do not go to an enormous firm. By contrast, if you see your business as having enormous growth potential, then choose a firm of solicitors large enough to handle your likely requirements.

5   Do give your solicitor all the facts. Do not be embarrassed about confiding all the gruesome details of the mess in which you find yourself. Your solicitor can only help you if you tell him or her everything.

6   Ask for an estimate of fees in advance of work done. You would ask for a quotation if you were employing a builder – why not for a solicitor?

Briefing a solicitor

Before going to see a solicitor on any matter, however trivial, do prepare for your meeting. Every time a solicitor lifts a telephone, writes a letter, or listens patiently to your ramblings, it is costing you money. Even a brief encounter with a firm of solicitors can prove enormously expensive. Work out precisely what it is you want your solicitor to do for you and what advice you need. It is often helpful to commit the various points to paper, so that your solicitor has a checklist against which to work (they do love everything in writing). Do as much of the spadework as

you possibly can. If you have some relevant documentation which your solicitor should study, copy it off for the solicitor before your appointment. You could double your fee hanging around the solicitor's office waiting for someone to finish the photocopying!

On the negative side, solicitors, like everyone else, get things wrong occasionally. If you do feel your solicitor has been negligent in any way, or is charging you too high a fee, then you do have some redress. Contact the Law Society – 113 Chancery Lane, London WC2, telephone number 01 242 1222 – and state the nature of your complaint. In theory, if the Law Society believes that the solicitor in question has been guilty of malpractice, then it will intervene on your behalf. In reality, though, experience tends to suggest that the profession 'closes ranks', unless there has been a very serious misdemeanour. It is always worth threatening your solicitors with the Law

Society, though, if you feel they are not coming up to scratch.

On the positive side, solicitors can contribute a great deal more to your business than simply sorting out your legal requirements. Often you will find that they will head you in the direction of a business opportunity, by perhaps introducing you to another client of theirs; and a solicitor is far more likely to be your mentor when it comes to general advice. On the whole they are far less cautious than accountants and more inclined to state their opinion. Solicitors are hardly a sanguine bunch and rarely given to wild enthusiasms, but often their bird's eye view of your business can prove of invaluable help. However, do not lose sight of the fact that whilst you might find it tremendously therapeutic to talk through your business problems with your solicitor every few weeks, it could prove a very expensive luxury. And remember, solicitors are not there to make decisions for you – the buck stops with you!

Assessing Your Business 'Shape'

Deciding upon the shape of your business is largely a matter of common sense. Whether you are at the stage of vaguely contemplating the setting up of a business, have firm plans ready to implement, or are currently in business and considering expansion, it is a question of assessing, not only your requirements today, but what they are likely to be in five years' time. Undoubtedly there are limiting factors – both personal and commercial – which will affect your business structure and, up to a point, dictate the shape.

Personal limiting factors

◆ If you have a family to support, it is going to have a great influence on the extent of risk you are prepared to take.

◆ If you are an undischarged bankrupt you will need a partner in whose name all financial transactions will have to be made.

◆ If you have a dependent relative you may have to operate your business from home.

◆ If you have any sort of police record you will not be able to run a pub or a restaurant unless the licence is in a partner's name . . .

. . . the list is endless.

Commercial limiting factors

◆ Are you intending to operate as a solo concern?

◆ Are you planning to go into business with someone else?

◆ Will you be putting your own money into the business, or are you seeking financial support?

◆ If you have a partner or partners, how will you split the profits, and will you all draw salaries?

◆ How big do you intend the business to become in the next few years, in terms of staff, premises, sales and profits?

◆ Are you buying and selling a product, are you going into design, manufacture, providing a specialist service or acting as a consultant?

◆ Will you be buying or leasing premises, equipment and vehicles?

◆ Where will you be selling – in the immediate locality, nationally, overseas – and how will your product be distributed?

These are the sort of questions you need to ask yourself to determine the shape of your business.

Example: It is all very well saying that you want to operate as a solo concern, but if you have no capital and no collateral to offer the bank in order to obtain a loan, you are going to have to face the fact that someone else is going to need to be involved – a backer, a partner of some sort, who believes in what you are doing and is prepared to finance you.

Example: If you are having to operate your business from home, then it needs to be recognized that this is a limiting factor on the size to which the business can grow. In this instance, you might be well advised to keep it as a solo operation, growing slowly and keeping all the profits for yourself.

Example: If you live in the depths of the country and have absolutely no intention of moving to the city smoke, then the only way to distribute your product may be by mail order. If this is the case, you have to recognize that you are going to need a very large capital base to mount this sort of selling operation.

The main options open to you are: to operate as a sole trader, to set up a partnership, form a limited company or buy an exisiting business. In pages 36 – 47 we explore each of these trading methods.

However modest your initial business aspirations, it is vitally important that you do start trading from the right base. In the early days of setting up your business, your impatience to get started can lead you to make a number of snap decisions which, as the business develops, you will regret. It is easy, for example, to accept finance from the first person who offers it, or to go into partnership with the nice neighbour down the road, because you like him or her, not because you recognize your friend has abilities compatible with your own. What you do have to consider, in the setting up of your business, is that the decisions you make now will most probably be affecting you in fifteen or twenty years' time. It is difficult, but you must define precisely what you see as being your ultimate goal. The establishment of a business is not just a question of a few formalities. How well you anticipate the future shape of your business can greatly influence the prosperity of your whole venture. Take time, take trouble and take care – it is well worth doing so.

Case history

Barbara Bentley and Elizabeth Jennings went into partnership a few years ago, by opening a chic little boutique in Amersham. On the face of it they seemed an ideal combination. Elizabeth had flair, good dress sense and natural poise. Her home and her clothes reflected her tremendous skill with colour combinations, and everything about her was stylish. An intelligent, articulate woman, she could put across her ideas well. Barbara, by contrast, was a bit of a rough diamond. Her business background was exclusively rag trade, but rag trade at the bottom end – mostly on market stalls. Her skill lay in her ability to buy. She had a natural eye for a bargain and could smell a profitable line a mile off. So far as she was concerned, she knew that the success of their business venture lay in the difference between the price they could buy the goods for and what they could sell for. Colour, style, taste and quality were all very well in their place, but what Barbara wanted to do was to make money.

On the face of it, their partnership should have been a brilliant success, their skills being so totally complementary. Instead the venture was a disaster. The two women fought like cat and dog and in the end Barbara left. Elizabeth was free to concentrate on developing the image she felt appropriate for her business and within a few months she had gone bust. Without Barbara, the wheeler-dealer, Elizabeth was soon carrying too much stock of the wrong type of goods.

So, what was the problem? It lay in the strained relationship between the two women, which in turn was adversely affected by the fact that they were equal partners. It highlighted the differences between them and caused the endless rows. One of them should have been overall boss, the other should have been employed. Whoever was then in the subordinate role would have accepted it because she would have simply been doing a job. As it was, both women had money invested in the business and were both trying to protect their own interests. This is a clear case where business shape ruined what otherwise could have been an excellent business.

The moment you set down this book, you could start trading, and you would be in business, with few legal requirements and the minimum of fuss. Because it is the simplest, sole trading is the most common form of business entity. Provided you know what you want to do and how you are going to do it, and you have facilities available, you can start trading tomorrow – today even. It is natural to think of sole traders as one-person businesses, but as a sole trader you can employ as many people as you like and there is no restriction as to the size of your business. In fact there are a number of very large concerns who trade in this way.

For operating as a sole trader there are only three legal requirements.

1   You must keep an up-to-date set of books and records for tax purposes. The tax authorities have the right to inspect these and may do so from time to time.
2   If your sales are over the current limit, you have to register for VAT. If you are reasonably sure that your turnover will exceed the current VAT limit, you should register *before* you start trading. Contact your local VAT office to establish whether you need to register, and contrary, perhaps, to popular belief, you will find them very helpful. They will be able to advise you on which rules apply to your particular business.
3   If you are employing anyone, you will have to comply with the wide range of legislation relating to employment. You will need to familiarize yourself with the rules relating to hiring, firing, sick pay, maternity leave, sex discrimination, and the Race Relations Act. You will also need to make PAYE returns. For a full understanding of all that is involved, it is best to go along to your local DHSS department and Tax Office. They will provide you with all the paperwork you need and will explain to you exactly what is required. Again, as with the VAT office, they have something of a reputation for being tyrants, but in fact you will find them quite helpful.

Advantages

There are a number of advantages to be gained from being a sole trader, perhaps the most important of all being that you keep 100 per cent of the profits. It also gives you a direct one-to-one relationship with your customers and your suppliers, which in turn gives your business a very personal feel. As a sole trader, you have no shareholders or co-directors to whom you are answerable. Unlike in a limited company, there is no requirement to file your accounts for all the world to see. In a nation somewhat beleaguered by red tape, the sole trader will attract the very minimum. There are tax advantages, too. If you make a loss in your first year's trading – and many new businesses do – you can claim back tax paid in the previous year, when, most probably, you were employed. In other words, as a sole trader you can claim a tax rebate on previous earnings.

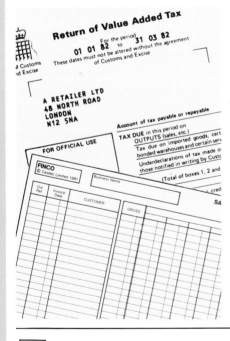

The other advantage is that the tax you are likely to pay in the first two or three years of trading will be assessed on the result of your first year of trading. Therefore, if you either make a loss or a very small profit, this pattern will be reflected in the next two or three years' tax demands.

Finally, if you are attracted by the concept of running your own business, then clearly it is because you want to be your own boss. As a sole trader you are most certainly this.

Disadvantages

Whilst you are the sole recipient of whatever profit is made, you are also 100 per cent responsible for any debts you incur, unlike in a partnership or limited company. If your business is in trouble and faces closure, unsatisfied creditors can pursue you, not only for the assets of your business, but also for your personal assets as well. For this reason, before embarking on a business as a sole trader, it might be sensible to transfer your major assets, such as your house, into your spouse's name, so that in the event of failure, at least your home is protected. This advice is not intended to encourage you to have a cavalier attitude towards your debts, but any business venture you undertake, if at all possible, should not jeopardize the family home – particularly where children are involved.

The other major disadvantage of being a sole trader is the difficulty of being recognized as a business entity in your own right. On the whole, banks prefer lending money to limited companies, landlords prefer granting leases to companies, private investors are more attracted to investing in a company rather than an individual. The inference is that as a sole trader, although you may have built up a sizeable business, the business remains dependent upon *you*, the proprietor. In the minds of backers and bankers, if something happens to you then

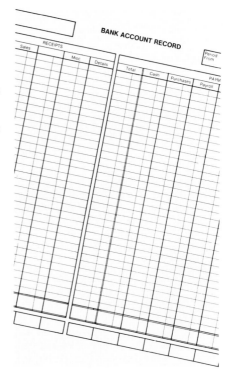

there is no business left. Investing money in a business is a demonstration of faith in its future. When its future appears to be bound up with one sole individual, it does seem to give the investor pause for thought. There may well be no justification for this attitude, but it is a view which is prevalent and worthy of consideration.

There is a lot to be said in favour of operating as a sole trader, and certainly if you are not wishing to expand your business greatly in the future, it is very tempting to suggest you should operate in this way. However, if you are going to commit yourself to heavy borrowings, or a large cash outlay, it is probably unwise to operate as a sole trader – you need the protection, structure and discipline of a limited company.

Partnerships

There are a number of reasons why you might want a partner –

MONEY

SKILL

MORAL SUPPORT

PREMISES

Of course all of these can be obtained from other sources but, without doubt, there are a number of attractions to going into business with someone else.

Be careful in your choice of partner

A golden rule – avoid going into business with friends. The ideal relationship is one where two people get together to form a business because, commercially, it makes sense to do so. Having established the business, if the partnership is successful, then chances are friendship will follow. However, going into partnership with someone because you enjoy meeting them for a drink is the worst of all possible motives for choosing a partner. Each partner has to contribute to the business, different but compatible skills and assets, so that your business has a wide pool of resources upon which to draw. Whatever each partner puts into the business should be drawn out on a pro rata basis. If one of the partners is doing 90 per cent of the work then, subject to recognising the capital put up by each partner, that partner should receive 90 per cent of the profit. An imbalance here causes untold resentment.

Beware of the sleeping partner

One of the most difficult relationships between partners is where one is a sleeping partner. If you have the business idea and the skill, but do not have the money, it may be possible to find someone to finance you,

who will take no active part in the running of the business. In the early days, of course, this is wonderful. You behave as though the business is your own, and apart from sending your sleeping partner monthly figures, you have no interference from the partner. Gradually, however, the business prospers and the time comes when you are in a position to make distributions of profits or dividends. Suddenly you realize that your sleeping partner is drawing as much as, if not more than, you are from the business, and yet *you* are doing all the work. It is your skill that has built up the business, while the partner has done absolutely nothing . . . except lend you the money. It is at this point that you have to remember that without your sleeping partner, you would have never had a business, so you should be grateful for the partner's continuing trust and support. It is not easy to adopt this attitude, and you should be aware of the problem before you take on a sleeping partner.

How to set up a partnership

The simplest form of partnership is merely an extension of the sole trader. Instead of one of you reaping the profits and carrying the responsibility for the debts, two or more persons are involved. There is no legal requirement for a written partnership agreement, but you would be extremely foolish not to have such a document – yes, even if your partner is your husband or wife. Without being unnecessarily pessimistic, the best relationships fail and the object of a partnership agreement is to make provisions for that possibility – you and your partner/s need protection in case something goes wrong.

Any solicitor can help you draw up a partnership agreement. A standard agreement probably will need to be adapted to suit your own particular case. Once the document is signed and sealed, you will probably never refer to it again, but it is there in case you need it.

In the image, on the desk/wall signs and speech bubble:

BUSINESS PARTNERS GUIDANCE COUNSELLOR

ARE YOU SLEEPING PARTNERS WITH ANYONE ELSE?

Questions you and your partner need to ask yourselves

- What drawings will you each take? – the maximum per month should be agreed.
- Cars – maximum value?
- How long will the partnership run – indefinitely, or for a fixed term?
- Will you allow for the admission of a new partner?
- How will you allow for the withdrawal of a partner?
- What happens if you grow to hate the sight of your partner, or he is no longer contributing to the business – can he be expelled?
- How will you distribute the capital on the dissolution of the partnership or on retirement of one partner?
- How will the voting rights be divided?
- What happens if one of you is chronically ill, or dies?
- What happens if the premises burn down?
- What happens when the business gets into terrible debt?

In a partnership, partners normally share the profits on an equal basis, and accordingly are jointly responsible for the liabilities of the business. However, you can create a limited partnership. In this event, one or more of the partners can opt for **limited liability**. This means that if things go wrong, a partner with limited liability is only liable to meet the creditors' claims up to the amount he or she has invested in the partnership. For instance, if the business fails with your firm owing Brown & Sons £3,000, if your limited liability was, say, £1,000, it would be up to your partners to find the rest. This could be a very useful device if you have, for instance, the responsibility of a young family. It should be noted that in every partnership, at least one partner has to be prepared to accept unlimited liability; and limited partnerships must be registered with the Registrar of Companies. There is a small amount of stamp duty payable on their formation.

The main disadvantage of a partnership is that the success of the business can so largely depend upon the relationship you have with your partner. People change, circumstances change, and when times are difficult particularly, even the best relationships can go sour. Remember, too, that you are entirely responsible for each other's actions. While your bank account can be controlled by you and your partner having joint signatures on all cheques, there is nothing to stop one partner ordering, let us say, £30,000 worth of goods on behalf of the partnership. Failure to pay for these goods would be your joint responsibility, whoever had placed the order.

In most groups of people, whether you are looking at the playground, the workshop or the boardroom, human beings tend to relate together best when there is an overall boss, somebody who is in charge – the ultimate authority guiding the direction in which everyone else moves. Constant decision by a committee can be unwieldy, time consuming and inefficient. Think very carefully before committing yourself to a partnership.

Limited Companies – Formation

A completely separate legal entity is created by the formation of a limited company. Company law is fairly technical, but the setting up of a small private company can be done quickly and simply, for a comparatively small cost. In theory, you can approach the Registrar of Companies yourself, fill out the necessary forms and establish a company without any legal advice. However, it is far more sensible to employ the services of a solicitor to ensure that the company is properly set up.

Your solicitor probably will recommend that you buy an established company '**off the shelf**'. To form a company, you need a minimum of two directors, one of whom will also need to be company secretary – unless, as in many cases, your solicitor volunteers for the appointment. There are considerable advantages in your solicitor acting as company secretary, as there is a degree of paperwork associated with the job, such as the drawing up of minutes and filing of annual returns.

One of the problems you are likely to experience with the formation of a limited company is its name. If you buy a company 'off the shelf', it will have been given a name by a registration agent. The names allocated to 'off the shelf' companies are extremely odd and it is unlikely that you will be given a name which you will want to use. It will be necessary for you, therefore, to file a new name which is acceptable to the Registrar of Companies – in other words one which is not already in use. This legislation varies from the sole trader or partnership, where you are perfectly entitled to call yourself what you like, regardless of how many other businesses there are of the same name.

Advantages of a limited company

◆ A limited company is a 'person' in its own right. It can own property and assets, can enter into contracts, sue and be sued.

◆ If the company becomes insolvent, it does not affect the personal status of the shareholder, nor indeed a director, unless he knowingly allows the company to trade whilst insolvent. This means that the company member's home and personal assets will be safe, whatever happens to the company, unless they have been pledged by way of personal guarantee.

◆ Within a limited company structure, it is possible to build up profits more tax-effectively than can be done by the individual or partnership.

◆ It is possible to borrow money more easily as a limited company than as an individual.

◆ If a shareholder, or for that matter a director, becomes bankrupt, seriously ill, or dies, it need not affect the company's continuity of business.

◆ It is generally believed that your likely relationship with the Inland Revenue is easier when trading as a limited company – particularly where personal expenses and costs are involved.

◆ A more structured environment, as provided by a limited company; has to be an advantage for trading and

CERTIFICATE OF INCORPORATION
ON CHANGE OF NAME
No. 1712439
I hereby certify that
BRITEBLACK LIMITED
having by special resolution changed its name, is now incorporated under the name of
THE PEN AND INK BOOK COMPANY LIMITED
Given under my hand at the Companies Registration Office, Cardiff the 1ST SEPTEMBER 1983
an authorised officer

employment purposes. Internal management reporting, the control of staff and various trading disciplines are more easily adhered to within a company structure. This also applies to personal discipline. Within a company structure, you are more likely to behave in a businesslike way.

Disadvantages of a limited company

◆ A limited company is less confidential in that accounts have to be published annually and details of shareholders and directors are available for inspection.

◆ A limited company is more costly to form than either a sole trading business or partnership.

◆ The need to make annual returns and prepare audited accounts will involve you in a continuing cost.

◆ By the very nature of the limited company structure, other people have to be involved, and this limits your independence – yet independence may be the main reason why you want to run your own business.

Although your solicitor will handle the establishment of your company for you, there are various terms connected with limited companies which you should understand.

Memorandum of association

This is the basic document required to form a company and will need to be signed by two directors/shareholders. It states the company's name, the address of the registered office, and the share capital. It also defines the objects of the company, i.e. the type of business in which it will be engaged. It is important that this description accurately covers your type of business.

Articles of association

This document, too, is required for the formation of a company and deals with the internal regulations of the company, and also requires the directors'/shareholders' signatures. Most Articles of Association are those set out in Table A of the Companies Act, and only occasionally will they need modification.

Share capital

Share capital is the money a company obtains by issuing shares to its members. The capital of the company is described as follows:

Authorized Capital - this is the nominal value of the shares which the company is authorised to issue at the time of its formation. The amount of capital involved will be partly determined by the amount of money the shareholders have to invest, and partly by the likely future needs of the company. The authorized capital can be increased from time to time, as necessary.
The Issued Capital - this is the name given to that part of the authorized capital which has actually been issued to members.
Paid Up Capital - this is the name given to the amount of issued capital which has actually been paid for by members.
The Uncalled Capital - this is the name given to the authorized capital which has yet to be issued.

In general terms, if your business is going to become involved in a considerable capital outlay – either at the time of its formation or as a result of expansion – then you would be well advised to form a limited company. Not only does a company look more permanent and reliable to customers and suppliers, *it actually is*, because it depends for its future not solely on one person, but on a combination of talents, skills and experience. If your business is going places, then you should seriously consider forming a limited company.

Limited Companies – in Practice

The job of the directors is to manage the company in all its day-to-day affairs – buying and selling assets, hiring and firing, manufacturing and selling, raising money, making a profit . . . To report on their achievements each year, the directors present the company accounts to the shareholders, for approval, at an annual general meeting.

Company meetings

At an AGM, Ordinary Resolutions will be proposed for the approval of the accounts, the payment of dividends, and confirmation of the appointment of directors and the re-appointment of auditors. These Ordinary Resolutions are passed by a simple majority. Normally this takes the form of a show of hands, of shareholders present at the meeting on that day. Any shareholders present at the meeting can, however, demand a poll, which means a count of votes per share from all shareholders present, including any proxy votes. Here again though, only a simple majority is required. If, therefore, you hold more than 50 per cent of the voting shares in a company, you can exercise total control at the annual general meeting.

Major changes in a company's constitution need to be approved by a Special Resolution, which requires approval by a 75 per cent majority at a shareholders' meeting. A special meeting has to be called, giving twenty-one days' notice, to allow shareholders a reasonable chance of attending. These are the types of change which will require a Special Resolution:

◆ Any changes in the main objects clause, in the Memorandum of Association. This could be required if the company is going to change or expand the nature of its trading outside that described in the objects of the company.
◆ Change of company name.
◆ Altering the capital structure of the company.
◆ Issuing additional shares – occasionally a Special Resolution is not necessary here, as the directors may have already been given specific authority to issue further shares.
◆ Placing the company into voluntary liquidation.

Shareholders' rights

If you, or a collection of shareholders, hold more than 25 per cent of the voting shares, you can prevent the directors making any of these major changes, because you can block approval at the shareholders' meeting.

Even smaller percentage shareholders can exercise their rights. Any shareholder, or group of shareholders, representing at least 10 per cent of the voting shares, can force the directors to call a shareholders' meeting, at which minority shareholders can put specific resolutions to the vote. This provision allows dissatisfied shareholders to challenge the management of the company's affairs by the directors. They can call for change in the board, although of course the voting majority will still apply. A challenging minority might make a good display on a show of hands, but fail miserably if the chairman demands a poll, which, of course, will then involve large blocks of shares, rather than a majority of individuals.

Holders of more than 10 per cent of the voting shares have one other weapon in their hands – they can block the sale to a bidder of the entire share capital. If a bidder manages to purchase at least 90 per cent of the shares, that bidder can compulsorily acquire all of the rest on the same terms. But if the bidder fails to get 90 per cent, the non-assenting shareholders have the right to continue to hold on to their shares.

Any shareholder, or group of shareholders – even a member owning just one share – can approach the court under Section 459 of the 1985 Companies Act, if he considers that the company's affairs have been conducted in a manner unfairly prejudicial to some part of its members. If the court agrees that this is indeed the case, it may make an order to redress the position. The most usual order would be that the majority shareholders should purchase the shares of the complaining minority. As an alternative, the court could order the company to be wound up, for the benefit of all the shareholders. This right is very useful for minority shareholders finding themselves locked into what they consider to be a bad investment in a private company, although the legal costs involved in such an action need to be considered very carefully before proceedings are started.

Directors' responsibilities

The Insolvency Act of 1985 has imposed additional responsibilities on directors – and, potentially, additional personal liability. If a company is being wound up, after going into insolvent liquidation, the liquidator may apply to the court for an order holding the directors responsible for the company's wrongful trading. If this is upheld, the directors will be required to contribute personally to the company's deficiency, if it can be shown that they knew, or ought to have known, that there was no reasonable

prospect of the company avoiding insolvent liquidation. This Act, quite obviously, is aimed primarily at those people who, in the past, have formed a company, run up debts, gone into liquidation, abandoned their creditors, and started trading all over again in the same type of business – sometimes repeating their actions several times over. However, as a director of a company, it is important to recognize the implications of this Act. It is up to you to ensure that regular monthly accounts keep you abreast of the company's development and that if the company starts to make substantial losses, and is heading towards insolvency, you must take action – either to put things right or at least stop the company from acquiring any further credit.

Traditionally, boardroom squabbles are all part of commercial life, and certainly the relationship between directors and their shareholders is often tense, based on their inability to understand one another's problems. Shareholders can be very quick to criticize the directors' actions, tending to see the trading of the company in simplistic terms, which is often impractical. By contrast, directors feel that they are doing all the work, while shareholders are just sitting back waiting for dividends to be paid and moaning when things go wrong. For this reason, if you are planning to run, or are running a small company with no grandiose ideas for massive expansion, keep your shareholding structure as simple as possible. If the capital requirements of the company demand that you need to bring in additional shareholders, try and keep yourself in the position of holding the majority of the shares – more than 50 per cent – and, of course, if possible more than 75 per cent, which in essence gives you complete control. Choose your shareholders as much for their personalities as for their pockets. You are looking for someone who has confidence in you, and will let you get on with the job, without constant interference.

Buying an Existing Business

The purchase of a business can, of course, vary enormously in scale. It could be that you commit yourself to a substantial investment involving the purchase of property and equipment, and taking on the obligation for a large pay roll. Alternatively, it may be just a question of buying what you consider to be a valuable name, plus the goodwill attached to it. Your motives for purchase can be equally varied. Let's consider these.

Why do you want to buy a business?

◆ To acquire expertise you do not have yourself.
◆ To acquire a market sector at the moment denied to you.
◆ To enhance the range of your existing business so that you can offer additional products or services.
◆ To make your business more efficient – perhaps you might consider buying an existing sub-contractor or distributor.
◆ To wipe out a competitor – if you cannot beat them, why not buy them!
◆ As an investment – to you, the buying of a profitable company might seem an infinitely preferable investment to dealing on the stock exchange or putting your money in a building society.

When you buy a business, however small, you do need professional help – an accountant to go through the books and a solicitor to check out the legalities. If you do not know the trade, then you also need to retain someone who does, to help you establish the true worth of the business. Knowing the worth of what you are buying is vital, regardless of what you end up paying. Be wary of picking up a business cheaply – very often a business, or a part of a business, becomes available for purchase because it has hit financial difficulties. What you have to ask yourself is WHY? Buying a business is all about carefully examining the assets and liabilities, setting one against the other and then seeing what you have left.

Assets

◆ *Freehold property* As well as establishing the value of any freehold attached to the purchase of a business, check out planning use, and whether the property conforms to the Health and Safety and Factory Acts with regard to the number of people you wish to employ – both now and in the future. Make sure the premises are not subject to any mortgages and that there are no prejudicial local development plans.

◆ *Leasehold property* The same conditions apply to leaseholds as to freeholds, with three important additions. You need to check out the rent review position, and see that there are no onerous clauses in the lease which will restrict your use of the premises for commercial purposes, and you need to make sure that the landlord will not be looking to you for major dilapidation costs at the end of the lease – or if so, that this is reflected in the price you pay.

◆ *Equipment* Original purchase price, less fair wear and tear, may be the right way to assess the value of the equipment. Equally it may not. Has the equipment been correctly serviced and maintained? Is it properly installed to conform with Health and Safety? Has it long-term use, or is it shortly to be made obsolete by more up-to-date technology? Above all, is it the equipment that you actually *want*? If not, it is worth absolutely nothing.

◆ *Stock* Again, it is not simply a question of assessing the value of stock – the point is, do you really want it? This is a particularly valid question if the business you intend buying is in financial difficulties, since, almost certainly, it will be carrying too much of the wrong stock.

◆ *Debtors* Very often in the acquisition of a company, you will inherit the trade debts. Before you allow that debtor figure to form part of the purchase price of a business, you need to make sure that the debtors are good for their money. It is advisable to demand an indemnity from the vendor so that if you are unable to collect the debts, you will be compensated.

♦ *Vehicles* Before taking on any vehicles, check out the HP position. It sounds incredibly obvious advice, but you would be surprised just how many people get caught by this.

♦ *Patents/trademarks/trading names* You may consider that a particular patent, trademark or trading name is one of the most valuable assets of your proposed purchase. These assets are not worth a jot unless they are currently registered – so do check.

♦ *Intangible assets* These include people, perfected services, knowhow, goodwill and a track record of profits. You have to decide not only what they are worth now, under current management, but what they will be worth under yours – and how badly you need them.

Liabilities

♦ *Mortgages and other loans* All loan agreements, overdraft facilities and mortgages need to be very carefully examined by your accountant, to make sure that the terms are not arbitrary, and that repayments can be made realistically from future trading.

♦ *Trade creditors* This is an area where you want to be particularly careful before agreeing to take on the liability. Are the creditors really fully disclosed and will you have sufficient funds to settle creditors as they fall due?

♦ *Tax liabilities* The same general comments apply as to creditors. Make sure your accountant has identified contingent tax liabilities, such as, say, hidden capital gains tax in the event of your selling assets.

♦ *Pension commitments* If you are taking over a company with a pension scheme, check it very carefully, since even with a small staff it can represent a big financial drain, especially if past service commitments have to be funded in the future. If in doubt, check with a pension broker.

♦ *Redundancy* Inevitably, if you are taking over a business, you are going to run it your way and your way will differ from the old régime. This will lead to staff changes and you need to establish, in broad outline, your redundancy liabilities if changes are to be made.

♦ *Contracts of employment* Check these out very carefully, particularly looking for onerous clauses with regard to length of notice, salary reviews, commission and profit sharing arrangements, etc.

♦ *Litigation* Satisfy yourself that the business is not involved in any legal actions.

Warranties

When you buy a business, you must obtain from the vendor a warranty that the assets and liabilities are what he says they are. Also make sure the vendor is good for the money – if not, withhold part of the purchase price for an agreed period, as a safeguard.

Buying an Existing Business – Case Histories

There are so many ways in which you can buy a business. You can employ someone who is keen, and he can bring his or her contacts, and therefore business, to you. You can take over an asset – say, a shop – and build your own business round it. You can buy a company, lock, stock and barrel, or the right to manufacture a product, or the right to sell it – nationally or in a particular area. You can take over a business with its proprietor and staff, but leave the tangible assets and liabilities behind. Here are four examples:

FOR SALE
Boulevard Restaurant, High Street, Exeter. Leasehold premises available, with all furniture and equipment, full licence. Only £35,000.

Three years later . . . Sidney and Gill Smith purchased the Boulevard Restaurant for the asking price of £35,000. The lease, at £5,000 rent per annum, only had two years to run, and their agent put a value on it of £7,000. He valued the furniture and equipment at £10,000. They therefore had paid £18,000 for goodwill. The lease was renewed after two years but the rent went up from £5,000 to £9,000 per annum, and the landlord charged them £8,000 for dilapidations. Sidney and Gill are still working seven days a week. They still have £40,000 of loans to repay and are earning between them about £10,000 per year.

Comments

A good buy? No. They overpaid for what they got. It would have been far better to have started from scratch.

FOR SALE
Entire share capital of OE Limited, a specialist office equipment company. Turnover £3 million, profits £200,000, freehold factory – home counties. Management/staff/workforce 70. £1,000,000 cash, or shares, required for a quick deal.

Four years later . . . OE Limited was acquired by a shopfitting group, with a view to broadening its marketing base. It borrowed the whole of the purchase money from its bankers. The deal went through quickly and with no problems, largely because the net asset value was virtually equal to the share price, so the bank had plenty of security for their lending. Since then, though, things have gone badly wrong. Within six months, almost all the senior management and staff had left. They liked the way the old family business was run, but could not accept the new tighter commercial control. Sales began to drop alarmingly and profits disappeared – the company's specialist product had been overtaken by the age of the microcomputer. In desperation, the new owners sold the freehold and took over production in their own factory, only to find that there was a liability of £250,000 of capital gains tax, which had not been expected.

Comments

A very poor investigation of the initial purchase. All the problems should have been seen and reflected in the price paid. The research done was all too superficial. No business purchase should be made on face value alone.

Two years later . . . Bob and Alan Cutler responded to James Rice's advertisement. They were in the same line of work and had a solid, but unexciting business. Bob had the green fingers and Alan was responsible for finance and administration. They had two employees. What they lacked was the flair and imagination of James Rice. 'He's a second Capability Brown,' said Bob. They paid James £10,000 for his goodwill and the three of them entered into an equal partnership.

'Our joint business has multiplied five times over in the last two years,' says Alan. 'We employ ten people and we are giving a really good service, making terrific profits, and we are all enjoying it.'

Comments

No comment necessary, these three got it right.

Three years later . . . Mr Bryan, a retired dentist, had an unexpected inheritance, hence his advertisement, to which he received countless replies. He eventually teamed up with a young couple, Anne and Tony, who had worked in the tourist industry and wanted to set up their own travel agency. Brampton Travel Limited was formed, with Mr Bryan holding 70 per cent of the shares and putting up virtually all the capital. After nearly three years, during which time Anne and Tony had been left alone to run the business, Mr Bryan began to get a little worried. He could not seem to get any regular management figures and the first two years' audited accounts showed a considerable loss. He was personally guaranteeing a £20,000 overdraft facility and the bank were getting anxious. What should he do? After all, he did not really know anything about the travel business. Fortunately, although tight for cash, the business was at last starting to make a profit and Anne and Tony managed to find a large travel group interested in buying the company. They were kept on as directors and Mr Bryan got his money back and was released from his guarantee.

Comments

He was very lucky. With no commercial business experience and no knowledge of the travel agency business, he had no idea how much capital was really needed when he made his initial investment. Furthermore he knew absolutely nothing about Anne and Tony. They meant well but they had never managed a company before. Mr Bryan lost three years and had many sleepless nights and he could easily have lost all his money. He should never have gone into the venture in the first place.

Franchising is just one word to describe a wealth of varying business relationships – some big, some small, some complex, some simple, some highly successful, some disastrous. Essentially, a properly constructed franchise involves a well-established company offering an individual the opportunity to trade under its corporate brand name and image. The company will also provide well-proven knowhow, a marketing programme, training, research and development facilities, and often bulk buying and administrative assistance. The individual, in return, pays for the privilege – usually by way of an initial fee, followed by a continuing levy, most often expressed as a percentage of sales.

A reputable franchisor can offer the would-be entrepreneur an excellent opportunity to establish his own business while protected by the umbrella of a big company. Particularly for people who perhaps have very little commercial experience, this can be a very attractive prospect. However, be careful – as well as good franchisors there are several who, it has to be said, are offering questionable value for money. Franchising represents a complex relationship and very careful consideration needs to be given before entering this field – in any capacity.

Being a franchisee

If you are considering buying a franchise, before you do anything else, contact the British Franchise Association, 75A Bell Street, Henley-on-Thames, Oxon, RG9 2BD, (telephone 0491 578049). The BFA is an organization whose main aim is to ensure that the franchise industry is run in an ethical way. From them you can purchase a *Franchisee Pack*, which contains some useful hints on being a franchisee and also includes an up-to-date list of those companies which are members of the association. The companies listed have been thoroughly vetted and you can therefore be confident about investing in the franchises they offer.

There are a number of franchising consultants around, but frankly you do not need them – far better direct any enquiries to the BFA. The one possible exception is the Franchise Shop, 6 Old Hillside Close, Winchester, Hants SO22 5LW (telephone 0962 55530). They describe themselves as an estate agency for franchising, and quite literally that is what they are, and they can direct you towards current opportunities.

In evaluating a franchise operation you need to go through all the same exercises as you would for starting your own business. You need to look at your personal circumstances with just the same amount of care, but you have the added requirement to very carefully vet the franchisor of your choice.

The pros of being a franchisee

- If you have a recognized skill or trade, but little or no commercial experience, then taking up a franchise could put you successfully and safely into business on your own.
- If you have the aptitude or inclination to run a particular type of business, of which you have no experience, then taking up a franchise could be the way to acquire that experience profitably.
- If you have the desire to run your own business, have some capital available but do not know what to do, or indeed, how to go about it, then taking up a franchise could give you the opportunity for which you seek.
- When you start a business of your own, however carefully you have done your market research, you cannot be sure it is going to work. Taking up a franchise – a good franchise – offers you a proven formula. If the business has been successful in Bradford and Truro, then logically it should also be successful in Swansea and Oxford. **You are investing your time and money in something that works, instead of something that you hope will work.**

The cons of being a franchisee

◆ What actually are you buying? Not a lot in many instances – mostly expertise, which you could acquire for yourself and which is often over-rated by the franchisor.

◆ If things go wrong, what will happen? You will lose your money, your business and your livelihood. In other words, you are no more protected than if you ran your own business.

◆ It is vital not to lose sight of the fact that although you take out a franchise, the business you are running is *yours*. Being a franchisee does breed complacency. Because Big Brother is looking over your shoulder, you assume you are safe and therefore have a false sense of security.

◆ The future is always dicey for the franchisee. Most franchise agreements only last five years and although, if you run a successful franchise operation, there is no question of not being offered a renewal, the terms may not be favourable.

◆ When you build your own business, if you are relatively successful, you are also building a fairly definite asset in terms of goodwill. With a franchise business the goodwill is not yours, it belongs to the franchisor.

◆ If you are attracted to the concept of running your own business, is it not partly for the joy and prestige of being your own boss? Without a doubt, there is a considerable amount of status associated with being a successful entrepreneur. If you are the franchisee of a company bearing a household name, you are still your own boss, but the rest of the world will not appreciate that. The public at large are surprisingly ignorant about franchising and as far as they are concerned, you simply will be looked upon as the local branch manager.

Being a franchisor

What can you franchise? In theory, almost anything. A product, a service, or even a concept. However – whatever you are offering, it has to be distinctive and above all a proven success. Perhaps you are a manufacturer, an importer or a wholesaler, and have developed a product, or range of products, which you feel is unique. Perhaps you have a specialist service to offer (look at Dyno-Rod) which could benefit from the franchise treatment. Either way, the ability to identify precisely what it is you are offering is very important. In theory, franchising your business gives you the opportunity to expand very much faster than you could do by opening individual branches, but you do have to bear in mind that you have to be able to pass on this attitude to your franchisees. Again, we would recommend that you contact the British Franchise Association, who have a *Franchisor Pack* telling you how to set about offering part, or all, of your business for franchise. They will prove very helpful in advice generally.

Franchising has a great future. In the right hands, it offers would-be entrepreneurs safe passage in their own small businesses, and the established company the chance to expand in a way that otherwise could only be the stuff of dreams. Without doubt, there are a large number of people in business today who would not be there but for the franchise umbrella. Similarly, there are companies who are wild successes – household names – who would have achieved no sort of prominence but for being able to expand by offering franchises. Whichever aspect of the business interests you, treat the world of franchising with respect and take time to get to know and understand it well before attempting to become a part of it.

Patents, Registered Designs, Trademarks, Service Marks and Copyright

In order to grow, industry must continually create and develop new ideas. Innovation is expensive and innovators need protection, to ensure that others cannot pirate their ideas. All of the items listed in the heading are known collectively, and rather pompously, as **intellectual property**, and with the exception of copyright, in order to register and protect your intellectual property, you need to contact The Patent Office. Their address is:

> The Patent Office,
> State House,
> 66/71 High Holborn,
> London, WC1R 4TP.
> (Telephone 01 829 6512)

While The Patent Office will be very helpful in bombarding you with leaflets and advice, unless you are thoroughly versed in design matters it is sensible to seek professional help from a registered patent agent. The list of registered patent agents may be inspected at:

> The Science Reference Library,
> 25 Southampton Buildings,
> London WC2A 1AY,

or purchased from:

> The Registrar,
> Chartered Institute of Patent Agents,
> Staple Inn Buildings,
> London WC1V 7PZ.

If you would prefer to deal with a local firm, you should find your *Yellow Pages* lists the patent agents in your particular area.

Patents

If you, your business or your company have produced what you believe to be a unique product or process, it is very important to register it as soon as possible, before disclosing your invention to anyone – especially your own particular industry. Essentially, the granting of a patent gives the patentee a monopoly to make, use or sell an invention, for a fixed period of time – which currently, in this country, is a maximum of twenty years from the date on which the patent application is first filed. In return for this monopoly, the patentee pays a fee to cover the costs of processing the patent. If a competitor tries to emulate your innovation while you have a current patent running, you can force them to stop trading and demand compensation, where applicable.

Registered designs

Have you created a new design for a particular product – this does not mean you have to have found an original product, just given it a new look? A new design, to be eligible for registration, will need to have a materially different appeal to the eye when the article is compared with the norm. To obtain a valid registration, the proprietor must apply *before selling or offering for sale in the UK* the article in question, though the design may be displayed at an exhibition. Designs can be registered for up to fifteen years.

Trademarks

A trademark is a means of identification. It is a symbol – whether a word or a logo – which is used in the course of trade in order to identify and distinguish to the purchasing public that the goods (or services) in question are yours. A good trademark is a very important marketing aid and you are strongly advised to register it. Initially, you can be covered for seven years, but thereafter renewal can be made indefinitely, broken up into fourteen-year periods.

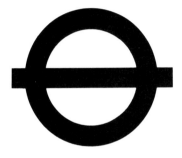

Service marks

This is a very new register which extends the trademark to cover not only goods, but services. If you are running a hotel, a hairdressers, a transport company – if you are a plumber, an insurance broker, or an actor – you can now register your service mark, if you have one, or if not, why not consider developing one? Full details are available from the Patent Office.

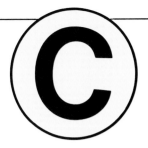

Copyright

Unlike the other four categories, copyright is established by evidence of creation, and protection is automatic. Proving that your work is your own is ultimately a matter for the courts to decide, if, in your view, there is any infringement of copyright. To safeguard your position, it might be sensible to deposit a copy of your work with your bank or solicitor, or send a copy of your work to yourself, by registered post, leaving the envelope unopened. This will establish that the work existed at a given time. Copyright is normally associated with the arts, but also applies to computer programmes and certain industrial articles – a drawing, a photograph, by way of example. It should be noted that there is no copyright attached to a name or title – it is the work itself that is protected. Further details from the Unofficial Registry of Copyright, at Stationers Hall Registry, Ludgate Hill, London EC4 (telephone 01 248 2936).

> Your business, particularly if it is relatively small, may depend utterly for its survival upon the marketing of one or two specific products. You cannot afford for these products to be emulated by anyone else and you must do your utmost to protect them, if at all possible. If your products, or services, are not eligible for any form of protective registration, would a change in the design or process make them so? This is seriously worth thinking about – protecting your innovation could be vital to the future of your business.

Estate agents, like all other professionals, have their uses, provided they are just that – professional. In using the term *estate agents*, it is important to be quite clear as to what that means. Any number of people set themselves up as estate agents, to handle the buying and selling of property. However, if you require anything more than this one simple function, then you should be dealing with a *fully qualified chartered surveyor.* Let us look at what an estate agent can do for you:

If you have a property – freehold or leasehold – an estate agent will

Sell your property, or find a tenant for all or part of it.
Value your property.
Act on your behalf in negotiating rent reviews with your landlord.
Act on your behalf in disputes with your landlord.
Act on your behalf in disputes with your neighbours.
Act on your behalf in negotiating with the local authority and with various officials and inspectors.
Act on your behalf in negotiating rating assessments/valuations.

If you want a property – freehold or leasehold – an estate agent will

Find you a property.
Negotiate price and terms if you are buying.
Negotiate rental/services/insurance terms if you are leasing.
Provide an independent valuation and survey report, to support a borrowing requirement.
Introduce sources of finance and negotiate terms.

If you either have, or want, a property, an estate agent will advise you also on

Planning permission.
Development potential.
Local road-building proposals, and all details relating to potential alterations, reconstruction or development of your premises and the surroundings.

Fees

Estate agents will charge you for anything they *do* in the negotiation or valuation field, and anything they *achieve* in both buying or selling on your behalf. If you ask an agent to find a property for you, giving them a description of what you want, you will be charged a fee for the purchase of any property to which the estate agent introduces you. This applies even if all the agent does is to send you some particulars, circulated by another agent.

Estate agent scale fees were abolished some years ago, but it would be helpful here, perhaps, to give you a rough guide as to what you can expect to pay. You will be charged approximately 1 per cent of the purchase price if an agent finds you a freehold property, or $1\frac{1}{2}$ per cent if the agent sells your property for you. If the agent is acquiring or selling leasehold property on your behalf, ask for a specific quotation, and indeed this applies to any sort of brief you propose giving an estate agent. This is particularly important because many agents, especially in major cities, have a minimum fee. During the research for this book, the authors were advised by one estate agent that it was not worth his while stepping outside his office for less than £500. Valuation fees can vary enormously – anything between $\frac{1}{4}$ per cent and $1\frac{1}{2}$ per cent of the value of the property.

As a general rule, only use an estate agent if you have no alternative.

Selling

Clearly, if you are selling a property, you almost certainly need an estate agent's help. Whilst you could advertise your property through the press, an estate agent quite literally offers you a better shop window, and provided you are quite clear as to what fees are going to be charged, you are best advised to use an agent. A word of advice here, though – never automatically accept an estate agent's valuation on your property. Estate agents make most money from quick deals, and as a result, even some quite well established firms have a tendency to advise selling at a considerably lower price than the market will stand, just to ensure a quick sale. If you and your agents do not see eye to eye on what your property is worth, why not give them an additional incentive to achieve the kind of price you feel is justified? Try offering them a scale of commission rates. If you believe your property is worth £100,000 and the estate agents are suggesting you should sell it for £90,000, offer them a 1½ per cent commission on a sale of £90,000 and, say, an additional 5 per cent commission on every thousand pounds they get over and above £90,000. Chances are they will sell it for £100,000 plus!

Buying

If you are looking for a property, it is very debatable whether you need an estate agent at all. Inevitably, although you brief them very carefully as to your precise requirement, you are liable to receive details on innumerable totally unsuitable properties. It is a question of valuing your own time and circumstances. If your business is based in Caithness and you are intending to set up a factory in Truro, then clearly you are going to need an estate agent to find suitable premises for you – it has to be cheaper than the alternative of buying a helicopter! If your every hour is already catered for by the demands of your business, and you do not have a member of staff whose judgement you trust, then again, an estate agent might be useful in helping you locate an appropriate property. However, if you are starting a new business, probably you would be best advised to do your own searching – why incur unnecessary fees? Indeed the very process of searching may well prove useful in providing you with an understanding of the locality in which you intend to work.

It is worth repeating, in conclusion, that you should only deal with a fully qualified chartered surveyor. Qualified agents are professional – they know about bricks and mortar. Buildings are their business and therefore the advice you receive from them is likely to represent value for money.

THIS PROPERTY WILL ALLOW FOR EXPANSION IN YOUR CYCLE REPAIR BUSINESS SIR

TO LET

Finding the Right Premises

These are the primary factors you need to consider when looking for business premises.

1 Location

Your customers

To be within easy reach of your customers may be vital or it may be totally unimportant. If you have a retail business, location is a major consideration. If you are in mail order, you can operate from anywhere in the country so far as your customers are concerned. If you are a wholesaler, do you require a showroom? If you are operating a factory, do you anticipate the requirement for a factory shop? Is it simply a question of being conveniently located for your customers, or are you relying on passing trade? It is vital that, in assessing the right location, you first clearly define the extent to which you need to make yourself accessible to your customers.

Your staff/workforce

Your employees have to be a top consideration. Clearly, you will find it easier to recruit the right type of staff if your business is located in a town with plenty of public transport and shopping facilities, rather than on an isolated estate. If your business is in the wilds, then you are going to have to provide appropriate facilities – for example, you may have to allow for a canteen, a recreation room and additional car parking spaces.

Certain regions/cities provide a hard core of skilled personnel in a particular field. If you are going into the advanced electronics business, you would be better placed to do so in Berkshire rather than Devon. If you are going into the clothing business, you would be better placed in Lancashire than Berkshire. It depends how much you rely on a high level of skill, but it may be worth while planning to locate your business quite specifically where you will enjoy the highest possible density of skilled labour, appropriate to your particular industry.

Your suppliers

If you are closely tied to an industry and require a specific raw material or a particular source of contracted goods or services, you may need to locate your business within easy reach of your suppliers. While the country is linked by a reasonably efficient network of transport, the closer you are to your suppliers, the more control you can exercise over your stock levels, the lower your transport costs and the more efficient your business is likely to be. Convenience can play an enormous part in business success.

You

Why drive fifty miles to work each day if it is *your* business we are talking about? Time spent travelling is time wasted – it leaves your nerves frayed, and it is exhausting and inefficient. Your home and business should be as near as possible to one another.

2 Size and shape

In an ideal world, you need to acquire the right accommodation for your scale of operation today and for your expansion plans this year, next year and some years in the future. This applies whether you are looking for a shop, an office, a workshop or a factory unit. However, it needs to be recognized that most businesses cannot afford to spend money on space that cannot earn its keep immediately, and this applies whether you are renting or purchasing. Before you start looking for new premises, work out very carefully just what it is you need *now*:

How many square feet of offices/storage/workshop/showroom?
How many square feet of employees' facilities?
How much car parking space?
How much outside storage for deliveries, storage and packing?

If you are uncertain as to what precisely you need, or you feel that the shape of your business is going to alter substantially and in the short term, do not commit yourself to a hefty purchase, or even as much as a five-year lease. Go instead for a temporary solution, while you determine what your long-term requirements are likely to be. In other words, never enter into a lengthy commitment unless you feel the premises are going to suit you in the long term. This applies not only to the length of a lease but also the terms under which you rent premises – i.e. whether you are required to give a month's notice or more. Do bear in mind that the cost of chopping and changing is vastly expensive – telephone installation, carpets, decorating, printing and stationery, staff disruption, removal costs, legal expenses – it is a horrific catalogue of expense which you should do your best to avoid. As a general rule, do not buy premises into which you *hope* you may ultimately expand, but which in the meantime you intend to sub-let. If you genuinely plan for, and anticipate rapid expansion then certainly buy more space than you need. However, expansion plans need to be quite specific since sub-letting surplus space is always a difficult task.

3 Cost

Whether you are buying a freehold or acquiring a lease, **take independent professional advice on value.** Hire a surveyor who will tell you whether the asking price, or rent, is fair. Whatever your business, the cost of your premises is going to represent a major overhead. If you get it wrong, if the overhead is too top-heavy for the size of your trade, you will go out of business.

4 Planning

It is essential to establish not only that the property can be used for the purpose for which you want it, but also that the planning consent will cover any future business

development. If you are intending to run a warehouse, that is one thing. If that warehouse is going to be visited by members of the public, you may find your neighbours up in arms, demanding that you either cease trading in this way, or apply for retail use – which, of course they will enthusiastically oppose. Use your commonsense. There is no point in moving into a small industrial unit, adjacent to a housing estate, if part of your manufacturing process involves excesses of noise, smell, dirt or mess. Be sure, the residents will drive you out in the end – if not legally, the weight of their wrath eventually will wear you out and moving will seem an easier option.

5 Environment

A great deal of nonsense is talked about working environment, and certainly a number of designers have got very rich on mad schemes – allegedly geared to making the working area more user-friendly. However, it is a fact that environment does play a large part in encouraging us to work efficiently, and this aspect must be taken into account. You will get more from your workforce if their surroundings are pleasant.

As a piece of general advice, it is always very helpful before committing yourself to premises, to see how operations similar to your own are catered for. A little industrial espionage is worth its weight in gold! If possible, visit your competitors. Ask members of their staff how suitable, or unsuitable they find their working conditions and what can be done to improve them. Use your eyes and learn from others' mistakes.

Particularly if you are starting a new business, the idea of working from home is very attractive. It enables you to keep your overheads to a minimum, allows you to work the long hours usually necessary in the establishment of a business, and leaves your options open – if the business does not work out, you are not committed to an industrial property. It needs to be recognized, however, that working from home can cause considerable problems.

Legislation

Strictly speaking, if you plan to run a business from your home, almost certainly you will need approval or permission either from *someone* or from *some authority*. Whether in fact you actively seek that approval is something you will have to judge. Many businesses run successfully from the dining-room table for years, without causing any inconvenience or concern to anyone. However, if your business becomes very obvious to outsiders, or is in any way a nuisance to your neighbours, or if something goes wrong – a fire or an accident, then lack of permission can rebound and can result in fines and even closure.

There are two kinds of restrictions which may affect your ability to run your business from home. The first is a series of contractual relationships which you may have already entered into without even being aware of them. If you own your own house, it is possible that at the time you purchased it, you accepted a covenant limiting its use to domestic purposes. Alternatively, you may live in a leasehold property, in which case you need to establish whether the lease (or any tenants' agreement which may exist) prohibits the use of the premises for trading purposes. If you have a mortgage, you are likely to find that there is a restrictive clause concerning the use and occupation of the house.

Of course, it may be possible to renegotiate any one of these agreements,

but if you are at all uncertain where you stand, contact your solicitor who will be able to clarify the position.

The second kind of restriction is that imposed by the main local authorities – Planning, Highways, Health and Safety. Assuming you live in a predominantly residential area, it is obvious that – for example – you cannot put petrol pumps in your front garden, nor can you convert your whole house to a hotel, or start an engineering works in your garage. However, it is also a fact that many much less obvious changes still need consent from the authorities, and here again there are two facets to that consent.

Planning permission

If you want to make a significant alteration to your house in order to accommodate your business, you will need planning permission or building regulations approval. This includes building an extension, putting rooms in the loft, or erecting a garage – in fact anything except extremely simple alterations requires you to make an application for planning permission.

Change of use

The second consideration is with regard to change of use. The authorities state that consent has to be sought for any **material change of use**. Interpreting material change of use is difficult, although the fact is that almost any business activity could be deemed to qualify. For example, if you are a farmer and put out a notice saying 'farmyard manure for sale – £2.50 per bag', then that will be material change of use if you have no authority to run a retail outlet from your premises. This aspect of change of use is very restricting and what you have to decide is whether your proposed use is of such a nature that approval should be sought.

General advice

If you are not proposing to make any

physical alterations to your property, if you are not going to have customers calling, if you are not going to employ any staff on the premises, if you are not wanting a notice board outside your house proclaiming who you are – then it could well be that no permission of any sort is needed. Certainly, by tradition, there are a number of occupations which are normally acceptable in a domestic environment – writers, artists, home teachers, designers, to name a few. It is a point worth noting, though, that the common denominator between these people is that they have a virtually non-existent nuisance level.

This, then, is the crux of the matter. Whatever type of business you intend running from home, it must be, for want of a better word, *neighbourly*. Try putting yourself in your neighbour's position and see whether your activity will affect them in any way. This is not for purely altruistic reasons – if your neighbour complains to the local authorities, they are bound by law to follow up that complaint, and if you have not sought prior permission, you could well find yourself on a slippery slope.

It is a fact that planning officers are taking a far more lenient view of home-based businesses, particularly bearing in mind the current unemployment problems. The authors were informed by one planning officer that he would be horrified if everybody who strictly needed planning permission to operate a business from home actually applied for it – his department simply could not cope.

Certainly, if you do proceed with change of use, it must be said that you are likely to become involved in some costs in order to satisfy specific legislation. For instance, your office layout might be quite adequate for you, but the fire officer may insist on an independent means of escape, in case of emergency. Also, formal approval for a change of use by the planning department will certainly trigger off a re-valuation of your house for rating purposes. As a result part of your house will then attract commercial rating, which is higher than domestic rating. In addition, when you sell your house, if part of it has been allocated for commercial use, you will suffer capital gains tax on a portion of any profit realized, because part of your house has ceased to be your own residence.

Insurance

Whether you are seeking planning permission or not, it is essential to check your insurance cover very carefully. Almost certainly, your existing house policy will exclude business acitvities, but you must be covered for these. Insurance companies will dispute claims when full information has not been disclosed. If, for example, your kiln was responsible for burning down your house, and you had no cover for the commercial activity of making ceramic mugs, then your claim would not be met and you would end up living in a tent.

Food hygiene

Many catering businesses start operating from home and they attract particularly careful scrutiny from the local authorities – quite rightly. If you are considering any form of catering business, you should apply to your local HMSO and acquire a copy of *Your Guide to the Food Hygiene (General) Regulations 1970.*

Working from home, in many respects, is not as simple as it seems and it may be that you recognize that there is no way your activity is going to be acceptable to the environment in which you live. There are alternatives – perhaps for a nominal rent you could find a few square feet within a compatible local business. Very often workshops, garages and offices have space which is not really being used and which could be leased in the short term while you establish your business.

Subsidized Premises and Locations

Depending upon the precise area in which your business is located, you may be entitled to receive assistance in the form of grants or subsidies from national or local government sources. This assistance can greatly influence where you choose to establish or expand your business.

Nationally available help

Across the nation, there are local authority 'nursery' units – partly funded by the ratepayers to assist local industry and employment. These nursery units are small and are aimed specifically at the new business. The rental is low with less restrictive leases than would be required by a typical private developer or institutional landlord.

Help applicable to inner urban areas

Under the Inner Urban Areas Act, there is assistance available from local authorities for improvement within designated districts – the essential aim being to provide local employment by encouraging local industry and trades into a specific urban area. This assistance takes the following forms:

90 per cent mortgage loans on commercial terms for periods of up to thirty years – this includes the purchase of land, buildings and the cost of building works.
Loans and grants for improving amenities – from renovating and demolishing buildings, to landscaping, tree planting and providing parking areas.
50 per cent grants towards the cost of converting and improving commercial or industrial buildings.

Urban development grants are also available from the Government to assist projects undertaken jointly with local authorities. This applies within certain inner urban areas and designated enterprise zones. Developments within enterprise zones are in fact free from many normal planning constraints and are exempted from local rates for several years. They also are entitled to attractive tax incentives in the form of 100 per cent industrial building allowance.

Help within assisted areas for expansion, as designated by the Department of Trade and Industry

In development areas, regional development grants are available to encourage industrial expansion. The grant payable for approved schemes is either 15 per cent of eligible capital expenditure, or £3,000 for each new job created – whichever is the greater. In some areas, the government has built advanced units, for sale or lease, on attractive terms, in order to foster local employment. In these areas, government-owned land may be available for development either by an outright purchase or on lease.

In the assisted areas a number of specific schemes are operating to encourage new job creation, or to help secure existing jobs. These schemes include:
Project grants towards the capital costs of expansion programmes for all sections of industry and commerce – both manufacturing and services.
Grants of up to 80 per cent of training costs.
Grants for small firms in areas particularly affected by job losses in the textiles, steel and shipbuilding industries.
Loans from the European Investment Bank and the European Coal and Steel Community.

For detailed help and guidance on all subsidized premises and locations, talk to your local authority, or contact the Department of Trade and Industry, 1–19 Victoria Street, London SW1H OET.

See map for details of assisted areas.

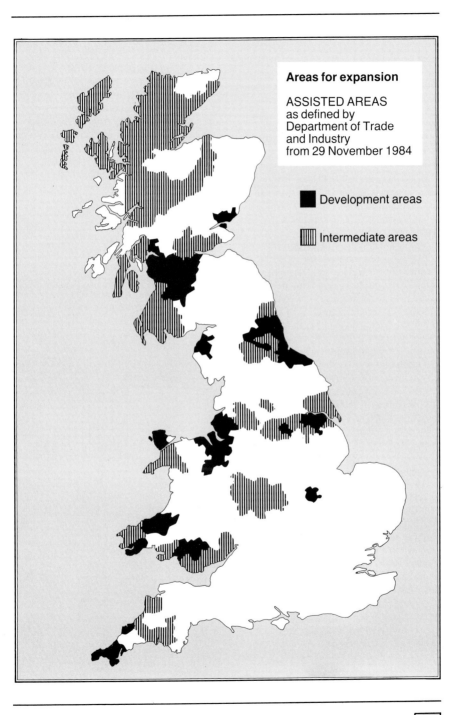

Areas for expansion

ASSISTED AREAS
as defined by
Department of Trade
and Industry
from 29 November 1984

■ Development areas

▥ Intermediate areas

Leasehold (i) – Acquiring a New Lease

Most people in business are likely to favour a modern purpose-built property, which in turn suggests leasehold, rather than freehold. Certainly, the costs of maintaining and, in many instances, converting a freehold property to suit your particular commercial requirements can be both inflated and inconvenient. The growth and development of industrial estates now means that there is a very wide variety of leasehold properties to choose from, in terms not only of size, but also of quality and location. Let us look in this section at what is involved in entering into a new lease.

The golden rule in taking on a new lease is to remember that your prospective landlord will ask for more than he expects to get. The name of the game is to negotiate. Except in very sought-after areas, a great many landlords today are having difficulty in filling their industrial units and you must not lose sight of this fact. Most property developers in the industrial sector are fairly astute, robust characters, and it is easy to find yourself pushed into accepting a lease of their property *on their terms* – not yours. The old chestnut which will be quoted at you is that they have a standard form of lease for all their property, which cannot be altered. Rubbish! Do not accept the standard wording of a lease unless it suits you to do so.

What follow are the main points which you should check out most carefully, to see whether they match up with your requirements. If they do not, ask your landlord to amend the lease accordingly. If the landlord refuses, and you know your demands are not unreasonable, then you do not want to rent the premises anyway, because your landlord is likely to be intractable throughout your relationship, which in turn will do your business no good at all.

Be prepared to negotiate on

- Cost of rent per foot. Do not simply accept the rate quoted – compare it with like premises and make sure you are not being overcharged.
- Rentalization of extras – be careful here. If you ask your landlord to put in extra fittings or facilities for you, in return for an additional rent charge, make sure you are not overcharged, as this is highly likely. Ask for a quotation in advance. The landlord shouldn't charge you more than about 10 per cent of the cost of additions and extras in the form of higher annual rent.
- Size of outside area – this is often poorly defined, particularly on industrial units.
- Number of car parking spaces. Are they really adequate for your staff and customers?
- Length of lease.
- Period between rent reviews.

- Rent-free period – particularly on a new unit, ask for this.
- Lighting, heating, carpets, office contents – make sure you know exactly what is included and what is not.
- Personal guarantee or rent deposit – most landlords will require one of these, particularly if you are a new business. You will have to accept it, but work out some sort of formula for release, so that, say, after three years' profits above a certain figure, your personal guarantee will be released and any rental deposit refunded.
- Assignment of lease. Landlords often try to incorporate very restrictive assignment clauses. Negotiate for a clause which says that assignment of the lease should not be unreasonably withheld – in the future you may have a very good reason for wanting to get out, and you do not want your hands tied.
- Sub-letting in whole *or in part* – try to make sure the lease allows for this – it could be vitally important to you in the future.
- Insurance terms – in most instances, landlords arrange insurance and then simply bill you for it. Make sure you know what the insurance cover is, that you are not being overcharged and that there are no conditions in the insurance which make the premium prohibitive. If, for example, your next-door neighbour on the estate is a firework manufacturer, you may find this adversely affects your fire insurance. These circumstances are not of your making and the landlord should pick up the additional premium – not you.
- Repair commitments – make sure you understand exactly what you are expected to do in order to maintain the building, and make sure this is in writing.
- Reinstatement of building at the end cf lease. Make sure you have a detailed written statement as to the current state of the building – if necessary supported by photographs. Do not assume that what you consider to be an improvement will necessarily be considered an improvement by the landlord. Reinstatement means exactly that. For example – you put an extra floor into your warehouse space, but whilst you may have created a two-storey building, your landlord may not want one and you could be asked to remove that floor at the end of the lease. Certainly, before undertaking any major improvement or reconstruction, as well as needing the landlord's permission, you need to make sure that the landlord will not expect the work you undertake to be undone at the end of the lease. If this is the landlord's attitude, it could make the whole exercise prohibitive.
- Service charges – you can find yourself paying a considerable sum of money for nothing. If you are on an existing estate, ask other leaseholders whether the service charges are justified in their view. If not, negotiate a lower rate.

Do check, very carefully, the user clause in the lease. It should not be too specific, in case you want to widen your area of operation or in case you want to assign the lease at a later date. Also **check planning, and landlord's title** – you should take nothing on face value. Time spent in checking every detail before signing the lease could save you thousands of pounds in the years ahead.

Taking over an existing lease

You cannot vary the terms of an existing lease, so make sure that you have read very carefully, and understand, what you are taking on. If you are taking over a lease with only a short period to run – a year or less – it may be possible to sign up on the basis of an understanding with the landlord, that once you are the leaseholder, the existing lease will be scrapped in favour of a new one on which you have already agreed terms. If this is the case, do make sure that everything is in writing – it would be all too easy for the landlord to change his mind once you have signed the lease unless there is a written agreement between you.

Premiums

If you are taking over an existing lease, you may well be asked to pay a premium. This could be for one of four reasons:

1. The lease has a value, because of the low rental currently being enjoyed until the next rent review. Before paying a premium in these circumstances, make sure you are aware of the implications of the next rent review. Subject to any specific wording in the lease, the rent will be increased to the current market rate at the time of the review. You need to evaluate approximately what that will be, and you need to satisfy yourself that the premium asked sensibly represents the value of the lower rent you will be paying before the review.

2. The lease has a value, because a previous tenant has incurred expenditure on alterations and improvements to the property. A typical example might be a small industrial unit leased originally without heating or lighting, and with offices of 500 square feet. The first tenant built, at own expense, another 1,500 square feet of offices (with the landlord's permission, of course) and installed heating and lighting in the industrial area and within the offices. None of these improvements will be reflected in the rent charged currently or at any future rent review, so you will expect to pay a premium on the assignment of the lease. But remember, if you are near the end of the lease, those improvements will revert to the landlord at that point, and any new lease negotiated will be based on the whole property, inclusive of improvements.

3. A premium may be charged for the value of the existing tenant's fixtures and fittings. It may well suit the existing tenant to leave fixtures and fittings – what you have to ask yourself is whether you want them. If you do not, they are valueless and you should not pay a premium for them – at least nothing more than a mere token, i.e. their scrap value.

4. You may be asked to pay a premium if there is an element of goodwill attached to the premises. This is not 'goodwill' as in the purchase of a business – that is a completely separate issue. If, for example, you are buying restaurant premises, which you intend to run as, say, a cocktail bar, it can be argued that you will receive a certain degree of trade, based on the fact that the public is used to visiting the premises. Be careful here – if the former business has not been well run it could be a positive disadvantage to inherit its reputation. Be wary of premiums and always have them independently valued by your own adviser.

Reverse premiums

In certain circumstances a current leaseholder may be prepared to pay you for taking over his obligation. This is likely to occur where rental charges in a particular area have dropped and the leaseholder is committed to a lease with a fixed high rental. In these circumstances, make sure that any payment you receive is directly related to the amount of additional rental you are likely to have to pay up to the end of the lease. Most standard rent-review clauses only allow rent to go up – *not down*. So, never assume that a high level of rent will be lowered when the next review comes round.

Dilapidations

Do be very careful, if taking over an existing lease, that you are well aware of the dilapidation position at the end of the lease. Has the existing tenant looked after the property, or will you find yourself in the position of having to foot a large repair bill at the end of the lease to put the premises back into the condition they were at the start of the lease?

Do bear in mind that you have the automatic right to a renewal of your lease at the end of the term, and on that renewal, the landlord can only charge a fair rent. Your right to a new lease is set out in the Landlord and Tenant Act of 1954, a copy of which can be obtained from your local HMSO. Remember too what applies to any lease – all improvements you make to the property revert to the landlord at the end of the lease, and the landlord can actually charge you additional rent on those improvements, when granting a new lease.

Granting your own lease

If you have industrial premises which you wish to let, again it is important to refer you to the Landlord and Tenant Act of 1954, which will set out your precise legal position. There are two major factors to consider:

- ◆ If you own a freehold which is subject to a mortgage you will most likely have to obtain the permission of the lender, before letting any part of it.
- ◆ If you are intending to sub-let all or part of a leasehold, you must have your landlord's consent.

Loophole

It may be possible to overcome any arbitrary conditions placed on you by your mortgage company or landlord, by charging for monthly or weekly storage facilities, rather than rent. You would need to be sub-letting to someone you know well in these circumstances, since they could take advantage of such an unofficial agreement.

Take care

Do take particular care in vetting your would-be tenant. If your tenant gets into difficulties, it will take between six and nine months to actually get them out of your premises. Before signing a lease, insist on seeing a record of profitability for the tenant's business. If the tenant has none, ask for a personal guarantee, but make sure that guarantee is worth something. If your tenant goes bust while renting your property, you will lose rental revenue, your property is bound to deteriorate and you will waste a great deal of time, energy and possibly money getting the tenant out.

Comfort is probably the keyword when describing the main advantage to your business of purchasing a freehold. Certainly, any business with capital available should look seriously at the merits of investing in its trading property. To many companies, the property they own represents perhaps their most valuable asset, and it does act as a protection against escalating rentals. However, it has to be said, particularly with a new business, it is unlikely that the first priority is going to be the purchase of a freehold property. What capital is available in a business start-up is most likely working capital – needed for funding production and sales, for staff training, selling aids and the myriad other costs likely to be incurred in the early days.

A great deal also depends upon the nature of your business. Investigation shows, for example, that the average solicitor's office is more than likely a freehold owned by the partners, and this would be true of many professional partnerships. The reason for this is that whilst the partnership may grow, the business is essentially stable. The addition of a few partitions, or possibly a small extension, will more than cater for the firm's expansion requirements over, say, a fifteen- or even twenty-year period. If, however, you are in a more volatile trade, particularly manufacturing, it is difficult to see how you can possibly predict your requirements for premises in ten or fifteen years' time. Whilst buying a freehold property may be a sound investment, chances are that the building will need substantial alteration and conversion in order to cater for the needs of your growing business. Whilst property values may escalate, it may not be possible to amortize your costs fully, unless you are able to remain in the premises for a considerable number of years.

In certain circumstances, however, the need for a long-term stay does not apply, particularly where the property involves a fundamental change of use. Supposing, for example, you purchased a high-street house in a developing town, and obtained a full licence and planning permission to open a restaurant. Instantly, the property would acquire a considerable premium in value, without any attempt on your part actually to run the restaurant. In these circumstances, you would probably make far more money by selling on the property to a would-be restaurateur than actually running a restaurant yourself! A note of caution here, though – you have to ask yourself whether you are in *business*, or in *the property business*. Do not confuse the two.

Buying a freehold – dos and don'ts

DO take as much care with the purchase of your industrial freehold as you would with the purchase of your own home – only more so, there are far more potential problems to consider. DO get a copy of *Planning Permission: A Guide for Industry*, which you will find an invaluable help. It is available from HMSO. DON'T ever buy a residential property in the vague hope that planning permission will be granted for your business activities. Whilst planning authorities may look favourably at your application for a change to business use, their decisions are notoriously fickle – there are too many personalities involved to make any decision absolutely predictable. DON'T start trading in your premises without planning permission, or change of use. Whilst these permissions can be granted retrospectively, you will make an enemy of the planning authorities for life, which is not to be recommended. DO consider the size and capacity of the property very carefully. It may well be worth while seeking professional advice on how to adapt your premises to be as space-saving as possible. DON'T attempt to purchase the property without a thorough survey. Remember industrial premises often have special requirements, which the surveyor should know, such as the need for load-bearing floors and additional power. DON'T buy a

more expensive building than you can afford. Crippling your business by heavy mortgage repayments is short-sighted. Whilst the acquisition of a property may in itself be a sound investment, if your business crashes from its inability to meet its obligations, not only will you have lost your business, but its failure is likely to have an adverse effect on the value of your property.

Golden rule

As already stated, it is important to recognize that if you are buying freehold industrial or commercial premises, by inference you are probably making a long-term investment. This being the case, you do not want to upset the local authorities, nor infringe the various industrial regulations. Our next subject – Health and Safety at Work – offers advice on this, but

before committing yourself to the purchase, do discuss the property with your local authoritiy Planning Department, the Building Control Department and the Environmental Health Department. Explain exactly what you intend doing with the premises – particularly if substantial alterations are taking place – and seek their advice at the earliest possible stage. They can be very helpful if they are consulted but they can be very obstructive if their authority is ignored.

If you are looking for an existing industrial freehold purchase, it is well worth while contacting the Department of Industry – Headquarters: Millbank Tower, Millbank, London SW1P 4QU (telephone 01-211 6486) – who should be able to give you a list of suitable locations for expansion and development.

Health and Safety at Work

Whether you have your own freehold or are leasing your property, under the terms of the Health and Safety at Work Act, 1974, you have certain obligations to protect yourself, your staff, your customers and your suppliers. If you are likely to be employing a fairly large number of people and anticipate a largish commercial concern, then it would be helpful to purchase a copy of *Croner's Health and Safety at Work*, published by Croner Publications Limited, 173 Kingston Road, New Malden, Surrey KT3 3SS (telephone 01 942 8966). Croner's reference book deals with all aspects of the Health and Safety at Work Act and is a very useful guide to have in your office.

Inspectors

There are two types of inspector – local authority inspectors and fire authority inspectors.

Local authority inspectors

Under the terms of the Act, local authority inspectors are concerned with premises where the main activities are:

◆ The sale or storage or goods for retail or wholesale distribution.

◆ Office activities.

◆ Catering services.

◆ Provision of residential accommodation.

◆ Consumer services provided in shop premises.

◆ Dry cleaning in coin-operated units in laundrettes.

◆ The keeping of wild animals for exhibition to the public (this does not apply to circuses).

Fire authority inspectors

The fire authority requires that a place of work should have a fire certificate, and in order for your business to get a fire certificate, the premises need to be inspected. The fire authority will wish to see that there is adequate provision for a means of escape in case of fire, and the necessary amount of fire-fighting equipment. The fire authority inspectors will advise you if these facilities are inadequate, tell you how they can be put right and then re-inspect the premises when you have carried out the necessary work. You normally will be given a time limit, by which the work must be completed.

Power of inspectors

The power of local authority and fire inspectors is considerable. They have the right to enter your premises in normal working hours, without your permission. If they have reason to believe you may challenge their right, they may seek the help of the police to ensure entry. They may take samples, photographs, inspect books, documents and even demand that part of your premises be closed down while they make their inspection, if they feel it is necessary. In most instances, where any unintended contravention of the Health and Safety Act has been committed, the inspector is likely simply to point out the problem and make an appointment to re-inspect when the necessary steps have been taken to put matters right. However, in some circumstances heavier tactics are needed:

Cases of imminent danger

If an inspector believes that an article or substance, which has been found on the premises, is of imminent serious danger to the public, the inspector may render it harmless, either by destruction or by removing it from the premises. It is then necessary for the inspector to make a report as to why this step has been taken.

Improvement and prohibition notices

If an inspector believes that his advice will not be taken, he may issue an improvement notice, which demands that whatever contravention is taking place must cease within a specific period of time – usually twenty-one days. If the inspector feels that some activity is going on which must be stopped and believes that it will continue in his absence, the inspector will issue what is known as a *prohibition notice*, which demands that the activity ceases immediately.

These notices are normally served on the responsible person in charge of the premises at the time. If the requirements of the local authority are ignored, then the health and safety inspector will decide whether or not to institute proceedings against the offender.

A breach of the Health and Safety Act is a criminal offence and employees, as well as employers, may be liable for prosecution.

Fines can be as high as £2,000 and, of course, if the activities continue after prosecution, then the offenders are in breach of court, which will have further consequences.

It is sensible to highlight the implications of ignoring the Health and Safety Act, but at the same time it is important to stress that the local authorities are not ogres, and with current unemployment statistics, they are advised by government to do all they can to encourage local industry. They are not trying to look at ways of closing down your business and a great deal of the advice they give you is of real practical help – from experts. If they find that your electrical wiring is inadequate, putting it right may not only save you from a factory fire, it could also save you from your insurance company refuting your claim for compensation, on the grounds of your own negligence. If you are in the catering business, advice on hygiene might save your customers from salmonella poisoning and a resultant reputation from which your business might never recover.

Health and Safety Act – employees

Your obligations to your employees, under the terms of the Health and Safety Act, 1974, are dealt with under our section entitled Employing People. However, in this section on Premises it is important to remind you of the need to provide adequate facilities for your staff, which is not simply the provision of a male and female loo! As well as the basic requirement of tea and coffee facilities, and an adequate first aid kit, you should also look at areas such as rest rooms, lock-up facilities for personal possessions and possibly a crèche for parents of young children. Advice on all these facilities is obtainable from your local authority.

The Importance of Forecasting

Being in business is all about money. Yes, you need a good commercial idea, yes, you need the qualifications to put that idea into practice, and yes, you need to be sure that there is a market for what you have to offer. However, these ingredients, although vital, are only part of the story. Indeed, however ingenious your business idea, it is as likely as not to fall flat on its face unless you do your sums properly, and this involves *detailed financial forecasting.*

To run a business successfully, you need to have a proper understanding of the financial implications. This means establishing the viability of your business idea. This, clearly, is an exercise which is essential in setting up any new business. It also provides the structure within which an up-and-running business should operate. Forecasts must be worked out annually, be constantly updated and must form the basis against which any major decision is made – whether it be an expansion programme, new capital expenditure or some form of diversification. It is a discipline which must be adhered to, whatever the size of your operation.

You always have to produce a forecast if you are going to borrow money, since all financial institutions will require a detailed analysis of how you see your business developing. However, it is just as important to go through a viability study if it is your own money you are using. Forget for a moment family, partners, bank managers, investment trusts and government grants. If your business goes wrong, their suffering will be only secondary. It is *you* who will bear the brunt of failure, and above all, therefore, it is vital that *you* satisfy *yourself* that your project is viable.

Whatever your type of business, the basic requirements are the same. Initially, it is a question of establishing a forecast of your anticipated sales and the costs involved in obtaining those sales – it is as simple as that.

In the next three sections of the book (pages 70 – 75) you will find, laid out, guidelines on how to go about producing your own forecasts. There are a multiplicity of words to describe the process – 'business planning, five year budget, resource forecasting' – the list is endless. What you have to do is to undertake three separate exercises. You need to produce a **profit plan**, a **cash forecast** and a **balance sheet forecast**.

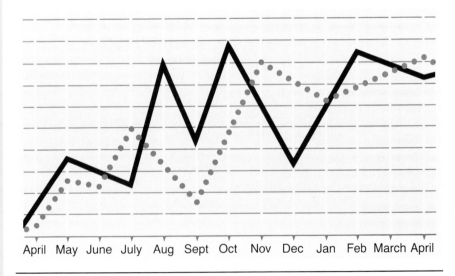

April May June July Aug Sept Oct Nov Dec Jan Feb March April

Profit plan

A profit plan represents your careful assessment of what you reasonably believe you will achieve, setting natural caution against natural optimism. Both words are important: *profit* is the reason you are in business, *plan* means just that – not an optimistic target, not the minimum achievable if virtually everything goes wrong, not a set of figures pulled out of the air, nor indeed what you think the bank manager wants to hear. Realism is what you are aiming for and this can only be achieved by a great deal of thought and by a careful study of what is going on in your particular market.

Cash forecast

A cash forecast is the second stage of the operation. Having satisfied yourself of the profitability of your project, via the profit plan, you must translate your findings into a cash requirement. Profits are all very well, but they can be expensive to achieve, and a cash forecast will tell you how much money you need, and when.

Balance sheet forecast

From the information set out in the profit plan and the assumptions made in preparing the cash forecast, you will be able to produce a balance sheet forecast. This will give you a projection of your assets and liabilities and thus highlight the shape of your business in the months that lie ahead. The balance sheet forecast will show you whether you have a healthy business or not. It will also determine the type of borrowing you need – whether you are looking for a short-term overdraft or a long-term investment.

Your forecasts need to be calculated on a monthly basis and you should plan ahead as far as possible – one, two or even three years are reasonable, depending on your circumstances. Less than a year is not enough, more than three years is likely to produce more fiction than fact. Certainly, if you are starting a new business, a year is the very most you can expect to forecast.

Read on for detailed information on forecasting.

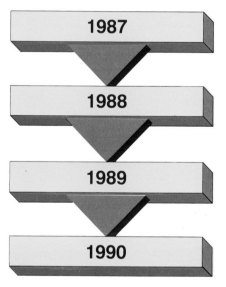

PROFIT PLAN	May	June	July	Aug	Sept
Sales					
Direct costs:					
labour (direct)					
materials/sub-contract					
transport					
Gross profit					
Staff costs:					
Salaries, wages (indirect)					
Travel expenses					
Car running					
Property costs:					
Rent					
Rates					
Light & heat					
Repairs & maintenance					
Admin. & Sales Expenses:					
Printing & stationery					
Telephone & post					
Legal & professional					
Insurance					
Advertising & promotion					
General expenses					
Finance costs:					
Interest & bank charges					
Depreciation					
Bad debts					
Total overheads					
Profit (Loss) Month					
Cumulative					
for Year					

Preparing a profit plan

1 Draw up a chart with twelve monthly columns for your year's trading, starting with the month in which you will begin trading, or from which you want the calculation to be made. Add an additional column for the annual total.

2 The first figure you put down, on a month-by-month basis, is **sales**, remembering to reflect the gradual build-up of trade which you may be expecting, and seasonal trends where they apply. Sales should be shown net of VAT. Particularly with a new business, where you don't have last year's figures to act as a guide, it is appreciated that monthly sales can be very difficult to gauge. However, you must be confident of a certain level of sales or you would not be attempting to go into business at all. Do remember that with a new business, and in many cases a new product or service, it does take a while for customers to make decisions. Allow plenty of time to reach your sales target.

3 You should then calculate your **direct costs** on those sales, again net of VAT. If you are manufacturing a product, your direct costs will be raw materials, components and productive labour. If you are merely buying and selling a product, your direct costs will be the purchase price of your product. In either case, you may need to recognize that transport is a substantial cost which therefore should be identified separately and dealt with as a direct cost. If you are providing a service, that element of your labour which is quite clearly productive labour should be shown as a direct cost. The difference between your sales figure and your direct costs is the gross profit.

4 The **gross profit** is a very important benchmark in any business. The gross profit margin, of course, can vary enormously from business to business, but suffice to say that you will generally sleep at night if your gross profit always exceeds your total overheads. An insurance broker may well need to have a turnover of £40,000 per month to earn £5,000 in

commission. By contrast, a retail fashion shop may well turn over as little as £7,000 to earn the same £5,000 gross profit. This does not mean, however, that it is better to be in retail fashion than insurance, for the overheads of running a shop and the capital employed are substantially greater!

5 This brings us to **overheads**. There are several pointers you need to watch in calculating your overheads on a month-by-month basis. First of all, do make sure you include *everything*. It is so easy to miss out items only to receive a nasty shock later on. Remember, too, that your overheads should be recorded, not as they fall due for payment, but spread over the period in which they are relevant. Let us take a simple example. Your rent is paid quarterly, but you should show the rent allocation monthly, so that the profit calculation for each month can be assessed with its full share of overheads. By contrast, of course, some overheads may be affected by the amount of sales you generate. An example of this could be salesmen's commission where, obviously, as your sales climb, so that element of your staff costs directly reflects this. We have listed on this page the typical business overheads but do not assume that these are all the overheads that exist. You may have additional ones relevant to your particular business.

Note the reference to **indirect wages**. As mentioned in stage 3 above, the element of your labour costs which directly involves the manufacturing process should be shown as a cost of sales, hence the term **direct labour**. However, those members of staff who are involved in general duties – your accountant, secretary, order processors, warehouse staff – should be shown as a fixed overhead, and they are known as **indirect labour**. Sometimes, particularly in a service industry, it is difficult to differentiate between the two, and you may have a single member of staff providing both direct and indirect labour – in which case the total wages of the individual should be split in appropriate proportions.

As with rent, your legal fees, your audit fee, your bank interest, insurance premiums, light, heat, telephone and stationery should all be calculated on a monthly basis, regardless of when these items fall due for payment. Sometimes there will be a considerable time lag between charging up the overhead and actually paying for it. Dealing with advertising and promotional costs is not easy. The most conservative accounting treatment is to write off this particular expenditure as and when it is incurred, with no attempt to compare promotional cost with the revenue it generates. Although prudent, this method of accounting can produce misleading losses if you are operating a business with high promotional expenditure – such as mail order. If you can apportion promotional and advertising expenditure to the month in which sales will be generated, this obviously would be preferable. Alternatively an annual or a season's total budget can be spread evenly over the period.

6 Net Profit/Loss. Having carefully listed the overheads for each month, you should deduct these from the gross profit, and the figure left is your **net profit** – or if the overheads are higher than your gross profit, then your **net loss**.

The profit plan calculation will show you whether you have a profitable business, and at what stage the profit will be generated. Obviously, in the early months of a new business, your overheads are going to be vastly higher than the gross profit. Some businesses take a year, or even two, to move into profit, but as long as the period of loss is expected and catered for, it does not represent a problem. Problems arise where instant profitability is expected and does not happen.

Consistent losses can, of course, prove the non-viability of your business. If your figures show a consistent loss, you have to decide whether it is because your overheads are too high, or your gross profit is too low. Are you being too cautious in your sales projections? Are you intending to charge enough for your product or service? If you are buying-in a product or components, are you getting them from the cheapest possible source? Looking at your overheads, can a cut-back in wages and the introduction of, say, a computer, reduce the overheads sufficiently? Perhaps your premises are too expensive, or perhaps your whole project is too ambitious and you should be thinking smaller – or perhaps twice as big! Realistically juggle around with the figures. Never manipulate the figures simply so that they look right. You must believe them. Hopefully you can produce a profit plan which makes sense. If you cannot, sorry – but scrap the whole concept.

Cash Forecast

CASH PLAN	May	June	July	Aug	Sept
Sales – credit %					
cash %					
Other receipts					
Total receipts					
Materials – credit %					
cash %					
Direct labour 70% wages					
30%PAYE/NI					
Indirect labour 70% wages					
30% PAYE/NI					
Transport					
Travel expenses					
Car running					
Rent					
Rates					
Light & heat					
Repairs & maintenance					
Printing & stationery					
Telephone & post					
Legal & professional					
Insurance					
General expenses					
Advertising & promotion					
Interest & bank charges					
Capital expenditure					
VAT payments					
Other payments					
Total payments					
Net cash out =					
Net cash in =					
BALANCE =					

As with the profit plan, the framework of this page shows you how your cash forecast should be set out. With the estimating done, the cash forecast is something that should flow naturally from the assumptions you have made in the profit plan. Basically, it is a question of taking each item of income and expenditure itemized in the profit plan, and judging which month the income will actually come into the bank and in which month payments will have to be made. **Please note that, unlike in the profit plan, all figures should be shown inclusive of VAT, since you are looking at the total cash in or cash out at any one time.** Here are some guidelines.

1 *Sales*
Depending on your type of business, your sales will be on a cash basis, a credit basis, or a mix of the two. If you deal purely in cash sales, then your figure for sales will be the same as the profit plan with the addition of VAT. If you are offering credit terms, then you must judge in which month you will actually receive payment.

2 *Other receipts*
In this column you should calculate, monthly, any income you receive which is not actually a sale. This could include VAT refunds, rent from sub-letting part of your property, commissions, disposal of assets – every item of money received must be recorded here.

3 *Total receipts*
Your sales figure, plus all other cash receipts during the month, should be totalled to show your expected total bankings for each month.

4 *Direct costs*
Direct costs in the form of material and sub-contracted items should be split between those purchases which are the subject of credit terms from your suppliers and those for which you have to pay cash. What you need to record is the actual **cash out** position, month by month. So far as labour is concerned, this obviously falls due for payment in the month in which i

is generated, but do not forget the PAYE and National Insurance contributions. These have to be deducted from staff wages and salaries, but they are not remitted to the Collector of Taxes until the following month. This effectively spreads about 30 per cent of the gross payroll into the following month.

5 *General overheads*
Your overheads will look vastly different when apportioned in cash-flow terms. As with direct labour, 70 per cent of indirect wages and salaries should be entered in the month in which they are earned, and 30 per cent spread over into the following month. Some overheads, however, will show an even greater variance. Suppose, for example, you are leasing a van. Three months' rental will most probably be required in advance, and then there is a full year's insurance premium to be paid, and the licence fee. All this expenditure will be made in the first month and therefore will show that month in complete variance with the carefully apportioned twelve instalments you have calculated your van will cost you in a profit sense. Working in your favour, of course, will be items such as bank interest and legal and professional charges, which, although entered on your profit plan on a monthly basis, will in fact tend to accumulate on the cash forecast, being paid in arrears.

6 *Capital expenditure*
In the cash forecast you will need an additional heading for capital expenditure, which in the first few months of a new business, or during a period of expansion, is probably going to be very high. As with every other item in the cash forecast, only reflect these items of capital expenditure in the month in which they are actually paid. Remember to include VAT. If you have any regular loan repayments, these can be recorded under the heading of capital expenditure.

7 *VAT*
As already stressed, unlike the profit plan, the cash forecast must include VAT on all items of income and expenditure. As a completely separate exercise, you then have to calculate when you will be required to pay over VAT on a quarterly basis and when, if appropriate, you are likely to receive a VAT refund. If you are starting a new business, or are involving your existing business in an expansion programme, it may well be that you are indulging in a fairly large capital outlay. This being the case, you may find that you will be receiving a VAT refund, since the amount of VAT you are paying on your capital items and routine purchases exceeds the VAT you are receiving on your sales. Either way, plot your VAT position carefully and show any expected refunds under **other receipts**, with the regular quarterly payments being recorded under the specific VAT heading.

The mechanics of cash flow

If you are starting a new business, you will find that your cash forecast probably needs to begin several weeks, if not months, before your profit plan, and initially the cash forecast will all go one way – OUT – more than likely in the accumulation of an overdraft. Gradually, however, once you open the doors for business, you will start feeding in sales and, as the year develops, you will see your bank balance swoop up and down, reflecting the peaks and troughs. In a cash forecast, you are not concerned with profit. It is purely the money in the bank in which you are interested. Having totalled your receipts, you similarly total your outgoings as they fall each month and you will end up with either **net cash in** or **net cash out** for each month. This, added to or subtracted from your opening cash balance (or overdraft), will give your new end-of-month bank balance. The size and trend of this end-of-month balance figure will indicate your working capital requirement.

On the face of it, the cash forecast may seem like an awfully tedious exercise, but it really is vital. So many potentially good businesses fail through being under-capitalized, and this occurs simply because they have not appreciated the time it takes to move into profitability and produce positive cash flow. In an expanding business, a continuing build-up of stock, debtors and capital investment may well produce an adverse cash flow for some months or even years, despite the fact that profits are being produced. If this situation is not catered for, the result can be quite disastrous. A cash forecast tells you how much money you need and when you need it. It is a truly vital business tool.

The Balance Sheet Forecast

The balance sheet demonstrates the shape of your business, showing whether it is healthy or sick, and how much capital is employed. It will also assist you in analysing whether your financial requirements are short- or long-term.

Below you can see typical headings which go to make up a basic balance sheet, together with coded letters to show the relationship between the various totals. Balance sheets should be prepared monthly by every trading company. New and established businesses, having prepared a profit plan and cash forecast, should also produce a balance sheet forecast, based on exactly the same figures and assumptions. Let us look at the preparation of the balance sheet forecast.

Opening position

A balance sheet forecast has to have an opening position. You will need thirteen columns, spread across the sheet, as before, but the first column is for the opening position – a summary of your present assets, liabilities and funding at the start of this new financial year.

If you are just starting your business, there may be little to enter in this first column – '£10,000, Cash in the bank', and '£10,000, Loan from father', for instance. You might have gone one stage further, before commencing to trade – purchased some machinery, bought a car on HP, put £3,000 into the bank yourself – all this needs to be reflected in the first column before you can start to introduce all of the movements over the

next twelve months from your profit plan and cash forecast.

Fixed assets

Fixed assets are those items which are necessary, on a permanent basis, in order for your business to function. They include goodwill you have purchased, your premises, your vehicles and equipment, and fixtures and fittings. These assets all appear on a balance at their original cost, less depreciation written off to date. As a guide, typical depreciation rates are:

Goodwill – 10 years or 10 per cent per annum
Freehold property – 50 years or 2 per cent per annum
Leasehold expenditure – the unexpired period of the lease
Plant and equipment – 10 years or 10 per cent per annum
Motor cars – 4/5 years or 20/25 per cent per annum

In preparing your profit plan and cash forecast you will already have worked out your asset depreciation and your capital expenditure programme, so you can now spread your opening figures through into each of the next twelve months' columns – reducing each subsequent month's asset items for that month's depreciation and incorporating new assets as you plan to purchase them.

If at any stage you want to introduce an independent valuation of your property into

BALANCE SHEET

Fixed assets
  Goodwill
  Property   A

Current assets
  Stock
  Debtors
  Cash in the bank   B

Current liabilities
  Bank overdrafts
  Tax
  Creditors   C

Working capital   B – C
Total capital employed   A + (B – C)

Funded by
  Proprietor's capital
  Accumulated profits
  Loans
  Hire purchase   SAME TOTAL

your balance sheet, the property figure is increased in the fixed asset section of the balance sheet and the surplus is shown as a re-valuation reserve in the funding section, together with the accumulated profit. But don't forget – you will need to increase the amount of annual depreciation.

Current assets

In making your trading projections, you will have identified your stock purchase requirements (the direct material costs in the profit and loss account). You need to assess how much stock you need to buy initially, and how much you then need to hold to support your forecast growth or sales. These figures can be spread across the twelve months of the balance sheet forecast.

The debtor forecasts are easy – you have, again, already done the work. In making your cash forecast, you may have assumed that all of your customers will take two months' credit. If that was your assumption, your forecast debtor figures will always equal the last two months' sales, plus VAT.

Cash in the bank – comes straight from your cash forecast.

Current liabilities

Overdraft – again, straight from the cash forecast.

If you are in a start-up phase, you can provide for a tax liability to build up from the time your profit plan starts to show a cumulative profit. If you are already trading, tax on current profits will be added to the opening liability. Any anticipated payment of tax will have been entered in the cash forecast under "other payments". So, again, you have the information to enter in the tax liability figures to the monthly balance sheet forecast.

Creditors – this will be a balance figure, which we explain below.

Funding figures

Proprietor's capital – that is what you, or your partners and shareholders, have put into the business on a permanent basis. The figure stays constant through the twelve months' forecast, unless you have assumed further cash subscriptions in your forecast.

Accumulated profits – the opening figure, if there is one, plus the monthly profit on the profit

plan. Cumulative losses need to be entered in brackets and deducted from the total funds.

The figures for loans and hire purchase will be made up from any opening position, plus new money, less repayments – as anticipated within the cash forecast.

The balancing act

If you have carefully completed every relevant line on the balance sheet forecast, apart from the totals, you will be left with one, incomplete – **creditors**. If you have stuck rigidly to all of the assumptions incorporated into the profit plan and cash forecast, you may now take a short cut and enter creditors as a balancing figure. (Add together capital, profits, loans and HP in the funding section – that total equals total capital employed i.e. $A + (B - C)$. Add fixed assets to find A, and current assets to find B. This then enables you to work out C. Insert each month a creditors figure so that the current liabilities add up to C.) Creditors in fact consist of all the amounts you owe for purchases and expenses, but rolled into this figure will be accruals created by estimating expenses in advance of payments, carrying forward rent in advance, providing for VAT, etc. You can work out the figures in detail, but "the balancing act" saves time.

Reading the balance sheet

A few points to look for:
◆ Profit compared to total capital employed – less than 15 per cent might raise a query on viability.
◆ Working capital – very small net figure, or even a negative figure suggests a strain on resources. Is the overdraft being used to support fixed assets or losses – do you have sufficient facility to cope with expansion – do you need more permanent capital?
◆ Stock – is it too high in relation to sales – can you afford it?
◆ Debtors – are they too high in relation to sales – or in relation to creditors?
◆ Creditors – are they too low – can you negotiate longer credit terms with suppliers?

Having prepared your balance sheet forecast, take it to your accountant or bank manager and discuss its implications with them. It provides an invaluable picture of how your business looks today, and the shape of things to come.

Looking for Finance

Borrowing money is easy. If you have some of your own, it is a great help, but even if you have none at all, it is still possible to borrow sufficient sums to start your own venture – *provided it is truly viable.* Most people, at some stage in their life, dream of starting their own business, but few actually put these dreams into practice. Ask why not and they will tell you that they cannot start their own business because they do not have sufficient money. The same excuse is often given as a reason why an existing business cannot be expanded. Neither argument stacks up. Money is *not* the major stumbling block along the path to success. If your project is sound, and you can demonstrate that you know what you are doing, then you will *always* succeed in obtaining the necessary finance.

Let us consider your position regarding the financing of your business.

If you have money

It may be that you have surplus capital – an inheritance, a nest egg for a rainy day, savings or redundancy money. It may be that you have some personal assets – for example, you are able to borrow money against the shares you hold, or take out a first or second mortgage on your house. It may be that your business partner has money or that you have a relative or friend who is willing to back you.

How much of these existing personal resources you are prepared to commit to your venture depends very largely on attitude of mind. Whilst stressing the need for you to be convinced of the viability of your business idea, you do not have to demonstrate this by stretching your personal finances to such an extent that you are in a perpetual state of panic. For example, supposing your project needs £40,000 to launch and run successfully. You may well be able to raise £20,000 by a second mortgage on your house, in which case your bankers might be prepared to loan you a further £20,000 against a

personal guarantee. The advantage of this situation, of course, is that the business remains yours and yours alone – all the profits are yours, but so are all the risks and therefore all the worries. There is little point owning 100 per cent of a business in which the proprietor is heading for a major nervous breakdown. The message here is that just because you have the ability to raise the money personally, it does not mean that you should necessarily do so – it may well be worth while involving a partner, or a financial institution, to share the risk.

If you have no money

If you have no money, then obviously you are going to have to rely entirely on outside finance. It is possible, these days, to find funding for your project without having any money of your own. There are a number of schemes available, perhaps the best of which is the Government Guaranteed Loan Scheme – more details in a later section. It is true to say, however, that in order to persuade a banker or institution to lend you

BUY

SINCE PION

THE ART OF MA

BUY-OUTS, WE'V

OVER 600 CC

START FROM A

FINANCIAL

BASE

A WEALTH OF
EXPERIENCE

100 per cent of the finance required, your approach is all-important. You need to be able to demonstrate that you are highly skilled and experienced in the trade of your choice, and your presentation of the facts and figures surrounding your project will need to be very professional. In other words you are going to have to work an awful lot harder than the guy with money!

The alternative, of course, if you have no money, is to team up with someone who has. Thanks to the Business Expansion Scheme, there are tremendous advantages these days to anyone investing money in a new business, and if you have the right backer, it can be an extremely rewarding relationship. After all, a person who has cash usually has considerable experience in how to acquire it, and you may also benefit enormously from the backer's advice as well as money. The problem, of course, comes with striking the right balance in a relationship. Ideally you want a backer who will not interfere with the day-to-day running of your business, but who will take an interest in the business and share in your personal sense of pride and achievement.

A guide to outside finance

These are the main options to you for the financing of your business.

- ◆ Investment by an individual, either in the form of capital or a loan.
- ◆ Institutional investment, from organizations such as Investors in Industry (3i) – again, either by way of capital or loan facilities, or combination of the two.
- ◆ Bank loans and overdrafts.
- ◆ Grants, loans and assistance from government or official sources – organizations such as CoSira, the Department of Industry and local authorities
- ◆ Payment of the Enterprise Allowance for up to a year – a scheme designed to help unemployed people start their own business.
- ◆ Hire purchase or leasing of plant, equipment and vehicles.
- ◆ Mortgage or rental of property, rather than outright purchase.
- ◆ Factoring of debts and invoice discounting.
- ◆ Loans against endowment and pension policies.
- ◆ Loans from suppliers within specialist industries.

Any of the above categories of financing may be suitable for you and your business – more likely a combination of several. Remember, whether you are starting out in business, or looking at ways of financing an existing business, every business decision has a financial implication. Finding the right type of finance for your particular business is, without doubt, the difference between make and break. Read on for a detailed look at the various types of finance available.

FINANCE

The Banks

Traditionally, banks are the places to which one goes to deal in money, and certainly, for most individuals – whether business people or not – an ordinary high-street bank seems the natural place to start looking for finance. This being the case, you could do worse than follow your natural instincts.

Not only are banks in the business of lending money, but they are also an invaluable source of information when it comes to looking at the other various options available for funding any part of your business operation.

It is often said of banks that if you don't need their help, they want to give it, and when you really need them, they don't want to know. This is most certainly true, but only if you approach your bank in the wrong way. As with everything in this life, you cannot expect something for nothing. A bank is going to be very susceptible to lending you money if you can demonstrate that you are prepared to put some of your own personal funds into your venture. The bank will take the view that if you are prepared to risk your money then it is probably a safe bet for them to risk theirs. If you have no money to invest then you have to demonstrate in other ways that you have something to give – expertise, hard work, determination, a well-thought-out plan. It has to be remembered that a bank's first duty is to protect its customers' funds. Whilst, of course, banks do lose millions of pounds a year on advances which go wrong, they must be relatively certain that any venture they support has a good chance of success.

Another popular misconception in approaching a bank is the assumption that banks will provide permanent capital for a new business. This is not the function of a bank. A bank's job is really twofold:

a   to support your day-to-day trading, usually by means of an overdraft facility, and

b   to loan you long-term money for a specific project, such as the purchase of a property, plant or equipment.

Overdrafts

For the new small business, the most common form of funding is an overdraft facility. The main advantage of an overdraft is that, unlike a fixed loan, your borrowing will fluctuate according to the requirements of your business. Interest is usually calculated at between 2 and 3 per cent over base rate, so it is not cheap, but at least you are not borrowing any more money than you need at any one time. The disadvantage of an overdraft facility is that it is rather insecure – technically, repayable on demand. Normally, facilities are granted for a twelve-month period and are subject to review. A poor year's trading or a new branch manager can make review time somewhat nerve-wracking. However, assuming you can convince your bank that your business is healthy, no bank manager is going to alter seriously the basis of your borrowing to the extent that it will put you out of business. If you are going through a tight period, if profits have taken a dip, a short-sighted manager could make life difficult for you, though.

Loans

By contrast, a bank loan is far more secure. You agree with your bank to borrow, say, £20,000 over a five-year period, repayable by monthly instalment. Nothing – flood, famine nor pestilence – will change that agreement – it is the subject of a contract between you and your bank, provided, of course, you keep up the repayments! As already indicated, bank loans are normally granted for a specific purpose. You might well find, in the establishment or expansion of your business, that your bank offers a mix of facilities – a bank loan to finance the purchase of equipment and an overdraft to cope with your day-to-day trading

It is very difficult to summarize what you can expect a bank to offer you, since every case is different. However, if you or your partner are putting money into the business, a bank usually will be prepared to match it by lending you a similar amount. In exchange, the bank will almost certainly require a charge on the assets of the business and your personal guarantee. Sometimes you will be asked to support your guarantee by a charge on your personal assets – i.e. a second mortgage on your house, or whatever. Try and avoid this.

Government Guaranteed Loan Scheme

New banking horizons have been opening up in the last few years. The most significant is the Government Guaranteed Loan Scheme. This scheme is available to proprietors of new or existing small businesses. It works like this. If you go to your bank with a proposal to borrow, shall we say, £50,000, the bank's normal reaction will be to ask how much of this £50,000 you can raise yourself and what sort of security you can give to support the loan. In the past, if your answer to those questions was negative, you were politely shown the door. However, under the terms of the Guaranteed Loan Scheme, the government in effect provides the bank with security by guaranteeing 70 per cent of the loan, provided the bank is prepared to risk the other 30 per cent. Under this scheme, up to £75,000 can be guaranteed, although much smaller sums of a few thousand equally qualify. You will find that interest rates for borrowing under the scheme tend to be high, and there is a premium of $2\frac{1}{2}$ per cent payable on the amount guaranteed.

Thus described, and in spite of the high borrowing cost, the Guaranteed Loan Scheme seems a gift from the gods, but you will have to work hard to persuade your bank manager to put you forward for the scheme. Again, it comes down to presenting a viable proposition and convincing your bank manager that you have the necessary skill and experience to

carry through your proposal to a profitable conclusion.

Selecting your bank

When it comes to selecting an appropriate bank, do not be afraid to shop around. If your borrowing requirement is small, you probably would do best to go to your own local bank manager – who knows you and, if you are an existing account customer, is almost certain to grant a modest request for finance. However, if your borrowing requirement is large, you would be recommended to go to a major branch. The larger the branch, the larger the manager's personal discretion when it comes to the amount of money which he is authorised to lend. By far the best way to sell your project is to sell to the man who is going to make the decision. If the bank manager cannot make the decision himself, because the branch's personal facility is too small, then the manager has to put your project up to the bank's regional office. It is also true that managers in charge of a major branch will be used to handling large borrowings, whereas a requirement for £50,000 in, say, the branch of a small market town, would be quite a daunting prospect for the manager in charge.

Where possible, if you are applying to a bank which is not your own, try and obtain an introduction. Your solicitor or accountant may be able to help here, or perhaps a business colleague or a friend. It always helps if you can be recommended, rather than making the appointment cold. One final point, and this is important – never be fobbed off with anyone other than the branch manager. You do not want to see one of the manager's assistants, nor the Head of the Advances Department. You want to see the man in charge – no one else will do.

Government Schemes

There is a whole range of schemes designed to provide official backing, both for new ventures and for the expansion of existing businesses. For the Loan Guarantee Scheme see the previous section, on 'Banks'. The government does have millions of pounds available for funding enterprise, and the money being offered comes in the form either of cash grants or loans – often at a specially low rate of interest. In particular, the government is anxious to promote industrial expansion in so-called 'development areas', and certainly if you live in one of these areas your chances of receiving financial help are fairly high. There is a mass of legislation and a profusion of schemes available, but the main areas to consider are listed here.

Small Firms Division

The Small Firms Division of the Department of Industry have their headquarters at Abell House, John Islip Street, London SW1 (telephone 01 212 3395). There are, however, regional offices all over the country and it would be advisable to contact your regional office to see what funding is available in your particular area. Certainly, you will receive a great deal of encouragement and advice and some regions do offer risk funding – ask for details.

CoSira

CoSira (The Council for Small Industries in Rural Areas) has its head office at Queens House, Fish Row, Salisbury, Wiltshire SP1 1EX (telephone 0772 24411). Again, there are regional offices all over the country. As the name implies, CoSira concentrates its attentions on industries in rural areas, but this does not mean that they are blinkered to promoting craft industries. They are interested in any form of enterprise. They are a very nice bunch of people and can be terribly helpful in giving advice on a range of subjects. They do have available a small amount of cash for loans and grants, though

you should be thinking in terms of hundreds of pounds rather than thousands. If you are living outside England, similar bodies to CoSira are the Welsh Development Office, the Scottish Development Office, the Highlands and Islands Development Board, and the Northern Ireland Development Office.

Your local authorities

In certain areas, local authorities will help with specific projects, particularly if you can demonstrate that you will be providing employment. Contact your local authority offices and ask what help is available. The most usual form of assistance is with subsidized industrial premises, but a really imaginative scheme, which is going to be of benefit to the local community, may well spark off positive financial participation.

Investors in Industry (3i)

3i, formerly known as Finance for Industry, which incorporated ICFC, was founded by the major clearing banks and the Bank of England, although it is an independent commercial body. Its sole aim is to provide finance for the establishment, growth and development of small and medium-sized businesses. As an organization, it is very keen to get involved right from the birth of a

business. 3i offers loans from as little as £5,000 right up to £2 million, and the term could be anything from five to twenty years. It would be fair to say that 3i is not interested in the small business without ambition. It will be prepared to back a business in its infancy but will be attracted to the concept of growth and expansion. The staff are easy to talk to and they do realize the importance of the founder of the business remaining in control of the company. This means that they are not greedy in their requirements for equity, usually only taking a minority holding. In addition, experience would suggest that 3i does not interfere with the day-to-day running of the business. Provided local managers see monthly or quarterly figures which show that the business is stable, you hardly know they are there. Your bank manager will advise you as to your local 3i office.

Enterprise Allowance Scheme

The Enterprise Allowance Scheme provides financial help during the first twelve months that you are working for yourself. If you are eligible for this scheme you will receive £40 a week for fifty-two weeks and this can be quite a help in the early days. In order to be eligible for the scheme, you must be between eighteen and state retirement age, and have received Unemployment Benefit or Supplementary Benefit as a result of being out of work, for at least eight weeks. You must also be able to demonstrate that you have invested at least £1,000 in your business. This does not mean that you have to have £1,000 of your own money – you can raise the capital either by loan or overdraft. Contact your local Jobcentre for details.

Tourism

If you are running, or intending to run, a business which caters for tourists, then it would be sensible to contact the Tourist Board. In England and Wales there are

what is known as Stream-Lined Aid Schemes, providing funding for specific tourist projects, such as visitor attractions, hotels and guest houses. Funding can be up to £100,000. The Wales Tourist Board also run a scheme for projects costing less than £5,000, which is designed to raise the standard of resort accommodation. There are twelve regional tourist boards, but here are the main head office addresses:

English Tourist Board, Thames Tower, Black's Road, London W6 9EL (telephone 01 846 9000).
Scottish Tourist Board, 23 Ravelston Terrace, Edinburgh EH4 3EU (telephone 031 332 2433).
Wales Tourist Board, Brunel House, 2 Fitzalan Road, Cardiff CF2 1UY (telephone 0222 499909).

For the inventor

If you genuinely believe that your project is an original invention, it is possible that the government may sponsor you. Certainly they do say that they will sponsor British initiatives in new technology. There is a body which deals with this, though it is reputed to be extremely cautious about becoming financially involved. The body in question is the National Research Development Corporation, 66 Victoria Street, London SW1. A word of caution, though – they usually want 50 per cent of the action.

During the lifetime of this book, the authors sincerely hope that the government will continue to dream up more schemes to assist the funding of new and existing businesses. When looking for finance, it is always worth contacting your bank manager, your solicitor and your accountant to make sure you are not missing anything! And phone 100 and ask for 'Freefone Enterprise' to talk to the Small Firms Service.

Asset Financing

Take a look at your balance sheet or your forecast balance sheet, and study your assets. It may well be possible to raise finance using them as security, or indeed to acquire them in the first place by an asset financing deal. There are various types of asset financing.

Your property

You can lease your business property rather than buy it outright. If you have owned your property for some time you can free the money tied up by selling it and taking a long-term lease back. If you are buying a freehold, as with personal property, there is no reason why you should not take out a mortgage. A number of companies deal quite specifically with industrial mortgages and your bank manager will be able to advise you as to who to approach. The banks are themselves now offering medium- and long-term mortgage loans for business purposes.

Hire purchase and leasing

This is an expensive way of financing. Interest charges are considerably higher than the normal rate for bank overdrafts, but there are grounds for saying that sometimes it is advisable not to put all your financial eggs in one basket. If, for example, you have a fairly hefty overdraft with your bank, probably you would rather not approach them for a loan for equipment as well. Luckily, banks tend not to consider HP and leasing as having any effect on your credit rating, so if you are using this method of financing, you do not need to keep the fact secret from your bank. Certainly, having financial aid from several sources, rather than one, does give you a greater degree of flexibility and in this respect hire purchase and leasing are useful.

The difference between the two is not as self-explanatory as their description suggests.

Hire purchase

Under a hire purchase contract, you will pay a deposit followed by monthly instalments over the period of the agreement. Legally, the asset becomes yours only on payment of the final instalment. For accounting and taxation purposes, however, the asset is treated as yours, from the date of purchase, with the instalments being treated as the repayments of a loan, with interest. To confuse the position further, a finance lease (which is a rental agreement containing no element of service) is now treated, for accounting and tax purposes, as a hire purchase agreement under another name.

Leasing

In the case of leasing, you are not buying the asset, you are merely paying for its use over the period of the contract, by monthly rentals. A full leasing agreement will provide such things as routine service and breakdown cover. The rentals will be allowed as business expenses for tax purposes, but the asset will never be yours. At the end of the leasing agreement it will go back to the leasing company, unless you then agree terms for a new lease, or offer to buy it. The leasing concept has particular value if you are giving your equipment a fair amount of use. Take the case of, say, a sales representative's car. In all probability a representative will be doing about 50,000 miles a year. You can lease a car for your representative and pay a monthly sum, which will include not only the leasing costs, but also a servicing contract. This will keep your sales representative on the road, trouble-free, for, say, three years, for a fixed monthly sum. If the vehicle goes wrong then it is up to the leasing company to provide a replacement car while it is being repaired. At the end of three years, what car having done 150,000 miles of heavy motoring is worth much? You will have had your money's worth! For vehicles, you can read equipment, and certainly if you are unsure what sort of equipment you need, you would do better to arrange short-term leasing rather than make an outright purchase which you might later regret.

Your bank will be able to put you in touch with reputable HP and finance companies. Alternatively, at the point of discussing the purchase of your equipment, your supplier is likely to be able to introduce you to a reputable hire purchase or leasing company, with which they deal on a regular basis.

Debt factoring and invoice discounting

These are difficult forms of finance to recommend. They have their uses, but are not widely adopted by businesses because, without a doubt, there is a great deal of consumer resistance, they are not cheap and they do create extra administration.

Debt factoring

Debt factoring raises money instantly by the sale of your unpaid book debts to a factoring company. Normally, a factoring agreement would cover future invoice sales as well. The factors will advance to you up to 80 per cent of the debts in anticipation of payment direct to them by your customers. You receive the balance of the money on settlement of the debts, and you pay interest on the amount advanced to you by the factoring company, less the amount received by them from the debtors. Linked to this facility, the factors will offer you additional services – such as the credit rating of potential customers and the raising of invoices. In addition to the interest charge, you will pay a fee based on turnover. The obvious advantage of factoring is better cash flow – you can get paid virtually as soon as you raise an invoice. The factoring company also effectively provides you with credit insurance, by taking the loss if one of your customers fails to pay up. But check this carefully. The factors may require a recourse agreement with you, which will put the onus back onto you.

The problem with factoring is that you have to tell your customers, and by inference it suggests to the world at large that you have financial difficulties. This, in most instances, is a wholly unjustified view. Factoring should be considered as a means of finance, like any other, but the very real prejudice against it will tend to make your customers query in their own minds whether you are financially sound, and this in turn could affect future orders. It also does need to be borne in mind that any dealings with customers, if done direct by your firm, will help cement relationships and encourage future business, if properly handled. Are you really prepared to put your precious relationship with your customer in someone else's hands?

Invoice discounting

A far better way of handling the factoring concept is by invoice discounting. Here again, you sell your debts, in block, to a factoring company, but remain responsible for invoicing and collecting the money. This has the distinct advantage so far as your customers are concerned, that they are totally unaware of your being involved with factoring at all.

Contact your bankers for details of factoring companies in your area.

It needs to be stressed that, with the exception of mortgages, all asset financing is expensive. However, if you are already heavily borrowed, you may have no alternative but to resort to this method of funding. Do be careful, though. There is a tendency for asset financing to encourage a business to over-trade. If you are using a factoring company, for example, unrestricted by the normal problems of cash flow, you may take on more and more work. This in turn will stretch your other resources to the point where you start to be inefficient, your stock level becomes too high, your quality suffers, and you become more susceptible to returns, etc. Similarly, HP and leasing may make you a little trigger-happy when it comes to the purchasing of equipment – the feeling 'live now, pay later' may make you commit yourself to too much, too soon.

The Business Expansion Scheme

The Business Expansion Scheme (BES) provides an extremely tax effective method whereby those people with high incomes can provide small businesses with risk capital. It is already proving one of the most successful methods of raising finance around, and in its first year of operation raised over £1 million of new investment in UK industry.

Are you eligible?

Not all companies are eligible for BES. It is necessary for your company to be incorporated in the UK and for your main activities to be based in the UK. Your shares may not be quoted on the Stock Exchange nor traded on the Unlisted Securities Market. Certain types of trades are ineligible for BES – such as banking, leasing, hiring, property dealing and development, insurance, accountancy and legal services, together with all farming trades. However, most other manufacturing and service industries are eligible, including, since 1 April 1985, those companies involved in research and development.

How does it work?

Individuals paying UK income tax can receive tax relief by subscribing to new ordinary shares in companies with which they have no close connections. They can invest up to £40,000 in any one year and can claim the sum as a deduction from their normal taxable income. The minimum amount of money that they can put into any one company is £500 and the shares must be retained for at least five years in order to receive full tax relief. If the shares are sold too soon, relief may be withdrawn or reduced.

The benefits

Clearly, one of the main benefits in attracting BES money is the likely attitude of the investor. This scheme is offering a high-income earner the opportunity to avoid tax legally and this is likely to be the investor's primary motive for any involvement in your business. This being the case, by inference, the investor is far less likely to interfere with the day-to-day running of your business than, say, a friend or member of the family, offering you money for partly altruistic reasons.

However, by far the main benefit must be the advantage of equity capital – every small business needs it, since it carries no repayment requirement nor interest commitment, and is really an essential part of business funding. If you are just starting up or expanding your business, an external investment rather than a straightforward loan can prove to be a vital shot in the arm.

BES *funds*

A number of stockbrokers, merchant banks and insurance companies have jumped on the bandwagon of the Business Expansion Scheme by forming and managing portfolios of investments in private companies. Normally an investor is asked for a minimum subscription of £2,000 and this money is then invested, not in one company, but spread over a number of different businesses, so minimizing the risk. For people who have not a great deal of commercial experience, these BES funds are proving rather attractive, and it is well worth while investigating to see whether your company could benefit from such a fund.

A BES investment has to be a good thing for your business, provided you are ambitious and are looking for continuing growth. In other words, you must have an attractive proposition to offer the prospective investor. If the relationship proves satisfactory and your business is doing well, the investor might be keen to have an ongoing relationship with you, feeding surplus income to you on a regular basis. A prospective investor will also want a degree of comfort. If things go wrong, the investor will lose money and, to this extent, needs to feel your business has a secure future. Attracting BES money for a brand-new business may be relatively easy, provided your idea is a good one. Attracting BES money for an established, profitable

business wishing to expand should again present no problem. However, if you find that your business is in trouble through being under-capitalized and is making losses, BES money will be difficult to obtain. This only goes to emphasize the need for careful forecasting and planning to establish exactly what your financial requirements are likely to be.

To find potential investors, apart from asking your rich friends, speak to your solicitor, accountant, bank manager and also the Inland Revenue. More and more BES money is being handled by funds and, here again, it is worth contacting stockbrokers, merchant banks and insurance companies. Ask to speak to their BES fund manager.

Over the years, various governments have tried to introduce a wide variety of schemes aimed at helping channel funds into the new and expanding private company. It has to be said that many of these schemes have fallen flat on their faces, but not so the Business Expansion Scheme. The reason for this is that everyone wins. The investor benefits and so, of course, does the individual company. If you have the opportunity to acquire BES money, or think you may be eligible, do treat this form of funding as a top priority and look at it first before settling for a more conventional form of borrowing.

If you require a medium- or long-term loan or permanent equity capital of a substantial size, then despite all the more recent schemes that have become available, you are really looking to the traditional specialist institutions for your needs – i.e. the merchant banks, the pension funds, the unit and investment trusts and insurance companies. Whilst the major clearing banks have extended their traditional banking facilities and will provide medium-term loan finance of up to ten or fifteen years, anything longer is really out of the question, and certainly there is no possibility of equity participation. It is to the institutions you need to go for **big money** from share issues. Some institutions may take a direct stake in your company, others may take a stake as part of a consortium or a private placing. Alternatively, they might invest as a result of a flotation. Borrowing big money is easiest if it really is big. In the City, it is far easier to borrow £5 million than £50,000, and certainly a merchant bank will rarely be bothered with a £50,000 loan, it is simply too expensive to set up and maintain – £250,000 might just be worth while.

What can a merchant bank offer you?

To the uninitiated, a merchant bank sounds a rather mysterious, unapproachable kind of institution, and up to a point this is true. Much of the merchant banking world is operating on the 'old pals act' – everyone knows everyone, and certainly, the personal introduction still goes a long way. What a merchant bank really has to offer, apart from access to large, long-term finance, is people and expertise. The management of a merchant bank should be made up of highly skilled people, who can guide your business towards big success. The other distinct advantage merchant banks have is that they are small – at least they are compared to the major clearing banks. This gives them a great deal of flexibility and means they can move very fast. They are not hidebound by traditional methods and can be inventive and speedy.

Increasingly, merchant banks, like all other banks, are starting to offer specific facilities such as leasing, factoring and property loans. Provided your company is of a size and type which attracts merchant bank money, then there is a lot to be said for looking to a merchant bank for your finance.

Insurance companies, pension funds and investment trusts

These institutions are the major investors on the Stock Exchange. However, nowadays, with the added emphasis on private enterprise, many of these institutions are willing to consider investment in promising unlisted private companies. Again, through your bank manager, solicitor or accountant, it is best if you can obtain a personal introduction, rather than make an approach cold.

Qualifying factors for institutional money

Before making any approach to a merchant bank or other institution, you need to look very carefully at your company, to analyse whether it qualifies. These are the major factors you should consider:

◆ *Funding required*   Your loan or equity requirement must be in excess of £250,000.

◆ *Management team*   Your company must have a qualified team of people who have well-proven expertise in your particular business field, or in the field into which you wish to expand.

◆ *Proven product or service*   You must be able to demonstrate that your product or service is of the very latest and best in terms of technical development.

◆ *Market potential*   You must be able to demonstrate that you are in a growth market and that there is plenty of room for expansion over the next few years.

◆ *Return on capital*   You must be able to offer an attractive return on capital.

Flotations

One of the ways in which a merchant bank can help you raise money is by supporting your company in a flotation – going public. There is no point in even considering offering your shares to the public unless your company has an exciting future. In other words, if you have a well-established, profitable business and are content with the way it is, do not go public, there is no point. The reason for considering a flotation is to help you realize your expansion dreams, which could not be realized by raising money in the form of a loan. There are two types of flotation – you can either have a full listing on the Stock Exchange or a quotation on the Unlisted Securities Market (USM). USM attracts smaller companies, sometimes even new companies with no track record, but big ideas.

What are your objectives in going public?
For whom do you wish to raise money? If you wish to raise money for your company then you should be offering new shares to the market. If you want to raise money for yourself and your shareholders then you should place some or all of your existing shares on the market. In many instances a mixture of the two is offered.

What will it cost to go public?
The costs of going public are high. As a rough guide, a flotation on the USM will cost between £150,000 and £250,000. This compares with costs of a full listing of between £200,000 and £400,000. It sounds a great deal of money, but there are a great many services you will require – the merchant bank, stockbrokers, reporting accountants, auditors, solicitors acting on the flotation, your company's own solicitors, surveyors and valuers, advertising and PR, printing and postage. Basically you are launching a marketing campaign with extremely complex legal and tax implications. There are no short cuts, and you frankly cannot have too much advice before taking such a step.

Alternative Sources of Finance

There are a number of methods of financing your business which do not fall easily under specific headings, but which need looking at carefully. These are described in this section.

Using your own money

Almost inevitably, in the start of a new business, you will be using some of your own money to finance it. This is a good idea because it demonstrates your confidence and will please bankers and suppliers alike. It will also tend to leave you with a greater degree of control. Since one of the reasons you are in business is almost certainly that you like the idea of being your own boss, retaining control must be an important factor.

However, it is absolutely imperative that you treat any investment made by yourself in exactly the same way as you would treat a loan from a bank or financial institution. You must see a proper return on your money and you must budget for it. This, of course, applies not only to money you provide, but to that provided by other members of your family.

Clearly, the personal asset most often used in fund raising is your own home. You may have a mortgage but, because of escalating property prices, you probably will have spare equity in the house, and a second mortgage may well secure you additional funding. If this is the case, do consider borrowing money by way of a personal pension policy, which, provided that you are not in pensionable employment, is far more tax-effective than simply taking out a second mortgage. Say you wish to raise £20,000 – sign yourself up for a recognized pension plan, which will give you a minimum cash payout of £20,000 on your retirement. When you link this with a second mortgage, you will find your bank happy to lend you the money, because they have the comfort of seeing a definite repayment source as well as the security of the property. The advantage of borrowing money in this way is that both the capital repayment (in the form of pension premiums) and the interest payments are allowed against income tax.

Partners

If you have no money, one method of acquiring it would be to take on a partner. Avoid friends, and if you are looking purely for a financial partner, avoid anyone with a particular interest in your type of business – if they have a knowledge of your trade, they are bound to interfere with the running of the business. Such a relationship can best be described as having a sleeping partner. Despite the obvious advantages, this is a dangerous relationship and you need to recognize it as such right from the beginning. Initially, you will be grateful to whoever lends you money to establish your own business or to expand an existing one. However, once your enterprise is up and running as a result of your own hard work, you will start to resent the payments you have to make to your sleeping partner when he appears to be contributing nothing. As we stated earlier, it is vital to remember that if your sleeping partner had not come across with the money when you needed it, you would have no business at all.

Suppliers' deferred credit

Negotiating extended credit terms is often a very cheap and effective method of obtaining finance. If your major suppliers have sufficient confidence in you and your business, they may well be prepared to extend you sufficient credit in order that you can be paid for the goods you sell before you have to pay them. This could involve sixty days' credit or even ninety, and even though you may lose cash discounts, it may well be a cheaper method of finance than borrowing the same sum of money from a bank. In some industries, financial help from suppliers can take an even more tangible form. The most obvious example is the relationship between the publican in a tied house and the brewery. The brewery will finance extensions and provide equipment, against an undertaking from the publican to use their product exclusively – this could apply to your industry.

Customers' advance payments

You may be able to finance your business partially by persuading customers to pay in advance, or at any rate make a part-payment on account of the goods or services with which you intend to provide them. Here again, it is a question of establishing confidence, and you may well run the risk of losing your customer if your demands for up-front payment are too extreme. Again, certain industries traditionally operate in this manner. Mail-order companies, for example, often ask for cash with order, and this is also the case in certain industries where the product is quite specifically designed for a particular customer's requirements. In the exhibition industry, the commission of a specific custom-built exhibition stand results in the exhibitor paying 50 per cent of the total cost at the time of placing the order. If you are providing a product or service which has to be designed to your customer's particular requirements, it may well be possible to obtain an advance.

Money by acquisition

If you have an up-and-running successful company, it is possible that you might be able to raise money by the acquisition of another business, followed by an asset-stripping operation. What is meant by this exactly? Many companies get themselves into the position where they have assets tied up in the business, simply not earning their keep in terms of profit. Often, the directors do not recognize either the problem or the real value of the assets. It may be that you have the means of

unlocking such a situation, because you have the distribution or sales force to release cash by a rapid sale of surplus stock. Alternatively, you might merge your production and sell their factory. Acquiring a company in trouble, with assets which have become grossly undervalued, could be a way of raising money in the long term. Be careful, though – you need to be very confident that you can do a better job than the company you are buying.

Sale and lease-back

If, within your business, you have a substantial asset in which a great deal of money is tied up, you could consider selling that asset and leasing it back. The most usual asset to be disposed of in this way is a property. Most large insurance companies will look at such a deal. If your business owns its own property you can sell it to the insurance company, who will lease it back to you for your continued use. This same method of financing could also apply to major pieces of equipment and, say, company cars. If you have twenty sales representatives' cars, you could sell them to a finance company, who would lease them back to you.

With all the methods of finance discussed in this section, it is probably true to say that no one particular scheme is right for you in isolation. A mixed package is by far the best, and you would be wise to consider every option before deciding what is best for you and your business. Particularly in a business start-up, there is a tendency to feel so relieved at being able to finance the scheme at all, that the principal accepts the first offer that comes along, which may well not be the right answer. Shopping for money is like shopping for a pound of potatoes. You have to consider cost against quality and above all ask yourself exactly what you want from your purchase.

Presenting Your Case

Many people fail in obtaining finance for their business, not because their proposal is unsound, but because *they do not know how to present it*. You must recognize that you will be required to do a very heavy selling job and great care is needed to ensure that you stand the best possible chance of having your proposal accepted. Here are a few hints:

◆ Be prepared – it is essential that you provide your potential backer with a profit plan and cash forecast, but you also need some evidence to support your figures. Your backer will be primarily interested in your sales projections, since this is the key to your success or failure. Where possible, provide orders, enquiries and contracts to substantiate your claims, or if you have none of these, a market survey would at least show you have carefully studied the feasibility of your sales projections. Almost the first question your backer will ask you is how your sales forecast has been calculated, and you must know the answer.

Include with your paperwork any valuation that you have on property or other assets. It will also help a great deal if you can obtain a letter from someone, such as your Regional Development Board, pledging support and confirming the viability of your project. In other words, any piece of paper from an interested party, which can verify that in their view you are on to a good thing, has to be helpful. With all your documentation, take along not only the originals, but also a complete set of copies, which you can leave with your backer.

It may be that despite the advice in this book, you decide you need professional advice with the preparation of a cash forecast and profit plan. This is fine, but do **make sure that you really understand the figures. The best presentation in the world will be ruined if you are floored by the questions asked.**

◆ If you feel you need moral support, then take along your accountant or solicitor (always remembering their fees!), but only do so if you really feel it will further your cause. If you are confident enough to make your presentation alone, this is, without doubt, the best way. Too many people putting forward their point of view can be confusing, and a one-to-one sales pitch is by far the best method of presenting your case.

◆ Do not be upset if you are turned down several times. If your project is viable and you have the necessary tenacity to stick with it, you will find the finance you want – it is simply a question of time. Be positive about your rejections, think of them as a learning curve. Make notes of the criticisms that were made about your proposal and see what can be done to improve on it. If your potential backer or banker is vague about rejection, then without being aggressive ask them to spell out exactly why they have turned you down. If you have taken the trouble to offer them your business, you deserve a full explanation, which could prove of invaluable help at your next interview.

◆ However many times your proposal is turned down, do make sure the date on your presentation documents is absolutely current. Bank managers say they often are presented with documentation which is three or four months out of date. This immediately tells them that the project has been turned down by other banks, and is bound to influence their thinking. As far as you and your case are concerned, you must present it each time as though it is a brand-new, fresh proposal.

◆ Do be a good listener. Your potential backer may have a lot to offer you in terms of help and advice, but in your efforts to sell your case, you may not listen properly to what is being said. Be flexible. If your proposal is accepted in part, then ask your backer's advice as to how you should go about obtaining the rest of the money you need.

◆ Mutual trust and respect is the only basis on which you are going to be able to sustain a long-term relationship with your backer. It is tempting to exaggerate, to stretch the truth, to paint a better picture than in fact you believe to be the case. Do not be tempted to do this, for it will all catch up with you in the end. Borrowing money on a false premiss, even if the only person you are kidding is yourself, is a very dangerous thing to do. Only borrow money against a scheme in which you really believe, and if this is the basis on which you make your presentation, you can be sure that you will be successful in obtaining the finance you need.

The Role of Insurance in Your Business

No business can operate without insurance. Big or small, whatever your trade, you need protection. Often though, the wrong kind of emphasis is placed on insurance, with unimportant cover receiving far too much attention and absorbing far too much money. No business can afford to spend a fortune on insurance, and in all too many instances an attempt is made to cover for every conceivable risk. Is it really of any material significance that £20 of petty cash is stolen from your office? So – you have a number of plate glass windows which would cost £100 each to replace if they are broken – big deal! No, it is the broader issues that should be absorbing your time. What you should be insuring against is the catastrophes.

Whilst these are the basics, the size and circumstances of your business will greatly determine your insurance emphasis. For example, if you run a small business with a partner and one of you becomes seriously ill, it could well jeopardize the whole of your future trading. This being the case, insurance against illness for you and your partner is essential. However, if you run a large company, employing, shall we say, a hundred people, and you have a good management team, then your being ill is not the end of the world and will take a much lower priority in the list of necessary insurances.

If you have limited resources for insurance, these are the catastrophes against which you must insure:

◆ Fire – aircraft – explosions – riots – strikes – civil commotion

◆ Loss of turnover

◆ Public liability

◆ Employer's liability

Insurance brokers

Whatever your size of business, you do need the services of an insurance broker. So far as you are concerned, the services are free since an insurance broker's commission is paid by whichever insurance company provides you with the necessary cover. A broker is not employed by any one insurance company, which means that he or she is free to shop around. The cover obtained for you is unlikely to cost any more than you would pay if you approached an insurance company direct – indeed sometimes even less, since the broker has the experience and skill to do some interesting deals on your behalf. If you have never used an insurance broker before, it is quite likely that in reassessing your overall insurance requirements, he may be able to save you a good deal of money on your existing policies. As with most professionals, it is better to obtain the services of an insurance broker through personal recommendation. Your bank manager, solicitor or accountant should be able to help you. If all else fails, use the Yellow Pages.

Special note for small businesses

If you run a small business from home, do pay particular attention to your insurance policy. It is not enough that your house and contents are insured against loss and damage. The insurance cover you are likely to have is a householder's policy and simply does not apply to the running of your own business. Should your word processor blow up, or your kiln set fire to the house, you can be certain that the insurance company covering you will do their level best to prove that the accident was a commercial one. If they succeed and your household policy has not been extended for commercial use, you could be in serious trouble. Do not try to be clever and save money – if you run a business from home, take out commercial insurance.

Serious catastrophes, such as accidents to staff or customers, or the destruction of your premises and/or equipment, need insuring properly. Do not undervalue their worth, since the whole object of insurance cover is to protect your position so that you can stay in business whatever problem confronts you. Equally, do not over-insure trivia – employ a good insurance broker to help you sort out the wheat from the chaff.

Assets

When insuring your assets, these are the main risks which you can insure against:

◆ Fire – aircraft – explosions.
◆ Special perils – storm, tempest, flood, burst pipes, earthquake, impact, riots, strikes, civil commotion, malicious damage.
◆ Theft – breaking in/out (you have to prove that there has been a physically forced entrance or exit).

The main assets you need to cover are described in this section.

Property (buildings/tenants' improvements/commitments under a lease)

◆ The most important point to watch, with regard to property, is value. For insurance purposes, this has absolutely nothing to do with the market value of your property. What you need to consider is the cost of rebuilding your existing premises – including fees, demolition of the old building and inflation during the period of rebuilding. This sum may well be far higher than pure market value.
◆ Landlord's cover. If you are leasing your premises, your landlord is likely to ask you to pay for the basic property insurance, which the landlord will arrange. However, the landlord's interest in so doing is purely linked to protecting his own position rather than yours. You must have sight of his policy, to see whether the cover is too limited and whether in fact you should be taking out additional cover of your own.
◆ Tenant's cover. Are you obliged, under your lease, to insure for specific perils, and have you insured in accordance with your commitment? Be careful not to be hidebound by the minimum requirements of the lease. You need to look at your own situation and decide whether the cover specified is in fact adequate.

Equipment

This includes machinery, plant, furniture, fittings, contents – in fact everything excluding actual stock. Here again, the important point to watch for is replacement cost, allowing for inflation. Do make sure you keep this cover up to date; it is very easy to find yourself exposed by forgetting to include new items of equipment – particularly in a new or expanding business.

Stock and work in progress

In most businesses, stock tends to fluctuate considerably from month to month. Your policy, therefore, should allow for a monthly declaration of stock value, which will ensure that not only are you properly covered, but also that you are not over-insured either – in other words, you only pay to insure your actual stock figure in any one month. Do remember when valuing your stock that it will be insured at cost price, not selling price.

Computers

In all probability, computers will be covered against physical damage under your general equipment policy. However, what you have to consider in the event of, say, fire is: what will be the cost of re-writing your records? There are normally limitations and exclusions in a standard fire policy in this respect, so do check it carefully, and if necessary cover your software separately. Consider also accidental damage, and link the reinstatement of records to that. You need to set up your own 'insurance' whereby, as a matter of policy, a complete copy is made of your records every few days to be stored in separate premises. This does not need to be formally in your bank or with your solicitor. It is perfectly adequate to keep a spare set of records under your bed, so long as a separate record does exist. Such a company policy may well help reduce your insurance premium, as any catastrophe obviously can be put right far more easily if a duplicate set of records is to hand.

 ## Money

This is normally covered by an 'all risks' extension to one of your main policies. This is not something you need to worry about too much, unless you have a very heavy payroll, or your business is a cash business, such as a retail outlet or restaurant. In those circumstances you may need to make sure there are adequate arrangements for removal of the cash from the premises, or for storing it overnight.

 ## Engineering

This is a special cover for mechanical equipment, such as lifts, escalators, boilers and pressure vessels in general use, as well as machine tools in an engineering business. It may be provided by a specialist extension to your general policy, or by the issue of a policy in its own right. You will find that your premium will be most affected by safety aspects, and you can expect routine inspections of your equipment. In considering the dramatic effects of what can go wrong, do not overlook the more mundane – make sure you are properly covered for a simple breakdown and its effects.

 ## Motor vehicles

There are three types of motor insurance:
Third party This is the minimum legal cover and simply protects you against third-party claims.
Third Party, Fire and Theft This not only protects you against third party claims but also against fire or theft of

your vehicle – so there is an element of asset protection.
Comprehensive This, as the name suggests, covers all aspects – comprehensive insurance includes accidental damage as well as protection for third-party claims, fire and theft. If at all possible, it is recommended that you should go for a comprehensive policy. Like it or not, your staff will not look after your vehicles as they would look after their own, and the chances of damage are far greater.

 ## Goods in transit

If your business involves a substantial element of transport and delivery, a special policy will be necessary to cover your stock while in transit. If the element of transportation is fairly small, then you may be able to cover this aspect by an extension of your existing policy.

These, then, are the main areas of asset insurance. What you need to do is to look very carefully at your business and see where the emphasis should be placed. If, for example, your business involves the storing of food in a freezer because you are running a restaurant or shop, this will involve special treatment in your stock policy, to ensure cover in the case of a power cut or a possible breakdown of your freezer equipment. Do not let yourself become bogged down by incidentals – concentrate on the major issues. If any one of your major assets is destroyed by some form of catastrophe, how much money are you going to need to reinstate it, how long will it take to regain the status quo, and how will you cope while the reinstatement programme is going on? These are questions that only you can answer. Take time and trouble to make sure you get it right, and thereafter make sure you keep the assets insured, at the right up-to-date value.

Ask yourself why you are in business. The answer has to be to make profits and earn money. This being the case, it needs to be recognized that you should take out insurance to protect your business from any interruption in its ability to earn profit. There are a number of terms which insurance companies use to describe this type of insurance – **loss of profits**, **consequential loss** and more recently, **business interruption**. However, this type of insurance is basically divided into two quite distinct types of policy, which cover the two main areas of risk. Either may be relevant for your business.

Policy type 1 – actual loss of gross profit

Example A
Your factory burns down, you lose production for six months and your turnover drops. Your gross profit therefore plummets, but you still have to pay most of the wages and salaries and a large percentage of the fixed overheads.

Example B
Your major supplier's factory burns down. You probably can keep in production for a month, from your existing stocks, but supposing it takes four months to find an alternative supplier? The result is the same as if your own factory had gone up in smoke.

Example C
A landslide six miles down the valley destroys the main power cable to your works – no power, so no production for six weeks. You miss the Christmas market, which is your main selling period, and you lose 25 per cent of your annual sales and the gross profit that goes with it.

Examples B and C clearly show that insurance against **actual loss of gross profit** needs to cover not only self-inflicted dramas, but the dramas which may be imposed upon you by some outside

influence. You should not become too obscure in dreaming up potential catastrophes, but you must try and cover the vulnerable areas. Do bear in mind that with this particular type of insurance you are somewhat in a 'chicken and egg' situation. Your insurance company will need a great deal of information to convince them to cover you. Obtaining that information may either prove too difficult, or if obtained, convince you that you do not need insurance at all!

Policy type 2 – additional cost of working

Example
The office block in which your consultancy business is based is damaged by fire. Your business is on the top floor and escapes unscathed, records intact, but you have to move out for nine months while repairs are carried out on the whole building. You find temporary offices round the corner straight away, so your income is not interrupted, but you are involved in double rent, extra printing and stationery, telephone and telex installation costs, extra costs of staff transport, short-term replacement of the staff canteen, etc.

Policy type 1

This type of policy most suits businesses providing a service, rather than manufacturing a product. A service industry usually can be re-located quickly and effectively, without any major loss of gross profit/turnover.

Premiums are calculated by reference to the earnings that are at risk, so far as Policy 1 is concerned. For Policy 2, premiums are calculated by reference to the costs you might incur in the event of a catastrophe. If you can get adequate cover in that form of policy, obviously it is cheaper to cover for **additional cost of working** rather than **actual loss of gross profit**. An important point to note is that the cost of this type of insurance is significantly affected by the period of cover required. If you have a manufacturing business and believe it would take up to two years to recover from a fire, try and calculate if it would be possible for, say, 90 per cent of your problems to be overcome in one year. If this is so, insure for one year's cover, not for two. Taking the risk on the other 10 per cent of loss has to be worth while when balanced against the fact that insuring for half the period will nearly halve the premium.

Policy type 2

What you have to assess, when selecting which policy to go for, are the time and costs involved in making a recovery in the event of a disaster. Your business may be very resilient to change and disruption. Alternatively, you may feel that the location, the premises and/or the equipment you currently enjoy are absolutely vital for the success or failure of your business. If this is the case, make sure you are properly protected.

There are three specialist insurance covers which protect the earning power of your business, but which fall outside the two main categories:

◆ *'Key Man' policy* This can be taken out in respect of one individual – say, you the proprietor – or all the key management of a large company. What this policy provides is a lump sum, which is paid to the company in the event of the vital manager/executive dying. This policy is discussed in the section on 'Life, Health and Pensions'.

◆ *Fidelity Guarantee* This is an insurance against fraud within your company – i.e. fraud carried out by your management/staff/employees. You will need to be able to demonstrate that you have very tight systems of control in order to get this insurance.

◆ *Credit Insurance* You can insure against bad debts; certainly falling foul of bad debts is one of the major reasons for business failure today. However, it has to be said that the degree of tight control required by an insurance company in order to grant you credit insurance is sufficiently high that, if their conditions are met, then your customers must be fairly 'blue chip' anyway and probably worth the credit risk. Tight credit control should be the policy of every business. To a well-run company, credit insurance is one of the less attractive business insurance schemes.

BUSINESS INSURANCE

Liabilities

The degree of insurance cover necessary
for your business is largely a matter of
choice. There are two areas of exception,
though. The first is obvious – if you own any
motor vehicles, these have to be insured,
by law, for at least **third party cover**. The
other area of legal obligation is **employer's
liability**.

Employer's liability

If you employ any staff, either full-time or
part-time, on or off your premises, you
must take out **employer's liability
cover**. This covers your employees against
any injury that may take place while they
are carrying out their duties – which, of
course, may not necessarily take place at
work. The degree of risk, and therefore the
degree of premium charged. depends
largely on the type of employee. Clerical
staff are obviously cheaper to cover than
machinists, sales staff are cheaper than
miners. If you run a medium to large
company, your insurance broker will
introduce an insurance policy where you
project, for the year ahead, the wages and
salaries of each category of employee, and
you will pay an estimated premium. At the
year end, a declaration of actual wages and
salaries will be submitted and the premium
adjusted accordingly. It needs to be
stressed that there is no short cut to this
form of insurance. **If you employ anyone,
in any circumstances, you must have
employer's liability cover**.

Public liability

The other main area of liability cover is
public liability, but this is not a legal
obligation. However, if you are in business
in almost any way, it is a necessary practical
cover, because a claim could be an absolute
catastrophe. This applies however small
your business – irrespective of whether you
are supplying a service or a product, cover
is still necessary. Supposing, for example,
you are a freelance electrician and you
repair Mr Bloggs's electric kettle for him.
What happens if you get your wiring wrong
and blow up the poor unfortunate
gentleman? Perhaps you run a restaurant
and your quiche lorraine gives everyone
food poisoning. What happens when your
customers claim for lost days' work and
doctor's bills? One of your staff is painting
the window frames, on the outside of your
premises, and accidentally drops a paint pot
on the head of the passing postman . . . and
so on, and so on. The point about public
liability cover is it provides insurance cover
for your legal liability to anyone against
whom you or your staff inflict accidental
injury or damage.

In addition to the main areas of liability insurance, there are also four specific forms of liability cover:

◆ *Product liability* This covers any legal liabilities which may arise from your supply of faulty products.

◆ *Professional indemnity* If you are providing a service, it is very important to consider taking out a professional indemnity policy. Professional people, such as doctors, solicitors, accountants and their like, automatically take out this sort of cover, for it would be madness to operate without it. Advice which goes badly wrong could wipe out your personal and business resources. Having said that, professional indemnity is very expensive, since these days claims are so high. If you belong to, or could belong to, a union connected with your trade, or are a member of some sort of professional body connected with your industry, this may qualify you for a reduction in premium, or in some cases – particularly where a union is concerned – you may be automatically covered, simply by being a member. Explore this avenue first before you commit yourself to a hefty annual premium.

◆ *Engineering liability* This really is an extension of asset insurance. You may, for example, have covered your high-speed lift for accidental damage or breakdown, but you also need to insure against the liability claims arising from your lift plummeting from the twelfth floor to the basement, with half a dozen people on board. You need to insure against the possibility of your fork-lift truck going berserk and damaging both the warehouse and passers-by. And what happens if one of your central heating boilers explodes with a shop full of people?

◆ *Legal insurance policies* These policies cover you against prosecution under Acts of Parliament, such as unfair dismissal and fair trading. The sensible way round this particular conundrum is to make sure you stay within the law, so that you will not be subjecting yourself to the possibility of prosecution. Having said that, if you do operate in a particularly sensitive area, there is an insurance policy to cover you.

As with all other forms of insurance cover, it is a question of taking a long, cool look at your potential liability risks and seeing where your vulnerability lies. Concentrate on the big issues – minor liability claims you can cope with. It is the catastrophe you are aiming to insure against.

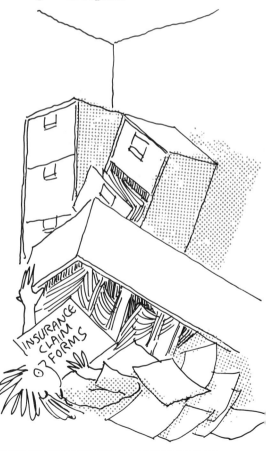

Life, Health and Pensions

Life cover

The 'Key Man' policy is the normal method of providing cover on the lives of directors and senior management for the benefit of the company. The policy can be applied to you alone, or to your more important staff – the effect is the same. If you or a member of your management team should die, then the company receives a lump sum in compensation. You need to think about this type of policy very carefully. If you run a large company, the most senior directors may well not be the key people in your organization. They may have founded the business, but it might be, say, your production director, or sales manager with specialist knowledge of your product, whose death would have a far greater impact on the company's profits. If you run a small business, perhaps even a solo operation, it is tempting immediately to assume that you need a 'Key Man' policy. What you have to ask yourself is what will happen if you die? Will a lump sum introduced into the business enable your spouse to continue running it, or safeguard it in such a way that there is something to sell? If, for whatever reason, neither of these circumstances applies, you might well be better advised to concentrate on making sure your family will want for nothing if you die and, frankly – to hell with your business. In other words, the message is that being 'top dog' in your company does not necessarily justify a 'Key Man' policy. If you do find it is justified, such a policy can be written in two ways, for tax purposes. If you want the sum assured to be received by the company free of tax, then the premiums paid will not be allowed for tax as business expenses. If you want the premiums to be treated as tax-allowable expenses, then any sum paid to the company under the policy will itself be subject to tax.

Health

Most established companies these days offer their top executives a private health plan, for themselves and sometimes their families – with BUPA or PPP or a similar organization. It is an attractive, but normally taxable benefit which goes with a top job, and provides a good deal of comfort for your members of staff and their families. In these days when unemployment is rife, there are grounds for saying this is one facility you do not need to offer staff, but in looking at private health plans you also need to consider the advantages to the company. If your top executives are covered by a private health scheme, they can be ill at the company's convenience. In other words, they can be treated quickly and efficiently and put back to work in the shortest possible time. The mere fact that your employees know they are covered by a private health plan will encourage them to take their symptoms to the doctor on a regular basis, which in turn should keep them fitter.

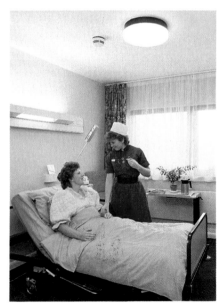

Pensions

Under the heading of pensions, there are two aspects to consider. First, if you run a very small business, perhaps are even self-employed, should you be considering providing for your own pension? Second, if you have a medium to large company, should you be introducing a company pension scheme? Let us look at the two aspects in more detail.

Self-employed

Open any newspaper on any day of the week and you will find an advertisement for self-employed pensions – and one has to say with good cause. If your business is starting to provide you with a reasonable, regular income, you would be advised to start looking at a pension scheme. There are a wealth of schemes available – which type of policy you take out depends entirely on your circumstances: your income, your age, your aims and ambitions. Plans are very flexible, and a personal pension plan can be virtually tailor-made to suit your individual requirements. For this reason, it is strongly recommended that you use not only the services of an insurance broker, but in particular a broker specializing in life and pensions. Personal pensions are allowed against your highest rates of income tax – normally up to a maximum of $17\frac{1}{2}$ per cent of your net earnings. You can elect for a premium paid in one year to be treated as having been paid in the previous year, or in some cases even one year earlier, to maximize tax-effectiveness. Conversely, if you do not pay the maximum premium allowed in any one year, unused relief may also be carried forward, up to six years. This does give you an enormous degree of flexibility in ensuring that the income you receive from your business is treated in the most tax-effective way.

Company pension schemes

There was a time when a company pension scheme was a good vehicle to introduce because it bred loyalty in your staff. Now, quite rightly, under government legislation, the kind of pension you are required to adopt is readily transferable to another company, should your member of staff leave your employment. None the less, providing a pension scheme for your staff does breed confidence. To any employee, or would-be employee, the existence of a pension scheme suggests that your company is here to stay. To set up your own pension scheme, you should employ the services of an insurance broker, who must specialize in life and pensions. All the major insurance groups will offer you the facilities for setting up a pension fund. Some companies do manage to fund their own, but this means the security of the pension fund may be linked to the stability of the company, which naturally makes it far more vulnerable. For small and medium-sized companies, a pension fund managed by, and under the control of, one of the leading insurance groups gives an enormous amount of security and confidence to the members involved.

The premiums payable for a company pension scheme will, obviously, depend upon the level of benefits offered and the age and length of service of the members. A reasonably generous scheme giving pensions based on final salary, with widows' pensions and life cover, may cost typically, between 12 per cent and 25 per cent of pensionable salaries, if not contracted out of the state scheme. Do ask the members to make some contribution towards this cost – even if it is as little as $1\frac{1}{2}$ per cent to $2\frac{1}{2}$ per cent of salary. Something paid for is something appreciated.

Life, health and pension covers are all optional – you do not have to offer them. Do make sure that the business can afford to meet these long-term commitments before starting. There is little worse than saying to your senior staff that you cannot afford to pay their pension premiums this year!

Employment and Its Implications

If you have the choice between hiring a man or a machine, hire the machine. This may seem a terrible thing to say in the teeth of so much unemployment, but for the good of your business do not take on staff, *any staff*, unless you absolutely have to. However, if you are committed to taking on extra people, take your time over recruitment. Repenting at leisure is an agonizingly costly exercise.

There is a great deal of evidence to support the view that once you start employing people your troubles really begin. Against that, of course, people make a business, people *are* the business. The fact that your venture has proved to be a viable one may be because you have a good salesman selling your products, a good production manager seeing that your customers receive good-quality items on time, and a good accountant making sure that the whole exercise is profitable. But employ the wrong people in these same roles, and you will find yourself in the position of having insufficient orders to cover your overheads, returned goods,

cancelled goods and your accountant cooking the books. If you have established that there is no alternative but to employ people to fulfil certain roles within your business, then recognize that once you start delegating responsibility, you are in effect at the mercy of your staff. This knowledge should in turn make you consider your own strengths and weaknesses. Some people are marvellous operators – perhaps you are one – but find delegation an impossible task. The need to interfere is just too great! If you suffer from this problem, you need to recognize that nobody in your employ will be able to do a proper job, because of your interference.

Owing to the current unemployment problems, actually finding somebody to work for you is no problem. In fact that may be part of the trouble – you are spoilt for choice and so often choose the wrong person. For everyone's sake, make sure you have identified a permanent vacancy before taking someone on, or if it is not a permanent position, then say so. Take a careful look at the most up-to-date

technology. Using the office as an example, consider the advance in computers, word processors, facsimile and telex machines. Rather than employ half a dozen people in your office, you might well be able to employ one – with the right equipment. If this is the case that person needs to be special, too, to be able to cope with the latest technology.

It has to be said that staff are one of the most draining overheads. Relentlessly, no matter what is happening to your business, the wage bill needs to be paid weekly, the salaries monthly. Whereas you can shut down a machine if it is under-employed, laying off people is a great deal more complicated, and rightly so. Over-staffing, too, is a terrible scourge – everyone works at half-speed and inefficiency becomes rife. People operate much better when they are stretched and know they are vital to the success or failure of an operation. Without being worked to death, your staff need to feel that their contribution is very important on a daily basis for the smooth running of the company.

However, whilst staff can be a tremendous burden, they can also represent the much-needed lifeblood. Recruiting your competitor's top salesman could mean he brings along a sackful of new business which will change the face of your company for years to come. Employing a highly technical production manager could mean he re-thinks your production techniques and doubles your gross profit. Setting up a mackerel-smoking business in Sheffield, or a steel plant in Cornwall, would be drastically reducing your chances of success, because you would not be taking advantage of the skilled labour in your area. The right staff can make your business, just as the wrong can break it.

There are a number of hidden costs involved in the employment of people, besides their salary.

◆ If you are employing anyone, you need Employers' Liability Insurance cover. It is a legal requirement.

◆ Staff get sick, need time off, have personal problems – all of which, to a greater or lesser extent, mean that while you are paying their salary, you are not getting a proper return on your investment. Indeed, you may even have to employ temporary help from an alternative source.

◆ It needs to be recognized that your staff will not take care of your equipment, plant and machinery, as you would do yourself. They will not be as careful about spending your money as they would about spending their own. This attitude may be restricted to their use of paper clips, or could be on a grand enough scale seriously to affect your gross profit.

The message is this – never employ anyone if you have an alternative, and if you do, take time and trouble to find the very best.

Recruitment

Having identified that you have a requirement to employ staff, what is your best method of finding them? It may surprise you that even with today's high unemployment figures, finding the right person for the job is not easy and, indeed, any personnel officer would confirm this in a more candid moment. When you consider the costs of redundancy or dismissal, it is imperative that you make the right decision when it comes to filling a job. Indeed, in many cases, employing the wrong person has far wider financial implications than simply the costs of getting rid of them. Take a salesman, for example. If you employ a useless salesman, not only do you have the costs of getting rid of him, you also have to bear the burden of reduced sales during the period the salesman is employed by you and is not bringing home the bacon.

Up and down our high streets, employment agencies abound. More discreetly, recruitment agencies, specializing in certain sectors of industry, bombard businesses with mailing shots advertising the services they have to offer. Frankly, you can do without any agency. They are fiendishly expensive and although their publicity suggests that they will screen and shortlist potential candidates for you, in most instances the kind of referral you are likely to get is positively indiscriminate. If you are looking for manual or clerical workers, you could do a lot worse than contact your local Jobcentre (apart from anything else, it is free), and for more senior appointments, place an advertisement either in your local newspaper or in a national paper, according to the calibre of person you are seeking.

Placing an advertisement

You have to be very careful with the preparation of an advertisement. Here are a few points to consider when advertising:

◆ You must take care not to infringe either the Sex Discrimination Act or the Race Relations Act.

◆ The wording of the advertisement is very important – keep it simple, quote the basic job description and details such as location, age of person required and salary range, if you are prepared to disclose it. Be specific – if, for example, the applicant must be able to drive, then say so. Stating your requirements clearly and concisely can save hours of sifting through useless applications.

◆ If you are advertising in the local press, it is not necessary to spend money on a large display advertisement. People who are looking for jobs read the small print, and you would do better to spend your money on running the advertisement over two weeks to give yourself the widest possible cross-section of choice, rather than splashing out on a big display for a week only.

◆ If you are advertising a top job in the national press, it is worth while considering a display advertisement. This way you will attract not only people who are unemployed, but

OUTSTANDING PRODUCTION ENGINEERS

THIS AD COULD CHANGE YOUR LIFE

If you're a first-class production engineer with the paper lucidly and quickly, Machinery and produ: like to talk to you about your future as a senior c one production engineering journal.

Applicants need not be experienced writer: unusual talent for understanding and commun must also possess an enquiring mind, energ Ideally, they will be aged between 30 and 40 tion engineering qualification and broad ex;

A sound knowledge of machine tools a: tial, while an understanding of the use environment would be an asset.

In return we offer a remuneration pa pany car, in the region of £12 000 to £1

Finan

Kent/Surrey

We are a progressive cons South East. Due to pro accountant with 2/3 years our small computerised statutory and management motivate others and roll up together with an opportunity profitability of this group would be an asset and a The group offer: contribu' people who are in work and may be only vaguely thinking of a change.

◆ Most newspapers, local and national, have special days for advertising jobs or types of job. Take the advice of the advertising manager and make sure you pick the right day.

◆ If you are in a tremendous hurry to fill the job and have a secretary who can handle calls, then you could quote your telephone number on the advertisement. As a general rule, though, it is far better to ask applicants to apply in writing, since a written application will provide the first stage of the shortlisting process. A number of applicants offering a poor standard of presentation letter can be instantly turned down. It is not easy to be so categoric with a telephone application.

◆ Having sorted through your applicants, shortlisted and called to interview those who you think are possible candidates, you are then ready for an interview. Whatever the outcome of your interview, do keep on file those people you have shortlisted. It may be that you have picked the wrong person initially, and if you come to this conclusion within a few months it might be worth contacting your former shortlist, before going to the expense of re-advertising.

If you would prefer an agency to handle recruitment for you, then do make sure you are aware of the financial implications. No agency charges less than two weeks' wages by way of an introductory fee. Some charge a month's wages, some much more. Make sure you give the agency a very precise brief, and if they start sending you unsuitable people, come down on them very hard. You are paying for their services because you do not have time to interview inappropriate candidates.

Whether you are planning to recruit via advertising or via an agency, do try and project a clear and *honest* picture of the job you have in mind. The more you can convey about the job at the recruitment stage, the more likely you are to find the correct candidate.

If you have a job vacancy coming up within your company, beware of taking on the relative of an existing member of staff – particularly if that existing member of staff is valuable to you. It is a trap into which many people fall. Whereas mother may be an invaluable accounts clerk, her son may be a hopeless salesman. If you are forced to sack him at some later date, it can cause untold ill feeling, and you may well find you lose two members of staff – not one.

Interviewing

Volumes have been written about interviewing technique – all too often making it sound complicated and rigid in structure. Every business is different, as is every interviewer and, of course, every interviewee. Each set of circumstances will spark off a different reaction, and flexibility of approach is the name of the game. Here are a few basic guidelines:

1 Before you even contemplate an interview, you have spadework to do. First, from your pile of applications you need to produce a shortlist. There is no easy route to this – it is simply a question of going through each application and gradually sifting out those people you know are inappropriate for the job. Write to them, telling them their application has been unsuccessful, and then concentrate on those who are left.

2 It is then a question of deciding in what order you should see your applicants. Understandably, we tend to have a natural prejudice against hiring the first applicant, or indeed the last, thinking in either case we are prejudiced. Certainly, if you have had a gruelling session of seeing, say, eight or ten people in a day, by the tenth you will be so confused and befuddled with details, you will find it hard to recognize if this is the right person. Bearing this in mind, it is advisable to put your most likely candidates somewhere in the middle of your interviewing programme. Do not cram too many into a day, or you will find yourself making the wrong decision.

3 Before seeing anyone, prepare a list of questions – general questions which relate quite specifically to the job you are trying to fill, and individual questions which apply to the applicant you are seeing. Prepared questions are very important. It is so easy in the heat of the interview to become sidetracked on a particular line of

conversation and then realize afterwards that you have not been thorough in your questioning.

4 In advance of the interview, study carefully your applicants' track records. These represent the most tangible indication of the type of person they are. Why have they had five jobs in as many years? There could be a good explanation – they may be highly ambitious and have found moving from job to job is the best way to obtain promotion quickly. As a general rule, though, be very suspicious of too many changes, and question this aspect very carefully indeed.

5 At the interview try and achieve a relaxed atmosphere. You want to see the applicant as he or she really is, and you are not going to do that if they are on their best behaviour. Use simple tools to help them unwind – a coffee, a

INTERVIEW ROOM

RELAX

cigarette, perhaps a drink at the pub if you have time. Find a common area of interest, unconnected with work, and steer the coversation in that direction for a while.

6   Above all, be a good listener. I am sure you have been to an interview where your prospective boss hardly draws breath in expounding the virtues of the company. You are then asked half a dozen standard questions and shown the door, leaving you wondering how on earth the interviewer can judge you from any other of the applicants – the answer is that he cannot. Yes, of course it is important to define the job clearly and describe the company for which the prospective employee may be working. After all, you are trying to find a round peg to fit in a round hole, and it is important that the applicant knows as much about you, as you know about him. However, do recognize when to shut up and listen.

7   If appropriate, introduce the applicant to the members of staff with whom he will be working, and then **leave them alone**. Give your staff time to make their own assessment of the applicant, uncluttered by your presence or any vibes they may be picking up from your reaction to the applicant. After the applicant has left, discuss the case with the staff concerned and really listen to what they have to say. However good you may consider the applicant to have been, he is of little use to you if the appointment is going to upset the existing staff.

8   Beware of anyone who speaks ill of a current or ex-employer. If they can rat on their former employer, they can rat on you. So, they may have been made redundant, that's tough, but it is all part of life's rich pattern. If they start whining, best forget them.

9   Ask for references and always take them up, but do not apply in writing.

Telephone former employers for information. These days the laws of libel in industrial relations make it very difficult for an ex-employer to be too derogatory. Not only that, with high unemployment, unless an employee has been dismissed for serious misconduct, the former employer is unlikely to be terribly frank if asked standard questions in writing. However, a telephone conversation is quite another matter – a few carefully worded questions should soon give you the full picture.

10 Do not be concerned about calling an applicant for interview twice, or even three times, before making a final decision. In these circumstances it would be a sensible gesture to pay for his expenses – travelling and meals – but for everyone's sake it is far better to ensure you are making the right decision, and first impressions are very difficult – for everyone.

A number of large companies use very complicated techniques for interviewing, involving a series of initiative tests, questionnaires and mock boardroom scenes. Like many ideas from the other side of the Atlantic, the concept is good in parts, but frankly the authors of this book do not feel it really suits the British psyche. The kind of aggressive individual who is likely to shine in these sorts of initiative test is not necessarily the sort of person you want working with you, on a day-in-and-day-out basis.

Appropriate qualifications, track record, pleasant personality, a tidy appearance, ability to get along with people, punctuality, reliability – perhaps not very original attributes, but undoubtedly the best.

Contracts of Employment

A contract of employment should be issued to every one of your employees who works for you for more than sixteen hours a week, and should be issued within thirteen weeks of the commencement of employment.

On the face of it, a contract of employment may seem to be yet another piece of rather onerous red tape, but in fact it is as useful to you as it is to your employee. Right from the outset of the relationship, it clarifies exactly what the terms of employment are and thus leaves no misunderstanding on either side.

On the facing page you will see a suggested contract of employment. It is shown in letter format since it seems preferable to make it as personal as possible, but there is no need for this – it can be a simple form. The suggested subjects covered are those standard items which should be mentioned, but your particular business may require added detail. For example, if you are in a seasonal business, the hours of employment may vary from summer to winter.

Some contracts of employment include such things as disciplinary rules relating to the job, grievance procedures for disgruntled employees and even a scale for minimum pay increases in the years ahead. Perhaps this is necessary in very large companies, but frankly it is not to be recommended. The contract of employment you are aiming to produce should strike a good balance between stating clearly the exact terms and conditions under which your employee is hired, and leaving a degree of flexibility.

The preparation of a contract of employment does concentrate the mind wonderfully as to exactly what you want your new member of staff to do and how expensive the whole procedure is going to be. It is worth considering actually drawing up a draft contract of employment prior to the interview, so that you are in a position to be very clear and categoric as to what you are offering a prospective employee.

In an ideal employer–employee relationship, once the contract of employment is signed, it will never be referred to again; any revisions in pay, conditions and benefits will from time to time be confirmed in writing, but the contract is always there, as a reference point in the event of disputes or misunderstandings arising.

SUGGESTED FORMAT FOR CONTRACT OF EMPLOYMENT

Dear

The following is a statement of the terms of your employment with the Company in accordance with the Contracts of Employment Act. Please be good enough to check these details carefully and sign and return the attached copy to me in due course.

DATE EMPLOYMENT BEGAN

TITLE OF JOB

REPORTING TO

EMPLOYMENT WEEK – For the purposes of the Social Security and Housing Benefit Act, the qualifying days are 7 days from Monday to Sunday.

NORMAL HOURS OF WORK – Monday to Friday   am –   pm with one hour for lunch. Saturday and Sunday by agreement from time to time.

PAID HOLIDAY ENTITLEMENT AND HOLIDAY PAY ON TERMINATION

(a) STATUTORY – All bank holidays
(b) ANNUAL –   working days to be taken in the calendar year by arrangement with your head of department. Holiday entitlement may not normally be carried over into the following year.
(c) IN YEAR EMPLOYMENT COMMENCED –   days with pay (to the nearest day) for each completed month of service. A day's pay for all purposes is taken as 1/5 of 1/52 of a year's salary.
(d) ON TERMINATION OF EMPLOYMENT – Holiday pay due on the date of leaving is calculated at   days for each completed month since the previous 1 January (termination taking place on or after 14 February or 15 of any other month being considered a completed month), less payment made for any holiday so far taken in the same period.

SICKNESS – In order to facilitate the payment of Statutory Sick Pay entitlement you should advise the Company if at any time you are incapacitated.

NOTICE – Employment may be terminated on either side by giving   months notice.

REMUNERATION – £   p.a. (paid monthly in arrears)

OTHER BENEFITS

(a) Membership of the Company's pension scheme in accordance with the rules of the scheme, a contribution equal to   % of your annual salary being deducted by instalments from your monthly pay.
(b) Use of a company car, a contribution of £   p.a. towards personal use being deducted from your monthly pay.
(c) Membership of the company health insurance scheme with
(d) Bonus or commission –

Yours sincerely,

MANAGING DIRECTOR

I acknowledge that the above is a correct statement of the current terms of my employment with the Company.

DATE

Staff Management and Promotion

How to be a great leader

Possibly the phrase most frequently issued from the lips of a desperate boss, is – "if you want a thing done properly, do it yourself." But just like the bad workers who blame their tools, ineffectual staff usually means ineffectual staff management.

If you have little or no experience of employing people, you are likely to fall into one of two traps.

◆ You may well expect too much of your staff. It is easy to be critical if they do not do things *your* way, but people need time to adjust to new jobs, and you need flexibility of mind. After all, your way may not be theirs and it is possible their way could be better.

◆ The other great mistake is to give staff too much responsibility, too quickly. This situation can all too often end in total disaster. You are resentful because the job is not being done properly. Your employee, aware that he is not giving you what you want, becomes tense and on the defensive. In no time at all the relationship breaks down and you are back recruiting again.

There are enormous adjustments to be made in starting a new job. Your employee has to get used to your business, to you, the other staff, a new travelling routine, a different pub for lunch . . . Much of this may seem trivial, but it is all very disorientating. Give your new staff time. You made the decision to employ them, so back your own judgement and give them breathing space.

Another major fault evident in many employers running small or medium-sized businesses is the inability to delegate. What is the point in keeping a dog and barking yourself? Maybe you can do the job better than the chap you are employing, but you cannot do everything. Develop your employees' skills as far as you can and then let them get on with it. If your business is to expand it can only do so by delegation. You simply have to know when to let go and concentrate on management.

In fairness, running a happy business is not easy. It is often very difficult to be sympathetic over staff squabbles when you yourself are battling away to keep your business alive. (They think they have problems, they should see yours!) It is very important, though, that you show genuine interest and concern and that you remember to praise good work as well as moan when it is poor. After you have been running your own business for a while, it becomes increasingly difficult to remember what it felt like to be employed. Particularly in these difficult times of unemployment, staff do feel very insecure. Do keep them fully informed. If your business is going through a good period, gather all your staff together and show them the rising graph. If you can afford it, give them a bonus – the more unexpected it is, the better for staff relations. Conversely, when things are going wrong, do not leave your staff to speculate as to whether they are going to be made redundant at any moment. Rumours and gossip are usually inaccurate and always damaging to the smooth running of a business. Keep your staff fully informed as to what is going on.

Above all, set a good example. You cannot expect your staff to work hard if you are not prepared to do so too. Do not arrive late in the morning, do not take three-hour lunches, do not leave early. Being the boss is not unlike being a parent – indeed the joys and sorrows come in roughly the same proportions. Be good to your staff and your staff will be good to you.

Promotion

Everyone, including you, has an optimum level of skill and ability to take responsibility, above which he or she cannot go successfully. All too often this factor is not recognized and never more so than when it comes to promotion. The wrong people, in the wrong jobs, can bring a business to its knees, but if you are expanding, and expanding fast, it happens all too easily. Perhaps you started your business from scratch, employing one or two people who would work round the clock to help you become established. The result – your natural inclination, as the business starts to grow, is to reward them for their loyalty and hard work. Your instincts are right, but it is all too easy for these rewards to take the form of over-promotion, well beyond their ability. This, in turn, will cause them stress and slow down the progress of your business.

The trap is a facile one. One of the most disastrous but frequent promotions is rewarding the brilliant sales representative by promotion to sales manager. Whatever you do, if you have a brilliant salesman never let him be anything else. If sales staff can sell your company's product or service then reward them by a better car, a higher commission, a cut of the profits . . . anything to keep them, but *never, never* take them away from the thing they are good at. You can bet your life that if someone is temperamentally suited to be a salesman, he will make a simply dreadful manager. Sales staff are very individual people – loners – they are totally unsuited to being in charge of others.

Of course, there are times when promotion is appropriate. You may well have taken one or two young trainees whom you are grooming for stardom because you recognized their potential early on. As a general rule, though, be wary of internal promotion – bringing in fresh blood may well be a better alternative. You can hinder the development of your business and cause a great deal of distress all round by heaping responsibilities on shoulders not broad enough to take them. If a job opportunity presents itself within your business, even if you think you already have the ideal person to promote into it, draw up a job description and then compare it with the known attributes of your existing employee. Look at it dispassionately – what you are looking for is the best person to fill that job. If that person does not exist within your company structure then go out, shop around and fill the vacancy from the outside. Remember, promotion is no reward unless it is really justified.

I WONDER WHAT CHANGES THE NEW BOSS HAS IN MIND.

In an ideal world, everyone you employ would be loyal and hard-working and would be prepared to put in whatever long hours were necessary for the benefit of your business. Attitudes *have* changed in recent years. The tremendous spate of business failures and the resultant high level of unemployment has tended to make workers look outside their own immediate requirements. Suddenly they are prepared to join in enthusiastically with a project which is going to ensure the future of the company which employs them. However, the fact is that most people respond best to some sort of tangible encouragement. Praise is all very well, job satisfaction is important, but an actual reward not only demonstrates their worth in their own eyes, but acts as the carrot for ensuring their hard work and support.

Before considering any type of bonus or incentive scheme for your staff, look first at what you are trying to achieve, and second – and more important – at what your business can actually afford. It is easy to introduce a scheme to boost sales, but when the new boosted sales become the accepted norm and the sales figure is still climbing, you can find yourself in the position of paying out vast sums of money to finance your business expansion. An incentive scheme, once introduced, rapidly becomes accepted as an entitlement and is very difficult to withdraw without causing a great deal of bad feeling. Wrongly calculated, it can prove to be an expensive and totally unjustified overhead.

Take the simple example of overtime rates. Perhaps you have a new contract, which involves a great deal of extra work. As a result, you encourage several members of your staff to stay on late at night, or work on Saturday afternoon, in return for which you pay them an overtime rate. Before you know where you are, that overtime will become a very expensive and regular habit, long after the contract is finished. Suddenly you will find that hard-working, but relatively unskilled, staff will

be earning more than your general manager. Your workload may be sporadic. Alternatively, you may need to operate a six-day week because your premises are not large enough to cope with the production demand within a five-day working week. Rather than granting overtime rates, you might be in a better position if you employed part-time staff.

Incentive payments can be offered as a direct reward for personal success, or they can be distributed on a pro rata basis from a common pool, based on a ratio of effort to results. Let us look at the different types of possible incentive.

◆ On a personal level, you can –
  a) offer piecework rates, perhaps linked to a bonus for reaching a particular production target, or
  b) offer commission linked to personal achievement, which in most cases would apply to sales staff, where the calculation can be directly related to their selling effort.
◆ General incentives can be offered where –
  a) A bonus is paid to a group of staff on the results of an individual department, office or division, or
  b) a commission or profit share is paid to all staff, as a result of the specific achievements of the business as a whole.

Rewards/incentive schemes should be regular and consistent. In other words, do not keep moving the goal posts. They should also be attainable. Little and often has a far greater impact than a huge 'pie in the sky' reward, which seems totally out of reach.

Where feasible, link the reward to net profit, rather than gross profit, and gross profit rather than sales.

Golden rules

◆ A salesman with any discretion on selling price should be paid commission on gross profit, not on turnover. If you base the commission on turnover it will be all too tempting to sell by discounting the price.

◆ Similarly, managers should receive a share of the net profit of their company/division/branch, since it would be all too easy for them to generate sales or even gross profit by excessive overhead spending. Their incentive must be linked to profitability.

When devising an incentive scheme, you do not need to be thinking purely in terms of cash. You could offer a holiday, a title – such as 'salesman of the year' – a dinner for two, a weekend break, a video . . . These sorts of relatively low-cost item can prove very effective. They inspire healthy competition amongst your employees, they are fun and much appreciated by staff.

Be warned: do be very careful about introducing any sort of incentive scheme which splits the company. In other words, if you introduce an incentive scheme into the production department, you may well have your sales and clerical staff up in arms, saying the business could not run without them, and why cannot they be included? In these circumstances, far from encouraging greater employee effort, you can end up with a divided and resentful staff.

Employee shareholders

You might feel that you can build a greater degree of management loyalty, or indeed workforce loyalty, by offering shares in your business. Alternatively, to encourage management, or perhaps to poach a top man from the opposition, you might feel it necessary to offer 'a piece of the action'. In theory, this is a good idea, and you can either issue shares or grant options. However, if yours is a private company,

you do need to be very cautious about taking such a step. Offering your staff shares in a private company can be both dangerous and ineffectual. What happens if your high-flying general manager/sales director leaves in three years' time with 5 per cent of the equity and goes to the opposition? From the employee's point of view, the shareholding cannot actually be sold without your help and so is not really worth a lot to him as an individual. However, the possible nuisance and embarrassment factor to you is considerable. Are you prepared to give away 5 per cent of your business, and for what? In a private company, it is far better to offer a percentage of the net profit, rather than a percentage of the equity. However, if you are considering issuing shares or offering share options to employees, make sure you obtain good tax advice, both for you and for them.

Employ in haste, repent at leisure. Hiring is easy, firing is difficult.

The legislation surrounding dismissal has to be treated with great respect. Many businesses fall foul of the section relating to unfair dismissal. These are the important pointers:

◆ Every member of your staff, part-timer or otherwise, who has been employed by you for fifty-two weeks (or two years in the case of a business employing less than twenty people) must be given a written statement of your reasons for dismissal.

◆ If you wish to dismiss someone who has been with you for more than a year (or two years, whichever is applicable) for some sort of unsatisfactory conduct or lack of performance, you must give three written warnings.

◆ These written warnings should clearly state your reasons for reprimand, what the employee must do to put things right, and what will happen if he or she does not conform.

◆ After three written warnings, he or she may be dismissed, but will still be at liberty to take the case to an industrial tribunal, to establish whether the grounds for dismissal were reasonable or not.

◆ You must give your employee one week's notice, or payment in lieu, if he or she has been with you continuously for four weeks or more, and after two years, one week's notice for every year of continuous employment. This, of course, is the standard requirement. The contract of employment you have agreed with your employee may well be different, entitling them to a month's or three months' notice – in which case this must be honoured.

Industrial tribunals

Industrial tribunals are perhaps a little more flexible when it comes to unfair dismissal than they have been in the past. For example, they do now take into account the size of the employer's business. If an employee is dismissed because he is unsuitable for a job, the industrial tribunal might say that a large business should make strenuous efforts to re-employ that employee elsewhere in the company. However, so far as a small business is concerned, it probably will be understood that this may not be possible.

So far as the industrial tribunal is concerned, the three main areas offering fair grounds for dismissal are **misconduct, incompetence,** or **genuine redundancy**. Redundancy we deal with specifically in the next section of this book, but let us look at the other two.

Misconduct
Assuming you have behaved properly towards your employee, misconduct is relatively easy to prove as reasonable grounds for dismissal. If a member of staff consistently has not turned up for work, or has taken three-hour lunch breaks, then this is misconduct, and provided that you have issued three written warnings, generally speaking the tribunal will uphold your decision.

Incompetence
Proving incompetence is not nearly so easy, because so far as most jobs are concerned, competence is a matter of opinion and is also greatly affected by other factors. You might dismiss a salesman for incompetence because he obtained no sales. The salesman could challenge this by saying that he has not had the necessary back-up, or that the product he has been asked to sell is over-priced, or of poor quality. With production staff it is generally easier to prove incompetence, because you can demonstrate that your employee has been

consistently turning out shoddy work. Here again, though, this is not so easy to prove if the person in question is part of a production line and maintains that it is others' work which is adversely affecting his standard of work.

There are other circumstances in which you may feel that you can no longer continue employing someone – if he is consistently off sick, or has some public duty – perhaps is on the planning committee of your local council. Then, of course, there is the additional problem of employing pregnant women. Let us look at these in more detail.

Sickness

It is quite unreasonable for an employer to dismiss anyone who suffers from ill health – clearly it cannot be morally justified. However, if you are running a small business, continual absence of a key employee can have a disastrous affect. The only grounds for dismissing someone who is consistently sick is your ability to prove that the absences are causing major disruption to your business.

Public duties

Whether it is a question of your employee being a member of the local council or being called to jury service, you are obliged to give reasonable time off to attend to these duties, though not necessarily with pay. Sporadic time off for public engagements would not be grounds for dismissal.

Maternity leave

Provided a woman works until eleven weeks before her confinement, and has been continuously employed by your business for two years or more, her legal entitlement is to take forty weeks off and then return to her original job, without any loss of seniority. This legislation does not apply to small businesses employing less than five people. It should also be noted that, regardless of length of service, or number of hours worked per week by an employee, if she is pregnant she must be allowed time off, with pay, during working hours, in order to keep an appointment at an antenatal clinic, if advised to do so by a doctor, midwife or health visitor.

In general terms, you do have to be extremely careful in all areas of dismissal. A case going against you could be absolutely ruinous to your business, since compensation awards can be quite high. Make sure you are meticulous in preparing your case for dismissal, and if you are in doubt, consult your solicitor before taking any action.

This, then, deals with the legal obligations of dismissal, but there are other practical considerations. Dismissing anyone, however justified the decision, is very disruptive for the other members of your staff, and will make them feel very insecure. Make sure when you have dismissed the employee in question, you explain what you have done and why to the other staff – not only because they deserve an explanation, but also because it may well stop them following in the same footsteps. Unless you have absolutely no alternative, never allow dismissed members of staff to work out their notice. Dismiss them, give the money in lieu of notice and get them off the premises immediately. There are very good grounds for making this point. An employee who has been sacked is bound to feel bitter and resentful, and in extreme cases may do actual physical damage to your premises or equipment. However, even if his or her reaction is not so dramatic, you can be sure that it will seriously undermine the morale of the rest of your staff. Your former employee will be critical of you and of everything your company stands for, and this is bound to rub off. Far better pay existing staff overtime or take on a part-timer while you find a permanent replacement.

Redundancy

Redundancy occurs when a job ceases to exist. You cannot make someone redundant one week and then employ someone else in a similar capacity the following week. Redundancy usually happens when a company is cutting back because of financial pressure, but it may also be necessary if a company is genuinely changing the direction of its trade and therefore requires a different type of employee. An employee is entitled to redundancy pay, based on a formula relating to the length of service and rate of pay, provided that he or she has been employed continuously by you for two years since the age of 18 and has not reached the age of retirement.

Redundancy payment is a lump sum of compensation for loss of job. If you are employing less than ten people, a sum equal to approximately half of the redundancy payments you make is recoverable from the Department of Employment, **who should** **be notified in advance** about anyone you intend to make redundant. We have included a ready reckoner for redundancy payments, which will enable you to establish what sort of money is involved in making someone redundant.

A genuine redundancy – whilst it can be expensive – will not attract a claim for unfair dismissal, but you do have to be absolutely confident that the job in question is really terminating, before making someone redundant.

For further details on redundancy payments, ask for the booklet on the 1965 Redundancy Payments Act, which is available from Department of Employment Press Office, 8 St James's Square, London SW1Y 4JB. If you are at all uncertain as to whether you are justified in making a redundancy, do consult your solicitor before taking any steps.

READY RECKONER FOR REDUNDANCY PAYMENTS

Read off employee's age and number of complete years' service. Any week which began before the employee attained the age of 18 does not count. The table will then show how many weeks' pay the employee is entitled to.

For a woman aged between 59 and 60, and a man aged between 64 and 65, the cash amount due is to be reduced by one-twelfth for every complete month by which the age exceeds 59 or 64 respectively.

SERVICE (years)

AGE (yrs.)	2	3	4	5	6	7	8	9	10	11	12	13	14	15	16	17	18	19	20
20	1	1	1	1	–														
21	1	1½	1½	1½	1½	–													
22	1	1½	2	2	2	2	–												
23	1½	2	2½	3	3	3	3	–											
24	2	2½	3	3½	4	4	4	4	–										
25	2	3	3½	4	4½	5	5	5	5	–									
26	2	3	4	4½	5	5½	6	6	6	6	–								
27	2	3	4	5	5½	6	6½	7	7	7	7	–							
28	2	3	4	5	6	6½	7	7½	8	8	8	8	–						
29	2	3	4	5	6	7	7½	8	8½	9	9	9	9	–					

30	2	3	4	5	6	7	8	8½	9	9½	10	10	10	10	–				
31	2	3	4	5	6	7	8	9	9½	10	10½	11	11	11	11	–			
32	2	3	4	5	6	7	8	9	10	10½	11	11½	12	12	12	12	–		
33	2	3	4	5	6	7	8	9	10	11	11½	12	12½	13	13	13	13	–	
34	2	3	4	5	6	7	8	9	10	11	12	12½	13	13½	14	14	14	14	–
35	2	3	4	5	6	7	8	9	10	11	12	13	13½	14	14½	15	15	15	15
36	2	3	4	5	6	7	8	9	10	11	12	13	14	14½	15	15½	16	16	16
37	2	3	4	5	6	7	8	9	10	11	12	13	14	15	15½	16	16½	17	17
38	2	3	4	5	6	7	8	9	10	11	12	13	14	15	16	16½	17	17½	18
39	2	3	4	5	6	7	8	9	10	11	12	13	14	15	16	17	17½	18	18½
40	2	3	4	5	6	7	8	9	10	11	12	13	14	15	16	17	18	18½	19
41	2	3	4	5	6	7	8	9	10	11	12	13	14	15	16	17	18	19	19½
42	2½	3½	4½	5½	6½	7½	8½	9½	10½	11½	12½	13½	14½	15½	16½	17½	18½	19½	20½
43	3	4	5	6	7	8	9	10	11	12	13	14	15	16	17	18	19	20	21
44	3	4½	5½	6½	7½	8½	9½	10½	11½	12½	13½	14½	15½	16½	17½	18½	19½	20½	21½
45	3	4½	6	7	8	9	10	11	12	13	14	15	16	17	18	19	20	21	22
46	3	4½	6	7½	8½	9½	10½	11½	12½	13½	14½	15½	16½	17½	18½	19½	20½	21½	22½
47	3	4½	6	7½	9	10	11	12	13	14	15	16	17	18	19	20	21	22	23
48	3	4½	6	7½	9	10½	11½	12½	13½	14½	15½	16½	17½	18½	19½	20½	21½	22½	23½
49	3	4½	6	7½	9	10½	12	13	14	15	16	17	18	19	20	21	22	23	24
50	3	4½	6	7½	9	10½	12	13½	14½	15½	16½	17½	18½	19½	20½	21½	22½	23½	24½
51	3	4½	6	7½	9	10½	12	13½	15	16	17	18	19	20	21	22	23	24	25
52	3	4½	6	7½	9	10½	12	13½	15	16½	17½	18½	19½	20½	21½	22½	23½	24½	25½
53	3	4½	6	7½	9	10½	12	13½	15	16½	18	19	20	21	22	23	24	25	26
54	3	4½	6	7½	9	10½	12	13½	15	16½	18	19½	20½	21½	22½	23½	24½	25½	26½
55	3	4½	6	7½	9	10½	12	13½	15	16½	18	19½	21	22	23	24	25	26	27
56	3	4½	6	7½	9	10½	12	13½	15	16½	18	19½	21	22½	23½	24½	25½	26½	27½
57	3	4½	6	7½	9	10½	12	13½	15	16½	18	19½	21	22½	24	25	26	27	28
58	3	4½	6	7½	9	10½	12	13½	15	16½	18	19½	21	22½	24	25½	26½	27½	28½
59	3	4½	6	7½	9	10½	12	13½	15	16½	18	19½	21	22½	24	25½	27	28	29
60	3	4½	6	7½	9	10½	12	13½	15	16½	18	19½	21	22½	24	25½	27	28½	29½
61	3	4½	6	7½	9	10½	12	13½	15	16½	18	19½	21	22½	24	25½	27	28½	30
62	3	4½	6	7½	9	10½	12	13½	15	16½	18	19½	21	22½	24	25½	27	28½	30
63	3	4½	6	7½	9	10½	12	13½	15	16½	18	19½	21	22½	24	25½	27	28½	30
64	3	4½	6	7½	9	10½	12	13½	15	16½	18	19½	21	22½	24	25½	27	28½	30

Pay As You Earn – PAYE

If you employ *anyone*, the salary or wages you pay will be liable to tax under Schedule E of the Income Tax Act. You, in your role as the employer, are obliged to collect that tax on behalf of the Inland Revenue, and pay it over to the Collector of Taxes each month. The UK fiscal year, for some highly obscure reason, ends on 5 April, and tax deducted by you from wages and salaries, paid up to the fifth day of each month, must be paid over to the Collector by the nineteenth day of that month. If you, as founder of your business, trade through a limited company, you will be regarded as an employee and subject to Schedule E tax, whatever you call yourself – a director, manager or simply an employee.

Therefore, even if you are a solo operation, if you trade as a limited company you personally will be regarded as an employee and will have to operate a PAYE system and deduct and pay over tax on anything you draw.

Conversely, if you are operating as a sole trader or in partnership, you will be taxed on your annual profit. This means that you are not taxed at the time you draw money out of business, but at the end of the fiscal year, when you make your tax return and submit your most recent accounts. In these circumstances you are taxed under Schedule D, but **before you begin trading** you must register your intention to be taxed under Schedule D, so that the tax office is aware of your situation.

Operating a PAYE system

Obviously a PAYE system costs money to administer – your time if you run a small business, or the cost of a wages/salaries office if you are in a medium to large business. However, it needs to be remembered that PAYE is not a tax on your business – you are merely acting as a collector and your job is to deduct the tax due from employees and hand it over to the Inland Revenue. Having said that, if you fail to deduct PAYE from *any* remuneration you pay which is properly subject to tax, you will be charged with the tax which should have been deducted and **you may have to pay an additional penalty**. This sort of situation will come to light during routine inspection of your PAYE records by the Inland Revenue – which happens to all businesses, every two or three years.

Example
If you pay £200 of casual labour and fail to deduct tax, it will be assumed that you have paid a gross figure of £274, less tax at 27 per cent – i.e. £74. You could end up by paying the £200 plus the tax of £74, plus a penalty of as much as another £100. Of course, in theory, you can go back to your casual labourer and recover the £74, but you are not likely to be very popular, nor enjoy that labourer's services again.

PAY ADVICE

Employee:
Employee no:
Contribution letter:
Period from:
Tax code:
NI no:
to:

PAYMENTS	HOURS	RATE	TOTAL
Regular hours:			
Overtime hours:			
Holiday:			

TOTAL EARNED:

DEDUCTIONS:

Income tax:
National Insurance:
Pension contribution:
Other:
Gross pay to date for tax purposes:
Tax free pay:
Taxable pay to date:
Tax due to date:
Tax refund:
TOTAL DEDUCTIONS:
TOTAL NET PAY:

KEEP THIS RECORD OF YOUR EARNINGS

PAYE administration is not difficult, but it is a chore. It involves you keeping records for each employee and dealing with weekly or monthly tax tables. Everyone is entitled to a tax-free personal allowance which is set off against income, and this may be increased by various allowable expenses, or reduced by reason of disallowable items. The effect is that virtually everyone has an element of income each year, which is not subject to tax. This free pay is notified to the individual and the employer in the form of a code number. You will be provided with tax tables which, with the individual's code number, will enable you to identify how much tax-free pay is allowed. Most new employees will provide you with a Form P45, which shows their current code number. This will be updated at the start of each new tax year. If your employee leaves your service, you in turn will then provide a P45 for the next employer. There are special rules (and needless to say, many more forms) for dealing with new employees who, for some reason, do not have a P45. While you are waiting for an employee to be given a code number, you will tax them on an emergency basis, under special rules.

Each time you pay someone, you have to
1   Calculate the cumulative gross pay earned in the current tax year.
2   Look up the free pay entitlement for the year to date, appropriate to the employee's code number.
3   Deduct the free pay from the gross pay, to arrive at taxable pay to date.
4   Look up, or calculate, the tax payable to date.
5   Deduct from this the cumulative tax already paid.
    Result = the tax payable this week, or this month!!!

At the end of each tax year you are obliged to submit a list of all your employees, showing the total tax deducted from each individual and reconciling the total deductions with the total paid over to the Collector of Taxes during the year. You also have to provide an annual certificate for each employee, showing gross pay in the year and the tax deducted, so that each one knows that the money you have collected has been passed over on his or her behalf.

Computerized payrolls

For the small business, computers are often of questionable worth. Here is a guide to the type of system you will need.
◆   If you have up to five employees use nothing more sophisticated than the Inland Revenue standard stationery forms.
◆   If you have five to ten employees, then invest in a small multi-copy payroll system – Safeguard is probably the best.
◆   If you have ten employees or more, you can choose one of two avenues. Either invest in your own small computer, plus payroll software – this can be done for under £400 now – or sub-contract the whole exercise to a local computer bureau, who will undertake the job for you and really charge very little for the amount of hassle they take off your shoulders.

The Inspector of Taxes, the Collector of Taxes – indeed the tax system as a whole – has a far from attractive image and as such, the average new business tends to look upon the tax system as the enemy. Certainly, so far as PAYE is concerned, this is not the case. You are doing a job on behalf of the Inland Revenue, whose wish is that you do it efficiently. Do not hesitate to ask for advice and training for yourself or for your staff. It is your right to do so, and surprisingly, perhaps, you should find the response you get disarmingly helpful.

National Insurance

Income Tax is not the only tax we pay. For many people, whether employed or working for themselves, National Insurance is another and sometimes more onerous form of taxation. Unlike PAYE, National Insurance is a tax on the **employer** as well as the **employee**. Once you pay anyone more than £150 a week (approximately £650 a month), the cost to the employer is 10.45 per cent of gross pay – without any upper limit. As a general rule, National Insurance is charged at the appropriate scale rate on the earnings actually paid in any one week, or month. An exception is made in the case of directors, where earnings are accumulated in each tax year, and National Insurance re-calculated by reference to cumulative pay. In other words, if for cash-flow purposes you have only been receiving £50 a week and then suddenly draw, say, £5,000 as a lump sum in September, the National Insurance due from you and from the company for the six-month period will be worked out on the total payments of about £5,600. The amount already paid will be deducted to find the contributions now payable on the £5,000. This does not apply to other employees.

There is a sliding scale of charges payable by employee and employer. The rates fixed in the March 1987 Budget are as follows:

The following examples will clarify the operation of these scale rates:

1 Gross pay in the week £99 – employee and employer each pay 7 per cent, or £6.93.
2 Gross pay in the week £101 – employee and employer each pay 9 per cent, or £9.09. (So the employee has earned £2 more, but is worse off.)
3 Gross pay in the week £350 – employee pays 9 per cent up to £295, or £26.55, employer pays 10.45 per cent on £350, or £36.57.

Married women
Provided that she chose to do so before 6 April 1977, a married woman, if she so wished, can have opted to pay the married woman's reduced rate of National Insurance contribution. This does reduce the married woman's benefits, but if her husband is amply covered by state and/or private benefits, this may not matter. However, whilst a married woman may have opted to pay a reduced rate, the employer is still responsible for making a full contribution.

Old age pensioners
Employees over pension age who are still working no longer have to contribute to National Insurance. However, their

	Rate Payable on all Earnings	
	Employee	Employer
Up to £39 a week	Nil	Nil
Between £39 & £64.99 a week	5%	5%
Between £65 & £99.99 a week	7%	7%
Between £100 & £149.99 a week	9%	9%
Between £150 & £295 a week	9%	10.45%
Additional charge over £295 a week	Nil	10.45%

employer's contributions must continue at the full standard rate.

Self-employed

The self-employed person pays a flat-rate contribution, normally by way of stamps, which is called Class 2. That person also will be expected to pay a profit-related contribution, which is payable at the same time as the income tax liability. This is known as Class 4.

HAVING A WONDERFUL TIME. NOT COMING BACK. YOU CAN KEEP THIS NATIONAL INSURANCE STAMP.

National Insurance can prove very expensive for the self-employed person, who is also employed. You can find yourself making contributions as an employed person and yet still being liable for classes 2 and 4, although you get a refund if you end up paying too much.

Voluntary contributions

Those people who are not in gainful employment can still opt to pay a flat-rate contribution, to ensure continuity of benefit. This is known as Class 3.

A few points to consider

◆ As an employer, it is better to employ two part-timers, at a rate of £38.50 per week or less, rather than one person at £77 per week. This is because if you are employing someone who earns less than £39 per week, you do not have to pay any National Insurance contributions.

◆ If you do not need the protection of a limited company, from a National Insurance point of view, it is better to be self-employed rather than employed. If you are employed by your own company, both you and the company will be paying National Insurance contributions. The total will almost inevitably exceed your self-employed liability.

◆ From an employee's point of view, it is better to have several low-paid jobs rather than one on a high salary, and certainly, if you can keep your wages below the National Insurance threshold, this is a great help.

For an employer it is necessary to keep records. These are, in effect, an extension of the PAYE system. Again, you will find your local DHSS most helpful in dealing with any queries you have with regard to National Insurance.

Statutory Sick Pay

All employers are responsible for paying Statutory Sick Pay (SSP) to their employees for up to twenty-eight weeks of sickness absence in any one tax year. However, as an employer, you can reclaim any SSP paid by deducting it from your PAYE and National Insurance liability each month.

SSP is payable to all employees, with these exceptions:

◆ Employees over retirement age.
◆ Employees on short-term contracts.
◆ Employees on strike.
◆ Employees earning less than £39 per week.

of SSP – i.e. the PIWs, the waiting days, the qualifying days and the SSP payments.

SSP is time-consuming and frankly will prove to be a natural irritant to you or your wages department. To a reasonably intelligent person the detailed SSP rules and regulations (contained within the DHSS *Employer's Guide to Statutory Sick Pay* and the annually published SSP *Rates and Notes*) are a nightmare of bureaucratic nonsense. It is important that proper records are kept, however, because there are penalties for employers who fail to administer SSP properly. There is no escape.

The current rates for SSP are as follows:-

Employee's weekly earnings	Weekly SSP benefit
£76.50 plus	£47.20
£39 to £76.49	£32.85

SSP is treated as earnings and is subject in the normal way to PAYE and National Insurance contributions.

How to qualify for SSP

SSP is only payable for periods of illness lasting four days or more and the term used for these periods of illness is PIW – **period of incapacity for work**. The first three qualifying days for a PIW are known as **waiting days**, and no SSP can be allowed for these. However, from the fourth day onwards, the employee is eligible for SSP. If two PIWs are linked by less than eight weeks, they can be counted together – in other words, you only apply three waiting days to the total period and SSP is payable on all other days.

There are two basic rules for SSP which need to be followed:

◆ Employees must report sickness promptly to their employers.
◆ Employers must keep a record of qualifying days for each employee. This means an accurate record of each stage

Maternity rights

Time off

First, regardless of length of service or the number of hours worked in any one week, an employee who is pregnant is allowed time off, with pay, during working hours, in order to keep an appointment at an ante-natal clinic, provided she has been advised to do so by a doctor, a midwife or a health visitor. However, the employer is only required to allow her this paid time off if she provides a medical certificate, or some other form of documentation, saying that an appointment has been made.

The right to return to work

If an employee is absent from work because of pregnancy and confinement, she has the right to return to work, provided that she has been continuously employed, by the same employer, for at least two years immediately prior to the eleventh week before confinement, unless –

- at the time she ceased work the employer employed less than five people.
- it is not possible for her employer to reinstate her in her original job, or offer her a suitable alternative employment.

It is also necessary for the employee to inform her employer as follows, in order to qualify for the right to return to work.

- She must inform her employer, in writing, at least twenty-one days before her absence, stating that she will be absent from work because of pregnancy and confinement.
- She must also inform her employer, in writing, that she intends to return to work.
- She must also inform her employer of the expected week of her confinement.

The employee has the right to return to work at any time before the end of the period of twenty-nine weeks, beginning with the week in which the confinement falls. She has the right to the job in which she was employed under the original contract of employment, and on terms and conditions no less favourable to her than those that would have applied if she had not been absent from work. The employer may write to the employee, not earlier than forty-nine days after the beginning of her expected week of confinement, asking her to confirm her intention to return to work, and informing her that unless she sends written confirmation within fourteen days of her intention to return, she will lose her right to do so.

As soon as you know a member of your staff is pregnant, take time and trouble discussing the situation with her and if she feels, at that stage, that she would like to come back to work after her confinement, begin planning how she can be eased out of the business without too much disruption and yet a place re-created for her when she returns. If you show willingness to co-operate, you will find that your employee is more than ready to be flexible if her role has to change slightly on her return.

Statutory Maternity Pay

Responsibility for the detailed administration of maternity pay has been transferred recently from the Department of Health and Social Security to individual employers, along very similar lines to the earlier transfer of responsibility for the payment of sick pay. Again, the detailed rules are complex.

Statutory Maternity Pay (SMP) is payable for a maximum of eighteen weeks, starting at the earliest in the eleventh week before the expected week of confinement, and at latest in the sixth week before the expected week of confinement week of confinement.

To qualify for SMP an employee must have worked for you continuously for at least twenty-six weeks, continuing into the fifteenth week before her expected week of confinement. This fifteenth week is known as the qualifying week. She must still be pregnant in the eleventh week prior to her expected confinement, and her average earnings must at least equal the lower earnings limit for payment of National Insurance contributions. She cannot work for you, or anyone, else, whilst you are paying her SMP.

There are two rates of SMP payable. The higher rate, equal to 90 per cent of average earnings, is payable for the first six weeks. A lower, fixed-scale rate is payable for the balance of the eighteen-week entitlement. To qualify for the initial higher rate, your employee must have worked for you continuously for at least two years up to and including the qualifying week, and she must normally have worked for at least sixteen hours per week. Alternatively, she may have worked for you continuously for five years at between eight and sixteen hours per week. You pay SMP after your employee has stopped work, but like wages or salary it is subject to tax and National Insurance. You recover the whole payment, plus compensation for the employer's National Insurance contribution, from your monthly settlement of PAYE and NI to the Collector of Taxes.

Trade Unions and Staff Associations

As an employer running your own business, it is very easy for you to take up the position of a trade-union basher. Yet it does need to be recognized that in today's industrial scene, trade unions do have a very important part to play and can be of enormous value to industry. All too often, the publicity that surrounds trade unions is geared towards the aggressive elements, completely ignoring the benefits a union can offer.

Having said that, if you are starting a brand-new business, value your independence very highly and are not in a particularly union-sensitive industry, then you would probably be best advised to employ non-union-members. This is a sweeping statement, because so much depends on your ambitions. If you are always intending to run a small to medium-sized business, then non-union labour is almost certainly the best answer. However, if you are ambitious for your business, wish to see it grow into a major force within your industry, pitching for the best contracts around, then you are going to be noticed. And if you are going to be noticed, sooner or later the fact that your staff are not union members may well rebound on you.

In certain industries, unions play a very small part, whereas in others they are very important. For example, if you are a commercial artist and decide to open your own art studio, you will know that in order to have your designs accepted by most of the national press, you have to have a union stamp. This is one instance, and there are many like it. There is absolutely no point in attempting to run a non-unionized company in such circumstances.

If you are acquiring an existing business, or already have staff who are union members, then the trick is not to aggravate your union. This should not be difficult, provided you play by the rules. If you treat your staff well and with courtesy, pay them the correct wages for the job and keep them informed at all times on the progress of your company, then your relationship with the union concerned should be relatively easy to handle. Unions can make a very useful contribution, and when there are staff problems, rather than having to negotiate with a number of different people – which can become very personal and emotive – you have just one body with

which to negotiate. Unions can be enormously helpful in such areas as industrial safety and maintaining standards of work. It is terribly important, though, not to operate in a vacuum and simply ignore the union rules. In most instances, for example, if you wish to make a union member redundant, you need to inform the union thirty days before you do so. This may not be very helpful from your point of view, but if you break the rules and do not inform them, not only do you upset them but you are also liable to have to pay the member of staff in question extra compensation.

If your business is involved with a union, wherever possible consult them about all aspects of the company's development – even those which do not directly affect the union members. When you open a new extension to the workshop or when you have a Christmas party, ask along the union officials. Like everyone else in a similar position, they need to feel that they are not being ignored and that the power they have is recognized.

Unions have moved with the times. Earlier in this century, without doubt management grossly exploited the workers. The backlash of this was that many unions for a while became all-powerful, militant and destructive – to the considerable detriment of our industries. The pendulum has swung again and this time has balanced out well. Unions expect a fair deal for their members but not at the expense of costing them their jobs.

Staff associations

A number of largely non-unionized companies have set up staff associations of their own. Certainly, if you have a very well-established company and feel that a staff association would be of benefit to your general staff relations, then there is nothing to stop you establishing one. However, it has to be said that if you are treating your workforce properly, you do not actually need a staff association, and certainly before setting one up, you do need to consider the implications of its not being successful. In a way, offering your staff this facility is suggesting that they actually need it, which in turn may make them suspicious as to their existing rights. If, for whatever reason, the association does not work, you may well find your staff turning to a recognized union instead.

A genuine staff association – i.e. one that has real power – is, to all intents and purposes, a union, which brings us back to our original comment. If you are not compelled to employ union people, then do not. Similarly, if you are not compelled to launch a staff association, then why do it? Certainly if you are not prepared to give your staff association real power then you are in danger of creating more resentment than if you did not have an association at all.

Every thinking person knows that in order to get a good job done, you need to employ the right people, pay them the right rate for the job and see that the conditions in which they work are pleasant and safe. It is also necessary to make sure someone you employ feels as confident as possible about his or her future, knows enough about your business, and can be enthusiastic about the overall achievements of the business. If there is a grouse or some personal trouble, there must be someone with whom to talk through the problem, and there must be a sense of job satisfaction. This situation is not a difficult one to achieve – all you have to do is put yourself in the position of your employees and see whether the conditions you have created for them are the sort of conditions in which you, yourself, would like to work. If they are not, then you must do something about it. Given this attitude to employing people, there is nothing any trade union or staff association can do to better the situation. Be good to your staff and your staff will be good to you, and the long-term benefits will be a prosperous business in which you all can work.

TAXATION

Income Tax

It is a fact of life that taxation plays a highly influential part in our financial planning, and as someone running, or intending to run, your own business, it is important that you have a rudimentary knowledge of the various taxes which you are liable to come across in the course of your working life. Let us look at income tax.

Income tax allowances

Everyone can enjoy income that is free of income tax, up to the level of the personal allowance to which they are entitled. The main personal allowances for 1987–8 are:

Personal allowance	Single Person	£2,425
	Married Couple	£3,795
Age allowance (applicable if either spouse is over 65)	Single Person	£2,960
	Married Couple	£4,675
Age allowance (applicable if either spouse is over 80)	Single Person	£3,070
	Married Couple	£4,845
Wife's earned income allowance (where both husband and wife are earning)		£2,425

The age allowance is a substitute for the personal allowance if either you or your spouse is over sixty-five – it is not an additional allowance. It is also reduced if your income (or joint income in the case of a husband and wife) exceeds £9,800. In fact it is actually reduced by two-thirds of any income above £9,800 until the allowance equals the standard personal allowance. This means that age allowance ceases to be of any benefit to a single person with an income of £10,603 (age 80 – £10,768), or a married couple with an income of £11,120 (age 80 – £11,375). All these allowances are adjusted annually in the Budget, to keep pace with inflation, and it is important that you check the up-to-date position.

Other allowable costs

A number of costs can be offset against income – in other words deducted from gross income to arrive at the net amount that is subject to tax. Your personal affairs should be organized to take maximum advantage of these allowances. These are the main allowable costs:

◆ Interest paid on mortgages or loans, to purchase or improve a property that is your only or main residence. You will be entitled to tax relief on loans of up to £30,000.

◆ Interest paid on mortgages or loans, to purchase or improve a property that is available for letting throughout the year and is actually let for at least twenty-six weeks each year.

◆ Interest paid on money borrowed to provide capital or loan finance for your business, or for a trading company in which you control at least 5 per cent of the equity.

- Investments under the Business Expansion Scheme up to £40,000 in any tax year.
- Pension premiums paid into an approved scheme, if you are employed – or into a personal pension policy if you are in non-pensionable employment or self-employed.
- Expenses necessarily incurred in carrying out your work – i.e. travel, meals, hotels. There are two areas here which are quite specifically not allowable. These are travel between work and home, and entertaining.
- Any fees or subscriptions payable to professional bodies relevant to your working life.
- If you are trading on your own account or in partnership, all appropriate costs, overheads and expenses specifically relevant to your business activities.
- Deeds of Covenant and payments of alimony or maintenance under a court order or decree.

Many, many people do not take full advantage of these allowable costs, which, bearing in mind the rate of income tax, is a ludicrous situation. Do check your outgoings very carefully and make sure you have included every possible item of expense on your tax return.

Rates of income tax

Rates of income tax for 1987–8 on taxable income are:	
Basic rate on first £17,900	27%
Higher rate on next £2,500 (i.e. £17,901 to £20,400)	40%
Higher rate on next £5,000 (i.e. £20,401 to £25,400)	45%
Higher rate on next £7,900 (i.e. £25,401 to £33,300)	50%
Higher rate on next £7,900 i.e. £33,301 to £41,200)	55%
Top rate of tax on income over £41,200	60%

These rates apply to single people, or to the joint income of a married couple. A wife may elect to be taxed separately from her husband, but if she does so, her husband will lose £1,370 of his earned income allowance. This being the case, there is little point in a wife seeking separate taxation unless both she and her husband have a fairly high income. To be more specific on this, it would be an advantage to be taxed separately if your joint income (before personal allowances) is over £26,870, of which the wife is earning at least £6,545.

This, then, summarizes the income tax position and certainly demonstrates that despite the gradual lowering of the top rates of income tax over recent years, high-income earners should still be looking at ways of investing their money to increase their capital, rather than their incomes. Certainly, if you are running your own business, it is better to keep your earnings as low as possible and maximize the expenses you can charge against your business. This, of course, is standard practice, but blatantly exploiting the expenses position will rebound on you. The tax people are no fools. In theory, the concept of owning a villa in Spain or a yacht in the Greek islands, charged to the company as a business expense, sounds ideal. In practice it is not. No inspector of taxes is going to wear that sort of ploy these days. Make sure you really are charging up every possible item of expense you can, but do not be silly about it. Once you have a reputation with your local tax inspector for trying to cook the books, that reputation will stay with you for ever and your records will be inspected far more regularly than is comfortable.

Capital Gains Tax (CGT)

Capital Gains Tax is payable at the flat rate of 30 per cent. It applies to the disposal of all or any of your assets, including gifts, except for specifically exempted items. Exempted items include:

◆ The disposal of your only or main residence.
◆ Transfers between husband and wife.
◆ Sales of government stocks and certain corporate fixed-interest stocks.
◆ Disposals arising from death.
◆ Personal belongings worth £3,000 or less at date of disposal, or having a useful life of less than fifty years when you acquired them.
◆ Gifts to charity and to certain national heritage bodies, museums and universities.

In addition, there is no Capital Gains Tax levied on the first £6,600 of capital gain in any one year, but this exemption cannot be carried forward. In other words, if you made no profit on the disposal of your assets last year, you cannot use that unused exemption allowance because you made £10,000 this year. Losses, however, can be carried forward indefinitely. For example, if last year you sold some shares for £3,000 less than the purchase price, you can, at any time in the future, deduct this loss from subsequent gains. There is a fair amount of rather similar and confusing jargon associated with CGT and it is worth listing these terms, together with explanations, in order to clarify their use.

PRINCIPAL AND PRIVATE RESIDENCE

IT WAS CALLED SAUCY SUE BUT I HAD TO CHANGE THE NAME FOR TAX REASONS

Chargeable proceeds

These represent the sale price or disposal value, less any disposal costs – e.g. stockbroker's fee in the case of shares, auctioneer's fee in the case of, say, a painting.

Chargeable gains

This is the term used to describe chargeable proceeds less allowable costs and indexation allowance (see note on indexation allowance below).

Allowable costs

This is the purchase price, plus any purchase costs and expenditure on the asset since acquisition.

Taxable gains

This is the term used to describe chargeable gains, less the annual £6,600 exemption and any losses brought forward.

Indexation allowance

Indexation of costs is allowed by reference to the Retail Price Index. The indexation rules are complicated, and professional advice is needed in complex situations. However, it is well worth referring to the Retail Price Index, for although you may have made a profit on the disposal of an asset, it could be that, when inflation is taken into account, no profit has been made at all – or indeed you might even have made a loss. Losses as a result of indexation can be carried forward against future years' profits.

CGT relief

There are several circumstances in which you may be able to qualify for CGT relief. One example is the disposal of business assets and investments in family companies on retirement. You do need to discuss this very carefully with your solicitor and accountant, because if you are passing on your business to a member of your family, or another director, you may well be able to avoid CGT.

CGT may also be deferred when an asset is gifted by an individual, or indeed, a trustee. You can make a formal claim for what is known as **roll-over relief**. This claim has to be made jointly by the donor and the recipient. What effectively happens is that the recipient takes over the asset at its original cost – in other words, he or she recognizes no increase in value from when the asset was originally purchased. CGT is therefore suspended until the recipient disposes of the asset, when he or she will have to pay full CGT on the difference between the original purchase price and the price at which he or she makes the sale.

There are fairly arbitrary conditions applicable to CGT which demonstrate the need of extreme caution when it comes to realizing investments and savings. As already mentioned, within the business structure you may well find that disposal of any assets or shares will not involve you in CGT, but it would be foolish to make that assumption. Check out the position very carefully well in advance of any disposal plans.

Inheritance Tax

Inheritance Tax was introduced in the 1986 Budget to take the place of Capital Transfer Tax. No Inheritance Tax is charged on an estate where the total value is less than £90,000 and so, on the face of it, it may appear that for many people this tax is not relevant. However, with the continuing spiral in house prices, it is relatively easy to find oneself in a position where one's estate is worth more than this figure – in which case it will attract Inheritance Tax.

Inheritance Tax is chargeable at the appropriate full rate on assets transferred at death and on gifts made within three years of death. Gifts made to individuals between three and seven years prior to death will suffer tax based on the value of the gift at the date it was given, at the scale rate applicable to the estate on death, but subject to a tapering percentage relief – more details of this in a moment. The effect of this is that lifetime gifts, made to individuals more than seven years prior to the death of a person making that gift, will be free from Inheritance Tax, although, of course, they may be subject to Capital Gains Tax. Where Capital Gains Tax has been paid on a gift made within seven years prior to death, it does not safeguard the estate from having to pay Inheritance Tax as well, so it does highlight the need to be very careful indeed.

The exemption of lifetime gifts to individuals over seven years before death, and the tapering relief, can also be applied to the setting up of specific types of trust funds, for the exclusive benefit of, say, a child or perhaps a disabled member of the family. However, in order to attract tax exemption, it is imperative that donors cannot benefit in any way from that trust.

Certain transfers on death, or made immediately prior to death, are exempt from Inheritance Tax, as follows:

- All transfers made to the transferor's spouse.
- The first £3,000 of chargeable transfers made in a fiscal year.
- Outright gifts of up to £250 to any one person in a year of assessment.
- The amount by which the preceding financial year's gifts fell short of the permissible limit of £3,000.
- Normal expenditure out of income. The transfer must be normal or regular and leave the transferor with sufficient income, after tax, to maintain his or her usual standard of living.
- Gifts in consideration of marriage to either of the parties of the marriage, up to the limit of £5,000 from parents, £2,500 from grandparents and £1,000 from any other person.
- Transfers in the course of a trade, provided the transfer is an allowable deduction for tax purposes.
- Certain gifts to charities.
- Unlimited gifts to political parties made more than one year before death. For gifts within one year the limit is £100,000.
- Gifts for national purposes to specific national institutions.
- Gifts for public benefit authorized by the Treasury.
- All assets that pass on the death of a person on active service.
- Death benefits payable to dependants under retirement annuity schemes and occupational pension schemes.

AFTER INHERITANCE TAX YOUR DESK SHOULD BE ABOUT THIS SIZE

Relief from the full impact of Inheritance Tax is given on both lifetime and death transfers of business assets. Provided that the asset has been owned for at least two years before transfer, the value transferred will be reduced as follows:

◆ By 50 per cent – for an interest in an unincorporated business or partnership, or a substantial (over 25%) interest of shares in an unquoted trading company.
◆ By 30 per cent – for a minority interest (not more than 25%) in an unquoted company.
◆ By 30 per cent – for land, building, machinery or plant in a partnership, in a controlled company or in a settlement.

Similar relief is normally available for agricultural property and forestry, but the position is complex and each case needs to be considered in isolation. Certain business assets do not qualify for relief; these include:

◆ Investment companies or property-dealing companies.
◆ Assets not used wholly or mainly for the business.
◆ Shares in a company in liquidation.
◆ Assets where a binding contract for sale is in force at the date of transfer.

If exempt assets are owned by a company, relief given on transfer of its shares may be restricted.

The rates of Inheritance Tax on the value of an estate are as follows:

On the first £90,000	nil
On the next £50,000 (i.e. £90,001 to £140,000)	30%
On the next £80,000 (i.e. £140,001 to £220,000)	40%
On the next £110,000 (i.e. £220,001 to £330,000)	50%
Over £330,000	60%

The relief applied to lifetime gifts is as follows:

Up to three years prior to death	nil
Three to four years prior to death	20%
Four to five years prior to death	40%
Five to six years prior to death	60%
Six to seven years prior to death	80%
Over seven years	100%

Gifts to trusts, other than the two already mentioned concerning children and disabled people, and also gifts involving companies, are subject to Inheritance Tax. These will be subject to tax at 50 per cent of the full-scale rates whenever they are made and then, if the gift is made by an individual, will be brought back into the estate on subsequent death and the tax recomputed.

As with any of the tax discussed in this book, but particularly in the case of Inheritance Tax, if you are making plans to safeguard an estate of more than £90,000, do discuss the matter with your solicitor or accountant.

The sort of problem which arises can be illustrated by a simple but typical example. Consider an estate comprising the family home, valued at £120,000, and the controlling interest in the family company, valued at £750,000.

Value of estate	870,000
Less 50% relief on shares	375,000
Chargeable estate	£495,000
Inheritance Tax payable	£201,000

Not only will the family home have to go, but a large sum will have to be realized from the company in one way or another.

Value Added Tax (VAT)

Unless the goods or services you supply through your business are zero-rated or your business is sufficiently small that your sales are below the VAT threshold, you need to charge your customers VAT. Generally speaking, you will find that VAT is charged to you on virtually all your purchases and expenses. The difference between the two – i.e. the amount of VAT you charge, as against the amount of VAT charged to you – has to be declared on a quarterly return, and paid over to HM Customs and Excise.

Before you start trading, you need to decide whether your sales are likely to exceed the VAT threshold (currently £21,300). If you think your sales will do so in the first year of trading then you should register with the Customs and Excise as a taxable trader for VAT purposes.

If you have decided not to register, because you think that your turnover will be below the annual threshold, you nevertheless must keep a careful check on the level of your sales, once you start to trade. If your turnover exceeds £7,250 in any calendar quarter (31 March, 30 June, 30 September, 31 December), you must notify the VAT office. Unless you still believe that your sales will be within the threshold for the full year, you will be registered for VAT.

There are two advantages to the small trader in being below the registration level:

◆ You save time and money on administration – no VAT returns – no special VAT invoices for your customers – fewer detailed records to maintain.

◆ You can actually charge your customer less (or keep more of what you do charge for yourself). This is of particular value when you are selling your goods or services direct to a domestic user (who will not be registered for VAT) – the plumber who charges £20 to mend a burst pipe, if not registered for VAT, will have to charge £23 if registered.

There is a facility to de-register if turnover drops below minimum annual levels.

Most goods and services are subject to VAT, but some are exempt. The principal exemptions are:

◆ Sale of land and certain works of art
◆ Insurance, postal services, finance services and betting, gaming and lotteries and sports competitions
◆ Health and education
◆ Professional bodies and trade unions
◆ Burial and cremation

The bulk of goods and services which are subject to VAT are chargeable at the standard rate of 15 per cent. Some, however, are zero-rated – the VAT is, literally, 0 per cent. The main zero-rated categories – affecting day-to-day business – are:

◆ Food and drink (other than confectionery, catering and hot food take-aways)
◆ Children's and protective clothing
◆ Books, newspapers and journals
◆ Drugs and medicines on prescription
◆ Equipment for the disabled
◆ Passsenger transport (more than twelve seats)
◆ Exports and services to overseas traders
◆ New buildings, large caravans and houseboats
◆ Cultural and entertainment services
◆ Gifts to charities

It is important that you appreciate the difference between zero-rating and VAT exemption. Zero-rating carries a theoretical rate of VAT, which just happens to be 0 per cent. Exemption means that no VAT applies at all. On the face of it, there appears no difference between the two, but there is a significant one. If the goods you sell are zero-rated, you can still reclaim VAT on your supplies. In other words, you register for VAT in the normal way and simply reclaim the VAT you pay. However, if your business is exempt, your status is far from desirable – you cannot reclaim the VAT on your inputs because you cannot register for VAT.

VAT returns tend to be looked on as things of dread, yet if you keep up-to-date records, your returns should not involve you in a great deal of extra administration. The problem comes when your own records are incomplete. At the end of each VAT accounting period (usually quarterly) you will have to make a return of all your outputs (sales), showing their total value and the amount of VAT charged. Against this you will have to calculate the total of your inputs (purchases) and the amount of VAT you have paid. The difference between the VAT on your outputs and your inputs is the sum payable to the Customs and Excise. Where the problems arise is in those types of trade where some items of sales are zero-rated and some are not. A small corner shop has vastly more VAT problems than some enormous companies with multi-million turnovers. In a corner shop, some items such as sweets are taxable, whilst other food items are not. A number of special schemes have been introduced for retailers to simplify the VAT records which need to be kept, and the completion of VAT returns. Your local VAT office will give you a lot of help (and a lot of complicated leaflets) when you register, to make sure that you know what you are doing.

Your VAT return will only show totals – to that extent you have to present no details whatsoever. However, the Customs and Excise have the right to make routine inspections and check the documentation which supports your VAT returns. When you are subject to an inspection, you will have to produce all the back-up records. As when you deal with other government bodies, if you establish a reputation for poor VAT returns, for inaccuracies or slow payment, that reputation tends to stick and you will find yourself constantly hounded by officials. If, by contrast, your returns are put in on time, your cheques are paid regularly and your books, when inspected, are found to be accurate, then you are likely to be left alone.

VAT has caused a great deal of resentment, because for the small business, it can mean some hours of extra work each week doing what many people consider to be the government's job. Having said that, VAT does inflict a discipline on the small business, which formerly was not there. You *have* to keep records in order to make VAT returns, and this discipline must be a good thing.

A word of warning. By law VAT returns have to be kept up to date, and there are fines and penalties for late payment and non-payment.

THE CAT SAT ON THE VAT.

MY FIRST VAT BOOK

Corporation Tax

Corporation Tax is only payable by limited companies. The provisions are somewhat complicated and, as with all other forms of taxation, it is sensible to seek professional advice. There are two separate rates charged – the full rate for companies whose profits exceed £500,000, and the small companies' rate for businesses whose profits are less than £100,000. Marginal relief is given in respect of taxable profits falling between the two figures, so that the effective rate of Corporation Tax gradually increases from the small company rate to full rate for profits over £100,000. It is important here to emphasize the word *profits*. Corporation Tax is a tax on company profits, not turnover. Corporation Tax is normally payable nine months from the end of each accounting period, but there is some leeway on this, depending upon when your accounts are finalized.

Dividends paid to shareholders are not an allowable expense against Corporation Tax, whereas salaries paid to employees – including the owners of the company – are deductible. On the face of it, therefore, if you have had a successful year and your company has made a big profit, it might appear better to draw additional salary than pay yourself a dividend. In practice, this is not such a straightforward decision. Certainly your salary will be allowable against Corporation Tax, the full rate of

which is at a higher level than the basic rate of income tax. Two examples will, however demonstrate the true position:

◆ Your company makes a profit of £40,000 before tax – you want to draw it all out –

a) You can take additional remuneration of just over £36,000 – do not forget that the company has to pay National Insurance – you will pay income tax, at higher rates on that £36,000 – the company will be left with no profit, and will pay no Corporation Tax.

or b) The company can pay you a net dividend of £29,200 (having provided for Corporation Tax @ 27 per cent – £10,800) which is equal to a gross dividend of £40,000, less income tax @ 27 per cent. Your gross income will have increased by £40,000, and you will have paid part of the ultimate tax liability by deduction. As in (a), the company will be left with nothing by the time it has paid over the tax on the dividend, in lieu of Corporation Tax. *But you will be over £3,000 less tax, better off.*

Your company is slightly larger, and pays Corporation Tax @ 35 per cent – you want to draw additional remuneration of £40,000, or the equivalent dividend –

a) You draw your £40,000, and pay income tax on it. The cost to the company (including the additional National Insurance) is just over £44,000, gross, or nearly £29,000 after Corporation Tax.

or b) You draw a net dividend of £29,200, equal to a gross dividend of £40,000, less tax @ 27 per cent. Your income is increased by the £40,000 gross. The final cost to the company is the amount of your net dividend.

The decision between additional remuneration and dividend also depends on the status and development of your company and its share structure. Many company directors feel it is more important to establish a profit record, and would actually prefer to show the company's true profit even though this attracts more Corporation Tax. This is particularly relevant if you are preparing your company for sale or amalgamation with another business, where the price you will receive for your business will largely depend on your profit record.

Below, we show the rates of Corporation Tax as they have applied over recent years. Also listed are details of Corporation Tax on capital gains, from which you will see that, until the March 1987 Budget, Corporation Tax was applied to a proportion of the capital gains realized by a limited company. The effect is to tax capital gains within companies at 30 per cent. From 19 March 1987, capital gains within companies will be taxed at normal corporation tax rates. Gains will be eligible for the small companies rate, where applicable, and will be taken into account for marginal relief.

RATES OF CORPORATION TAX

Financial year to 31 March	Full rate	Small companies rate
1982	52%	40%
1983	52%	38%
1984	50%	30%
1985	45%	30%
1986	40%	30%
1987	35%	29%
1988	35%	27%

CORPORATION TAX ON CAPITAL GAINS

The fraction of a company's capital gains brought into charge to the full rate of Corporation Tax has been as follows:

Financial year to 31 March

1982 and 1983	15/26	
1984	3/5	
1985	2/3	
1986	3/4	
1987	6/7	– for gains up to 18 March 1987
1987	Full	– for gains from 19 March 1987
1988	Full	

Capital Allowances

If you buy an asset for your business – a building, a computer, office equipment, machinery – you have to decide how that asset is to be written off in terms of depreciation. This is a personal decision, though it is in your interests to work it out as accurately as possible. Neither the total cost of the asset, nor the rate at which you decide to depreciate it, is allowed for tax purposes. Part of the cost, however, can be offset against tax each year, by applying specific rates of capital allowances.

Capital allowances tend to have been manipulated over the years by successive governments – all recognizing the need to encourage investment in business assets. Over the years there have been various forms of investment and initial allowances designed to give savings in Corporation Tax to stimulate capital investment. More recently, company profitability has been encouraged by dropping the rates of Corporation Tax and this has been accompanied by a simplification in capital allowances. Shown on the facing page are the rates of capital allowances on items purchased since 1 April 1986.

When calculated, capital allowances are treated as trading expenses in arriving at taxable profit. If there is insufficient taxable profit in any one year to absorb the allowance in full, they need not be claimed

YOU WOULDN'T BELIEVE THE CAPITAL ALLOWANCE WE CLAIMED ON THESE LOCKERS

in full. The unutilized allowances may be carried forward and set against future profits.

The calculation of allowances and their carry-forward, in general, is achieved by pooling the purchase and disposal of all assets. Expenditure on plant, equipment and commercial vehicles would all be put into a pool, for instance, for capital allowance purposes. A typical example of such a pool might be as follows:

		£
1 April 1986	Written-down value of plant and equipment, brought forward	46,000
31 March 1987	Sale proceeds of disposals in the year	(7,000)
31 March 1987	Cost of new purchases in the year	29,000
	Total	68,000
31 March 1987	25% writing-down allowance	(17,000)
1 April 1987	Written-down value, carried forward	51,000

Certain exceptions are made to the general pooling principle:

◆ Motor cars costing up to £8,000 – these form a pool separately.

◆ Motor cars costing over £8,000 – these are not pooled, but dealt with individually – the 25 per cent writing-down allowance is restricted to £2,000 in any one year – a balancing adjustment arises on the sale of each car.

◆ Assets which are expected to have a useful life of less than five years may be omitted from the general pool and dealt with individually – this means that a balancing adjustment has to be calculated when the individual asset is sold or scrapped. This provision is particularly useful for high technology assets, having a short life.

NUCLEAR POWERED

YOU CAN CLAIM 100% ALLOWANCE DUE TO A RADIOACTIVE HALFLIFE OF SIX MONTHS

RATES OF CAPITAL ALLOWANCES FOR EXPENDITURE INCURRED FROM 1 APRIL 1986		
Type of asset	*Type of allowance*	*Rate*
Scientific research, and buildings in enterprise zones	Initial	100%
Plant, machinery, vehicles, patent rights and knowhow	Annual writing-down	25%*
Industrial and agricultural buildings, hotels and dredging	Annual writing-down	4%
* Percentage applied to reducing balance		

Business Cars

The provision of 'company cars' within any organization is almost bound to stir up mixtures of envy, pride, resentment, gratitude and dissatisfaction in equal measure – amongst the favoured few who have them, because they need them, those who have them but do not need them or deserve them, those who need them and deserve them, but do not have them . . . and so it goes on. However carefully you handle the issue, however flexible you are, or however inflexible you are – there is always trouble.

But all that is another story. And business cars are so important and emotive an issue, we should look specifically at their taxation treatment, from the point of view of the business and of the individual user. There are also VAT considerations.

Company taxation

Cars purchased by a company, for use by its directors or employees, attract capital allowances, which are substituted for the commercial rate of depreciation in the books of account. The ultimate result is the same – the cost of a car (being its original purchase price, less its eventual sale or part-exchange value) is written off and allowed as a charge against taxable profits. The annual charge against Corporation Tax is a writing-down allowance of 25 per cent, calculated on the reducing balance. As

explained in the previous section, cars costing up to £8,000 are pooled together. Cars costing over £8,000 are dealt with individually, and the annual allowance is limited to £2,000 in any year.

All of the running costs of company cars are allowed as business expenses for Corporation Tax purposes. If a car is rented or hired at a price which includes maintenance, the rental costs are allowed as an expense. If a car is bought on hire purchase, or on a straight finance lease (exclusive of maintenance), the interest element of the instalments will be allowed as an expense. The capital element will be disallowed, because annual allowances will be claimed.

Personal benefit

A director or higher-paid employee (earning £8,500 p.a., inclusive of benefits) using a company car will be assessed by the Inland Revenue on the benefit enjoyed for its private use. This personal benefit is assessed on the basis of fixed-scale charges, which reflect the size of the car, its purchase price, and the extent to which it is used for business purposes. The general scale of charges for the personal use of a car for the 1987–8 tax year are shown here; they are made up of a charge for fuel and a separate charge for the supply of the car and other running costs:

Cars with an original market value up to £19,250 – size of engine	Fuel Benefit	Tax Benefit	
	Any age of car	Less than 4 years old	4 years old or more
1,400 cc or less	£480	£525	£350
1,400 to 2,000 cc	£600	£700	£470
Over 2,000 cc	£900	£1,100	£725
Original market value, if more than £19,250			
£19,251 to £29,000	£900	£1,450	£970
Over £29,000	£900	£2,300	£1,530

The fuel benefit is charged if *any* fuel is supplied by the company for the car.

All of the rates are halved if business use exceeds 18,000 miles per annum.

The rates are increased by half for a second car or where business mileage is less than 2,500 miles per annum.

Sole traders and partnerships

If you are in business on your own, the Inspector of Taxes may insist that you keep detailed records of personal and business mileage, in order to apportion all of the purchase and running costs of your car. This will either restrict the allowable costs which can be borne by the business, or identify your personal benefit.

If you are in partnership, you may be involved in a very similar situation, although cars provided for your employees will be

dealt with on a similar basis to cars within companies.

In the case of either the sole trader or a partnership, you may be able to persuade the Inland Revenue to deal with your car, in all respects, as if it was a company car – which does tend to simplify matters. This is entirely at the discretion of the inspector.

VAT and the Business Car

When you buy a private car, VAT is included in the purchase price. This VAT is not recoverable under any circumstances.

When you hire a car, inclusive of maintenance, the rental charges will be invoiced with VAT. This VAT is recoverable, as the rental will be treated as a business expense.

Since the introduction of new provisions in April 1987, VAT is now charged, on a scale basis, on fuel used for private motoring. If you provide fuel for private motoring, you can reclaim the VAT as input tax, but you must account for output tax in accordance with the following scales, depending upon whether you submit quarterly or monthly VAT returns:

Size of engine	Quarterly VAT charge	Monthly VAT charge
1,400 cc or less	£15.65	£5.21
1,401 to 2,000 cc	£19.56	£6.52
Over 2,000 cc	£29.34	£9.78

You will see that these charges represent the VAT content of the fuel benefit scale figures used for income tax purposes. In the same way that the fuel benefit scale is halved when business travel exceeds 18,000 miles per annum, so these VAT charges are also halved for the same minimum business mileage – equivalent to 4,500 miles per quarter or 1,500 miles per month. There is no adjustment to the VAT scale charges, however, for second cars or for business mileage of less than 2,500 per annum.

Accountants

If you are starting or running your own business – big or small – you need the services of an accountant. As a self-employed, freelance person, you can have a direct relationship with the inspector of taxes, and annually provide a full schedule of income and outgoings so that the inspector can assess your taxable earnings. However, unless you are genuinely experienced in tax affairs, even if you prepare your own return, you should at least talk it through with an accountant. Whilst the tax inspector can be very helpful – surprisingly so – and will give you a degree of advice, it is not part of the job to tell you how to reduce your tax burden. That is why you need an accountant.

If your business is a small one, it is also easy to fall into the trap of assuming that your accounts are simple, too. The fact is, if you are running very nearly a solo operation, you are already playing half a dozen roles within your business, and that of accountant is one you could well do without. Certainly, if you are not a particularly numerate person, it is well worth paying an annual fee to have all the worry and headache taken off your shoulders. You can use the extra time this creates to generate more business and make more money!

The type of accountant you select depends very much on the size of your business. If your business is small then you should be looking at engaging the services of a small firm – perhaps even a qualified accountant who practises alone. If you have a medium to large company, then you want a large firm of accountants which has specialist departments dealing in taxation, company law, etc. However, whatever the size of your business, the same rule applies – choose an accountant you like and trust. You must be able to be frank with your accountant, you must feel he is a person you can go to when you have problems, whose advice you trust and who is thoroughly experienced in commercial affairs.

The best method of finding an accountant is by way of recommendation – ask your bank manager, your solicitor or your chum up the road who runs a small business. However, do not be swayed into necessarily hiring the first firm you see – go shopping for an accountant.

If you are forming a limited company, then clearly you have no alternative but to employ the services of a firm of accountants, because you are required, by law, to prepare audited accounts. It is also important that you prepare audited accounts if you have a partnership, so that there can be no argument between you on the results of your efforts. Similarly, if you have offered anyone a share of the profits in your business – perhaps a valuable member of staff or a sleeping partner who has invested money in your enterprise – then again, it is important to produce audited accounts to form the basis for any payout, and thus avoid argument or ill-feeling.

In the earlier pages of this book there are details of how to prepare a profit plan, cash forecast and balance sheet forecast. In this section we look at management accounts. These are needed to help you keep track of how your business is developing. It is important that you do this, whatever your size of business, but particularly so if you are in a high-risk area – big turnover and small profit margin. If you and your staff cannot produce monthly management figures, then it is vital that you employ an accountant to produce them for you. It is no good reaching the end of your financial year and then finding you have made a crashing loss – in such circumstances, in all probability the information will arrive just in time to coincide with your going out of business. If you are making losses, you need to know quickly so that you can do something about it. If you are making profits you need to know quickly so that you can maximize them.

If you are wishing to borrow a substantial sum of money to start or expand your business, it is worth employing an accountant to help you prepare your profit plan and cash forecast. It may be helpful to ask your accountant to come with you when you make your proposal to the bank or financial institution. With the help of the right sort of man this can prove an excellent plan – you can dazzle the bank manager with the brilliance of your project, while your accountant is talking his language and putting up a good case as to why the bank is not going to lose its money by backing you.

Two golden rules

1   There are a number of people around who call themselves accountants, but who are not qualified. These people usually operate on their own. If you have your suspicions about a so-called accountant who has made an approach to work for you, you can easily check whether he is qualified. An accountant needs to be either a member of the Institute of Chartered Accountants or the Association of Certified and Corporate Accountants. Do not hire someone who is not a member of one of these.

2   Accountants are expensive, and the way to keep costs to a minimum is to do as much of the spadework for them as you possibly can. It is terribly important, for your own sake, that you keep proper records of your business activities, but it is also essential if you want to keep your accountancy bill low. Chucking a load of scruffy-looking envelopes at your accountant containing cheque stubs and bills, will, without doubt, issue him with a challenge, but can you afford for that challenge to be met? Before seeing your accountant, always work out precisely what you want done for you, and give clear and exact instructions, preferably in writing. Also, before giving the accountant the go-ahead on any major work for you, ask for a quotation. Of course, sometimes it is not possible for accountants to be precise as to the kind of fees that will be involved, but they should be able to give an indication. Some firms of accountants may suggest that you pay them a monthly retainer, for which they will handle all your business requirements. Frankly, this is not to be recommended – certainly not in the early days of a business. Most firms will bill quarterly, in arrears, on a time basis for the work they have done. This is preferable.

The very nature of the beast makes an accountant a cautious and precise person. Your questions are rarely answered with a decisive *yes* or *no*, and the advice tends to be cautious and peppered with reservations. However, a good accountant is a true friend to your business. Make sure you pick yourself a winner.

Basic Book-keeping

Whatever type of business you are running, you have to find a formula for keeping control. Book-keeping is a chore in most businesses, but it has to be done. Indeed, unless you are prepared to keep adequate records you should not be in business at all, since clearly you do not have a responsible attitude towards your trading. If you are already in business, or intend employing accounts staff from the start-up of your new business, then this section may not be particularly relevant to you. None the less, these are the basic rules of keeping control, which should be applied to every business – big or small.

Book-keeping falls into two categories – the requirements of the outside world and those internal controls which you need for your own benefit in order to manage your business. In dealing with the outside world you require records for your bank, your customers, your suppliers, the VAT people, the tax people – both for PAYE and business tax – and the DHSS for both National Insurance and Statutory Sick Pay. The records you require for internal use cover stock control, costing and general performance , your bank balance, creditors, debtors and – most important of all – whether you are making a profit or a loss.

Without attempting to take you through the details of double-entry book-keeping, here we give a few thoughts on the basic principles of control. Let us look first at accounting for your dealings with the outside world, under the headings we have already mentioned.

The outside world

The bank

To keep control of your bank balance, it is essential that you have a cash book which records on one side the receipts and on the other the payments you make. The cash book should be kept up to date every day – in other words you must enter cheques drawn and the takings as they occur. At least every month you must check these against your bank statement and reconcile the bank statement against your cash-book balance. Ask your bank for weekly statements – they make it far easier for you to keep control. Routine is what you need. You should work out the bank balance every Monday morning and you should never go home until the cash book is written up.

Customers

If you sell on credit terms, but only raise a few invoices each month, you can keep track of outstanding accounts by keeping a file of unpaid copy invoices in your top drawer. When you receive the cash, bank the money, enter the receipt in the cash book and place the invoice in a file of paid invoices, in your bottom drawer. If you are producing a volume of sales invoices, you need a sales journal to list and analyse your sales and a sales ledger to record the sales to each customer. It is worth mentioning here how vital it is that you invoice properly as soon as goods or services are supplied – not at the end of the month. You cannot afford to give anyone extra credit, so remember to send out statements within a week of the end of each month. You must produce a list of debtors at the end of each month, with outstanding balances listed against them, according to age. Outstanding debts need your personal attention.

Suppliers

As with sales invoices, if you only have a few purchase invoices each month, files in your top and bottom drawer will work well. Otherwise you need a purchase journal and a purchase ledger. The purchase ledger should be kept up to date at least weekly and agreed with suppliers' statements at least monthly. As far as possible, pay your suppliers against statements, not against invoices.

VAT

Unless your sales are below the VAT threshold, or your goods or services zero-rated, you need to charge VAT to your customers and pay it quarterly to HM Customs and Excise. Your cash book should be analysed to identify the VAT content of your sales. Likewise, the VAT charged to you on virtually all your purchases and expenses should be identified in your cash book and, if appropriate, your purchase journal, so it can be deducted from your quarterly statement.

Tax

PAYE is more of a nuisance than a difficulty, but it is unavoidable. If your payroll is five or less, simply use Inland Revenue standard forms for your records. If you employ half a dozen people, invest in a small multi-copy payroll system. If you are employing more than ten people then perhaps you should sub-contract the job to a local computer bureau. Tax on the business will be based on your annual accounts, but make sure your books and files are up to date, so that the information your accountants need is available without a major research programme being mounted.

DHSS

National Insurance administration is part and parcel of the weekly or monthly payroll routine and tends to be dealt with in conjunction with PAYE. The need for adequate personal records and files has been underlined by the recent introduction of Statutory Sick Pay, and you must now keep records of all your employees.

So, that is what you **have** to do, now let us look at what you **should** do. You need internal controls for your own benefit.

Internal controls

Stock

No outside influence requires you to introduce stock control. Some businesses, of course, do not carry stock, and in other cases the stock level is so small that any form or record would be a waste of time and money. However, it has to be said that

many a business has failed through too much of the wrong stock. If stock plays a significant part in your business, then monitor it carefully.

Costing

This is another area which is vital to the successful running of your business, whether you are involved with manufacture or service. The price you charge your customer may not be based necessarily on your costs. A pricing policy based on what the market will stand may well be more appropriate in your case. Remember, however, that you have to know what your costs are – gross profit is the all-important figure.

Performance

If you have an adequate and sensible set of books and records, what should you be doing with them? How can you use them to tell you what you need to know? Basically you should be able to use them to provide you with a performance record to measure what is happening and to enable you to plan ahead. When you start your own small business you do everything – you open the post, sign the cheques, sweep the floor. In two years' time, however, you may be employing forty people and it is then that you are in danger of losing control. You have to know what is going on, how many enquiries you received last week, how many orders, how much is owed to you by Bloggs & Co., what is the size of your overdraft, what sort of profit did you make on that French contract, how much did you pay for that latest batch of material. You need this information and, in order to obtain it, you need proper books and records. It is a fact that the more successful you are, the more vulnerable you are. The more you prosper, the more reliant you are on other people and the more remote you become from the action. So be prepared – however small your business, set up the controls now. They will still be standing you in good stead when you reach that first million!

Collecting Money

Every year a number of otherwise good businesses go to the wall because they have been unable to collect their debts. **Do not be one of them.** Here is a seven-point plan which you are recommended to follow in order to assist the collection of money from your customers.

Terms

Most customers want credit, but do not give it to them unless you have to. If you decide to offer credit terms, it is fairly standard practice to ask your customer to settle in full the value of the first order at the time of placing it. This will give you time to take up references and establish account facilities. Do this whatever the size of the company with which you are dealing. No business is sacred, and you are within your rights to insist on establishing their creditworthiness. Although they vary from industry to industry, normal credit terms are thirty days from supply of goods or services. Do not offer more, you cannot afford it.

References

You should ask for a banker's reference and two trade references. In the case of the banker's reference, you should ask your

own bank to check this out for you. If you are in a hurry for the reference, ask your bank to telephone your customer's bank direct. So far as trade references are concerned, we would suggest you telephone rather than write to the companies quoted. If you write you will tend to receive back a standard letter. Ring the sales ledger department of the company quoted as a referee, ask if the company settle their account regularly and without argument, or whether they need constant chasing. Friendly enquiries should provoke candid answers. Having obtained your references, only you can decide whether to proceed with credit terms. It is a risk you have to weigh up against the implications of losing the money. If you cannot obtain a banker's reference for a company, **under no circumstances offer credit**.

Invoicing

You cannot expect to be efficiently paid if you cannot efficiently invoice. Make sure your invoice goes out immediately the goods or services have been supplied, and make sure it is properly addressed. This applies particularly if you are supplying large organizations. Your invoice should be headed with the order or contract number and the name of the project. Where you have dealt specifically with an individual, mark it for his attention.

Making friends with the right person

In most companies, your invoice will be passed first to a director or senior manager, for authorization. It will be then passed down to the accounts department, where the purchase ledger clerk will have responsibility for entering it into the books and producing a cheque for signature. You must get to know that purchase ledger clerk. When dealing with big companies particularly, you will be told initially that you cannot have your cheque because it is in the computer system and the computer will not be producing cheques for, say, ten days.

This is rubbish – the system can always be bypassed. Cheques can be produced by hand, and daily, and often are. Making friends with the right person will ensure this happens if settlement is overdue. More important, it will help you get your money on time – regularly.

Chasing payment

So, you have issued your invoice to the right person, with the right information. Thirty days have elapsed and you have received no payment. Ring your friend, the purchase ledger clerk. Be kind but firm. Make a note on the file of whom you have spoken to and on what date, and then ring every two or three days thereafter until you have received payment. Standard chasing letters or invoices with jovial stickers do not work – phone calls do. Keep up the pressure.

Late payments

An invoice is seriously overdue if the customer is more than two weeks late in paying. You must then toughen your attitude. Be polite, friendly and understanding, but absolutely adamant that payment must be made. At this point one of two things will happen. In most cases, you will receive your cheque, but you should remember for the future that this customer has a tendency to be late in paying and therefore you should start chasing in earnest earlier next time. The second possibility is that your customer is in difficulty, and usually the signs stand out a mile. First, the person you normally speak to will not be in and will not return your call. Second, there will be a milliard excuses as to why no one can sign the cheque – everyone is on holiday, or whatever. The third and most dangerous sign is when you are told the cheque is in the post and yet it does not turn up. Once your customer starts lying, you do have problems. The moment you start getting these signals, threaten legal proceedings. A **seven days,**

or else letter from your solicitor will probably produce results, but if a cheque is still not forthcoming, issue a writ.

Legal proceedings

Any advice given on legal proceedings should be prefaced by saying that it is not cheap. You do need to weigh up the amount of the debt against the costs of pursuing it. Even if you are successful in obtaining judgement, your customer may already be in such trouble they are unable to pay you – in which case, you will have been involved in a costly exercise for nothing. It is a balancing act in which you should seek the advice of your solicitor and get an explanation of precisely what steps you can take and what each stage will cost. If you receive no payment before you obtain judgement for your writ, you are dealing with a very sick company indeed. Once judgement has been made, it is the job of the County Sheriff or Bailiff to collect the money. In some instances, the Sheriff or Bailiff may not succeed. If this is the case and the sum of money you are owed exceeds £1,000, use the ultimate weapon – a Winding-up order against the company. Every company, regardless of the seriousness of its financial state, will try at all costs to avoid a Winding-up order. If granted, this enables you to appoint a liquidator to dispose of the assets of the company.

It needs to be stressed that most of the gruesome steps outlined here it will not be necessary for you to take, but where a company is in serious difficulties, and you are aware of it, experience suggests that the one who shouts loudest gets paid. Be flexible with valued customers where you can. Remember that payment does not have to be made all at once. If your customer is finding things a little difficult, suggest instalment payments – there is nothing to gain by putting the company out of business.

Owing Money

Creditors' money in your business is the cheapest form of finance. This does not mean that you should irresponsibly run up big debts and make commitments you cannot honour, but clever handling of your payments can be an extremely profitable exercise.

Business start-up

When you start a new business it is always difficult to obtain credit from suppliers. You are in a 'chicken and egg' situation – your suppliers will give you credit when you have a track record and you can only obtain a track record when someone gives you credit. When applying to a supplier for credit terms, avoid if at all possible mentioning that you are a new business, unless you are asked the direct question. If a supplier insists on cash with order, or cash on delivery, agree to it but for a limited period only, saying you will pay cash for two consignments and thereafter expect normal monthly terms.

Trading relationships

In most industries, normal monthly terms of credit are thirty days from the date of invoice. If, however, you can negotiate with your suppliers for sixty or even ninety days, it can make a tremendous difference to your cash-flow. Look carefully at your major suppliers and plot the impact of an extra month's credit – you will be amazed at the difference. Try a little gentle persuasion – if you are dealing with a big company, an extra thirty days' credit will be of little significance to them. You will be surprised how many large companies will be prepared to give you a helping hand in the early days, provided you can prove your reliability. But ask for it – do not just take it.

This brings us to the golden rule with regard to taking credit. Negotiate as much credit for your business as possible, but whatever terms you finally agree, stick to them and **pay up on time**. Whether you are paying cash or enjoying credit terms,

always do what you say you are going to do. It is the only way to establish a good reputation and therefore a credit rating. You have to build up your suppliers' confidence – too many companies are caught by bad debts these days and once you have a reputation of being a poor payer within your trade, you will find it is a very difficult reputation to reverse.

Paying suppliers

A few practical hints on paying suppliers. Once you have started to build a reputation for paying properly, you can start taking advantage of your suppliers' inefficiency. This does not mean breaking the rules, or letting people down – it simply means that you only respond to requests. In other words, if a supplier is too easygoing or inefficient to send you a statement at the end of the month, do not feel worried about paying late. As a general rule, always insist on a statement – do not pay out against invoices. If a supplier asks you for less than you think you owe, pay the lesser sum and let them find their own mistake. On the other hand, if a supplier is asking for more than you think you owe, still pay the lesser amount. Always assume that your accounts are more accurate and more up-to-date than your suppliers'. Check off suppliers' statements very carefully against your records. It is so easy to over-pay if you are settling individual invoices and not paying against agreed statements. It is surprising just how inefficient people can be – it is not immoral to take advantage of that.

Good cash flow

If, as your business grows, you find you are flush with cash, remember that taking cash discount is the easiest way in the world of making profits, since it involves absolutely no effort on your part! In these circumstances, negotiate with your major suppliers. Ask for a discount for settling on time, ask for a bigger discount for settling in seven days, or bigger still, for settling on receipt of goods. If you are absolutely confident that your supplier is stable you can even offer cash with order, but you do have to be very sure about quality and performance before you commit yourself to this. Using a buoyant cash flow in this way can make you far more profit than simply placing the money on short-term bank deposit. It also lends your business credibility, so that if some time in the future you need extended credit, you are far more likely to get it.

Cash flow problems

Practically every business suffers from cash flow problems at some stage in its development. Owing money you cannot pay is a dreadful feeling. It is frankly terrifying, it saps your confidence and your immediate reaction will be to bury your head in the sand – anything but face the problem. Hoping that cash-flow problems will go away is the worst thing you can do. If you find it is going to be difficult to meet your commitments on time, tell your supplier you cannot pay on the day payment is due – in other words, **before they start chasing you**. What applies to suppliers applies equally well to PAYE, VAT or a reduction in bank overdraft.

This point underlines the need for good record keeping. You must be able to see a financial hiccup coming, and then you will find you are able to cope with it. It is when it hits you unawares that you have problems.

If you are being seriously chased for money, there is nothing that will cause greater aggravation than not answering your suppliers' letters or telephone calls. Explain your position carefully and ask for extra time to pay. Payments by instalment are usually best. Few suppliers like the idea of receiving nothing from you, but regular payments for an extended period are usually quite acceptable.

Do remember that it becomes increasingly more difficult to negotiate terms the further down the slippery slope you slide. It is relatively easy to negotiate with your supplier, it is far more difficult to negotiate with your supplier's solicitor, and it is extremely difficult to negotiate with the Bailiff! Avoid at all costs the debt going into legal hands – once that happens it gets increasingly more difficult and expensive to resolve the problem. However black things look, do remember that it is in nobody's interests to close you down or make you bankrupt, and most people realize this. The best way suppliers can get their money back is to see that you stay in business. Provided you are convinced that, given time, your cash-flow problems can be controlled and overcome, then you should be able to convince your creditors as well. If, however, you know that digging yourself out of your problems is just not possible, then the sooner you face up to it, the better.

Concentrate on building up sound relationships with your suppliers: they are quite as valuable to you as your bankers – probably more so, for they are less easy to replace.

Good stock control has to begin with good suppliers. If your supplier can be relied upon to let you have your materials on time, of consistent quality in the correct sizes and colours, then you are halfway towards good stock control. If, however, your suppliers are usually late on delivery, if 25 per cent of the goods supplied have to be returned, or the order is only part fulfilled, then you are going to compensate for these factors in the only way you know how – **and that is to over-order.**

A build-up of stock is one of the most dangerous things that can happen in a business. Yes, of course, having a good stock of current sales items – whether you are a manufacturer, a wholesaler or retailer – does mean that you can give your customer a speedy service, but what you also have to look at is what that stock is actually costing you. Convert it, for a moment, at cost, into money in the bank and imagine your total stock value is sitting where your overdraft now is. You may well

OH YES, WE'RE ALWAYS RUNNING OUT OF THAT ITEM, IT'S VERY POPULAR

find it completely changes the look of your business and, frankly, that really is the simple choice – you either have the money in the bank or sitting on the shelves, gathering dust.

The other major factor involved in a build-up in stock is that all too often stock that is accumulating is either slow-moving or – worse still – out of date. One of the industries most notorious for stock problems is mail order, and it is a good industry to demonstrate the kind of thing that can happen.

Example
Supposing a mail-order business is offering a dress for sale in blue and green, in sizes 10, 12, 14 and 16. The company starts off with a spread of, say, 500 dresses across the size and colour range. Their advertising campaign is a success. They take £80,000 worth of sales but by the end of the campaign they still have 400 dresses left. So, you say, what's the problem? It is obviously a good selling line. There is a problem, however, if there are that many dresses left at the end of the campaign. It means that someone has not been interpreting the orders correctly. If you took a look at the detail of those closing stocks, you would see that instead of a spread of dresses across the range of sizes and colours, they would almost exclusively be of one colour (the slow-moving one) and in the least popular sizes. In other words, those 400 dresses probably would be 360 green, 40 blue and only in sizes 10 and 16.

For mail order, read any industry. What you have to be careful about is to gauge your fast-moving lines, and stock accordingly, whilst trying not to build up unnecessary stocks of the slow movers. If, however, you reach a point where you know you have a great deal of stock which so far as your business is concerned is dead, then have the courage of your convictions – and offload it. Yes, all that stock does look good on the balance sheet – puffed up at some phoney figure – but you know the truth only too well. At some point you are going to have to grasp the nettle, so the sooner you do it the better. Turn your dead stock into cash – some cash, any cash – clear out the shelves, making room for fresh, merchantable stock . . . and make sure you do not repeat your error.

So, if you are starting out in business or expanding into new areas – choosing your suppliers is a vital ingredient for success. Being frank with them is the first step to a good relationship. If you are not sure precisely how much you are going to sell and therefore how much stock you are going to need, then tell them so. Ask for a degree of flexibility. Sell them your business ideas, your prospects – make them feel that if they get in on the ground floor, you could prove a valuable customer in the future, and certainly that is true. A supplier who has helped you in the early days of your business is likely to be someone who retains your loyalty.

Stock systems

Clearly, today, the most effective way of keeping control of a volume of stock is to computerize it. If your business is not large, there are many small computers available with the necessary software to keep track of your stock. However, it has to be said that if you are computerizing your stock, you should be looking at it as part of the accounting function, so that sales automatically reduce the stock levels and purchases increase them. We will be looking at computers in detail in the next section of this book, but suffice to say that if you have a stocking level which you feel needs computerizing, it would be most sensible for you to employ the services of a computer consultant to tell you what you actually need.

It may be that the items you stock are such things as nuts and bolts, which you feel are sufficiently low-cost that only rough stock control is necessary, and therefore computerization is not justified. This is fine – in fact any stocking system is fine provided it does the job it is intended to do. Here there is often confusion. When many businessmen are asked what they consider the main function of their stock control, they will say to stop pilfering. That is rubbish, unless you are in the industry which is manufacturing gold bars or cutting diamonds. Your job, as head of your business, is to ensure that you employ the kind of people who are not going to pilfer from you to any large extent. Yes, there will be some losses, but they should be at the level of the odd box of paper clips. No, the purpose of stock control is to ensure that you have the right materials or merchandise available to you in the right quantities when you need them. Stock control is all about predicting and recognizing trends and ensuring that, whilst minimizing your stock levels, you never lose an important order because you cannot supply the goods.

Stock insurance

A note on the insurance of your stock. Clearly you must make sure that your stock is adequately covered, but on the other hand you do not want to be paying insurance cover at a higher level than you need. Virtually all insurance companies offer the facility of insuring on a stock declaration basis. This means that your average stock over the year ahead is estimated, and you are charged a provisional premium accordingly. During the year, on a monthly or quarterly basis, you declare your stock value and an adjustment to the premium is then made. This is ideal, since it ensures that you are always covered but you do not have to pay for any more cover than you actually require.

Costings and Quotations

How much should you charge your customers for what you have to offer them? Should you take your cost and add on 50 per cent, or should you take the view that you will charge as much as you possibly can, or will you pitch your prices at the same level as your competitors? Alternatively, in order to establish your business, do you need to undercut the rest of the market?

All these avenues of approach are possible, but whatever your selling price, you are going to have to sit down and establish exactly what is the cost of your product or your service.

Whether you are manufacturing a product, selling something which you have purchased for resale, or providing a service – you first need to calculate your prime cost. If you are a manufacturer or contractor, your prime cost will be some combination of:

◆ Raw materials, components, sub-contractors' charges.

◆ Labour cost – including National Insurance and holiday pay.

◆ Packaging, transport, installation.

These need to be evaluated carefully for each job you do – whether the job is a one-off project or the manufacture of a batch of 2,000 of your standard widgets for stock.

If you are a retailer or wholesaler, your prime cost is unlikely to be significantly at variance from the purchase price of your bought-in stock – but you still need to be conscious of that current cost – and its relationship with your selling price.

If you are providing a service, you have to cost the direct labour involved, together with all outside costs. If your business involves quoting and selling each job you do, then you must accurately cost each job. If your service business involves charging your customers on an hourly basis, you are selling hours, so you must cost each hour, including the direct costs of transport, if relevant.

In each of these cases, your objective is to calculate your direct costs on everything you make, and sell. The difference between selling price and direct cost is gross profit. Your total gross profit in a week, a month or a year, less your total overheads for that period, will equal net profit. You need to find a formula which will allocate your overheads to your cost figures, so you know how much net profit you are making on each job, or each hour or on each product. In either a manufacturing or a service business the number of chargeable productive hours each week might be a starting-point, so you can compare your direct labour cost with your overheads, to find that overheads represent, say, 75 per cent of direct labour. Alternatively you might work out that you can do twenty jobs per day – in which case your weekly overheads could be divided by 100 and thus allocated to each job. In a retail business, overheads can be expressed as a percentage of sales value, or a percentage of purchase cost.

A point worth making in relation to your own time, if you are running your own small business – cost your own time accurately, from the moment you go into business. Even if you do not actually draw the money out, do not fool yourself. Your time is more valuable than anyone you employ, and you must build it into your costings, and charge it out.

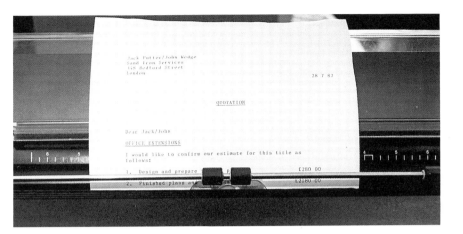

Jack Potter/John Wedge
Sand Iron Services
68 Bedford Street
London   28 7 87

QUOTATION

Dear Jack/John

OFFICE EXTENSIONS

I would like to confirm our estimate for this title as
follows:

1. Design and prepare   £ 280 00

2. Finished plans an   £2180 00

Preparing a quotation

You need to bear in mind that once a
quotation is accepted, it is a legally binding
contract between you and your customer. It
is therefore very important that you get
your facts right. Here are a few basic points
to consider:

◆ It is important in your contract to quote
the prices as being current ones and
give a time limit during which they are
appropriate. Although inflation has
been low during 1987, there easily can
be substantial variables in your costs of
raw materials, due to quotas/bad
weather/industrial disputes or
whatever, and you cannot afford to
have your quotation lying around over a
lengthy period without some qualifying
factor on time.

◆ It is not unusual for a customer to
change the original specification. In
your quotation you should allow
yourself the right to charge extra if the
customer asks for extras.

◆ Quote your trading terms, which
presumably will be thirty days net. Do
you require any money upfront?

◆ Timing. You may well be asked to
complete the job by a certain date.
Counteract this by stating the
circumstances beyond your control

under which you would not be able to
complete on time – such as the
weather if you are working out of
doors.

◆ You should make it clear that once the
quotation is accepted, you will be
proceeding with the work, and the
customer cannot cancel without being
liable for all the costs incurred to date,
plus your normal profit.
Never proceed on the verbal
acceptance of a quotation. Ask for
confirmation in writing before you
commit yourself to the purchase of any
supplies, or start work.

Continuous product assessment

Every few months you should sit down with
your sales staff if appropriate – and consider
your pricing policy. The marketplace does
change, requirements do alter, the goal
posts move. It could be that for virtually no
additional cost you could introduce a change
– perhaps a change of colour – for which you
could charge substantially more.
Alternatively, you might find that the
reason for recent poor sales is because your
goods have become over-priced compared
with competitors. Make sure you have a
costing meeting at least every month – you
cannot afford to do otherwise.

Measuring Performance

We have looked at the importance of planning and forecasting. We have looked at some important specific areas of control. What needs to be recognized, though, is the necessity for you to know how your business is performing – all the time. Last year's accounts – produced by you, your bookkeeper or your accountant – told you about last year. Your plans and forecasts will tell you about the future – how you should be doing. What you must have is regular information – day by day, weekly, monthly, quarterly – telling you about the performance of the business *now*.

You must look at today's information and compare today's information with what you expected to see today – your profit plan and the forecasts you made for it. There is no point in planning and forecasting if you do not then measure actual performance against the plan.

This is not a mammoth exercise. If you have already sat down with cold towels and prepared your plans – if you have a book-keeping system adequate for the smooth running of your business – you are 95 per cent there. You simply need to extract the right information from the books and records.

What we are talking about are **monthly management accounts** – and the appropriate back-up figures. They will obviously be less complex for the solo

plumber in the VAT section, charging £20 to mend a burst pipe, than for the high flyer in the Corporation Tax section, working out the best way to draw an extra £40,000.

At one extreme, our plumber knows exactly where he is. He or his wife answers the phone. He does the work. But is he charging what he intended to charge? Is his business doing as well as last year? Is his bank balance what he thought it would be? Why not?

At the other extreme, with three factories and 600 employed, is our businessman confident of the sales director's projections? Did they get that big, repeat order, from the States? How did that exhibition go last month? Why are the creditors so high this year?

The plumber needs simple information, simply presented – to enable him to identify how his business is performing – so that he can alter course if he needs to, and so that he has a guide to the future.

The high flyer needs complicated information, simply presented – for precisely the same reasons.

To prepare basic monthly management accounts, take the format of your profit plan (page 70), listing sales, direct costs, gross profit, all the overheads, and finally net profit. You will need six columns for figures, laid out like this:

Description	Month of November			Eleven months to November		
	Actual This year	Plan	Last Year	Actual This year	Plan	Last Year
Sales	1	2	3	4	5	6
Direct Costs						

Each month you will fill in, from your accounting records, all of the figures for the current month and for the cumulative period to date. The comparative figures will be extracted from your profit plan and last year's accounts.

Also take your forecast balance sheet and list exactly the same asset and liability headings, with three columns to show the month-end figures – actual this year, plan, and last year.

For a straightforward small business just these two sheets of paper, produced within a couple of weeks of the end of each month, will provide you with a good grasp of where your business is, and why. They will prompt questions and in some cases require detailed analysis for complete understanding.

◆ Why are the sales in November down on plan?
◆ Why is the gross profit margin up 2 per cent?
◆ Why have we spent so much on legal costs?
◆ Why is the debtor lock-up forty-eight days instead of the forty days planned?
◆ How did we manage to spend so much on new cars this year?

The smaller the business, the more summarized can be the information.

The larger the business, the more detailed will be the information required – but it will be available from a more sophisticated accounting system.

In addition to a full set of monthly accounts, most businesses will need to produce daily and weekly routine figures – recording enquiries, orders, number of jobs, etc.

General Assessment

Computers are changing the business world. Their development and the effect they can have on the way a business is run can be the deciding factor as to whether a business is successful or not. Virtually any business, however small, can justify using a computer, and costs continue to plummet, making the purchase of a computer within almost anyone's grasp. The rapid development has its drawbacks, though. A computer system installed today may well be obsolete in three years' time. What you have to decide is whether your business will truly benefit from a computer *now*, or whether you would be better advised to wait for next year's model – or perhaps even the year after's. There is no short cut to such a decision. What is needed is a great deal of careful and detailed study.

What is a computer system?

It is a combination of three things.

◆ *Hardware* This is the actual equipment, comprising a central processor, one or more keyboards, one or more VDUs (visual display units – i.e. TV screens) and one or more printers. Most small computers combine the central processor within the VDU.

◆ *Software* This is the programme of instructions which makes the hardware do what you want it to do. Your software may be a payroll programme, a sales ledger programme, a stock control/sales order processing programme, a word processing programme, etc. Software is recorded on tape, on a floppy disc or on a hard disc – depending on what sort of hardware is being used.

◆ *Back-up service* This is a vital part of the computer package. Hardware and software are useless without a competent back-up service – either from the hardware manufacturers or their selling agent, from the software house or dealer, or from an independent consultant who may be acting for you. Back-up service is essential to every business user in order to cope with faults on hardware, programming and updating of software – indeed any problems which may arise on the system as a whole.

Would your business benefit from a computer?

First, a generalization – if you are setting up a new business, you would be well advised to introduce all your administrative procedures manually. Do not put in a computer until you are absolutely certain that your procedures have settled down, **and they work.** You need a foolproof manual system before you attempt computerisation. The exceptions to this rule are –

a if you are a very experienced computer user and are in a field where manual systems just cannot cope (such as mail-order dispatch), or,

b if you need a computer for specific product design work or detailed financial assessment/planning, or perhaps to link up with an existing standard procedure within your industry.

Assuming you have an administrative system up and running within your business and you feel it is relatively efficient, what aspects should make you consider the introduction of a computer system – what are the benefits?

◆ A computer will help you carry out routine accounting tasks far more quickly and accurately than they can be done manually. This will reduce the amount of clerical work required, and in turn will allow you to train your staff to undertake more productive activities. It will also mean your business will be able to expand considerably without any increase in staffing levels.

- A computer will help you establish the right stocking level by providing an instant and accurate record, which can be constantly updated and enable you to develop a pattern against which you can calculate future ordering requirements.
- A computer can help you increase your sales and profitability, since you will have available at your fingertips up-to-date information about your products and customers which otherwise would take months of research to establish.
- A computer will help you improve your cash flow by providing faster invoicing and day-to-day control of creditors and debtors.
- A computer will help you to do a better management job, by providing you with regular management information.

Where to begin

Before you can even consider what types of computer are available on the market, first you need to make a detailed assessment of your own requirements. What exactly do you v ant your computer to do for you? Define your precise objectives first and then go shopping for the equipment to meet them. Look carefully at your present systems. How can they be improved? Where do the problems lie? Sit down and write out on a piece of paper precisely what you would like a computer to do for you, where you would like time saved and where you would like information you currently cannot obtain – in other words, what you would like to achieve in an ideal world. Try and sub-divide your current business into the following sections, which will help a supplier gauge the type of equipment you need.

- How much information you need stored – sub-divide this down into number of product lines, number of orders received in any one year, number of payments made and number of customers. Provide as much

information as you can.
- List the detailed information you feel a computer should be able to provide for you, highlighting those elements which are absolutely essential – i.e. customer details such as number of orders placed by a single customer in any one period, number of individual products sold in a specific period broken down into size, colour, etc., list of debtors with ageing analysis, list of stock which has not moved in the last six weeks . . . The possibilities are endless, but only you can highlight those elements of your business which need to be carefully monitored.
- Try and identify the element of non-standard procedures within your business. Do you need a specific facility to make refunds? Do you run a great many special offers? Do you produce a particular product at a particular time of year?
- Timing – How often do you require information – monthly, weekly, daily, hourly? Try and be specific on all the information you need.

This assessment should highlight in your own mind whether you actually need a computer, and whether the benefits will really justify both the investment and the inevitable upheaval involved in computerizing any part of your business.

Golden rule

Do give major consideration to the amount of computer experience of both yourself and your staff. If none of you have computer experience, you will have to employ someone with the necessary background to assist in the operation of the system. Whilst computers are becoming a great deal simpler, you should be aware that unless it is operated by someone with quite specific training and experience, your computerized system is likely to create more problems than it solves.

Identifying the Right Equipment and Software

In your search for the right computer, it is important to bear in mind that software and back-up are more important than hardware. There will be any number of types of computer hardware which will fulfil your requirements, but finding the right software package is the key to success. If you have a very large organization, with plenty of financial resources, you can consider having a package designed specifically for you. However, this is very expensive, and can involve a lot of teething troubles, and it is far better, initially, to look to a standard package to meet your requirements.

If you have decided to put in a computer, you should have gone through a detailed examination of the tasks you want it to perform and have evaluated the benefits to be obtained. As a result, you should have written down a description of the system you need – this is vital. Once you have this, your next task is to prepare a list of possible suppliers. Refer to specialist magazines, advertisements in the press, promotional literature, but also actively seek personal recommendation, particularly within your industry. Finding a supplier who understands your business is half the battle.

There are other considerations, too. There is little point in choosing a supplier who is geographically unsuitable. You must be able to lift the telephone and have instant help when you need it. Above all, you need a supplier who is well established and stable. Do not even consider buying equipment from a supplier until you have taken up references and have satisfied yourself that the company is very unlikely to go out of business. The implications of putting in a computer system, only to find that your software supplier has gone bust, are horrendous. You simply cannot afford for that to happen.

Having drawn up a list of potential suppliers, make contact with them and give them brief descriptions of what you are looking for. An initial talk will soon sort the sheep from the goats. The suppliers who are hell-bent on moving their equipment, and more interested in telling you about their product than listening to your needs, are not the suppliers you want to deal with. A little sifting should reduce your potential list to between three and six possible suppliers.

Send your written list of requirements to each of the companies on your shortlist and ask them to submit written proposals to you. When the proposals come back, compare them in terms of the software and equipment offered, ease of operation, number of administrative tasks that can be performed, growth potential and support training. Select the best two or three proposals and arrange for demonstrations to show you the system in use, with the functions you require. Take along your key personnel to the demonstration, get them all to make notes, and take time over your selection process. If you do not feel the demonstration has given you enough information, go back to your potential supplier for further information. It is their job to make the system clear to you. If they resent your need for information, then they are not the suppliers you want.

Having decided on your supplier, it is vital that you obtain from them guarantees that the system they will be installing will cope with your workload, as you have described. Using your statement of requirements as the basic document, get them to undertake in writing that these functions will be available to you. This is no simple piece of equipment you are buying. Until it is up and working, you have no way of knowing whether the supplier is really giving you what you want. Written guarantees are essential, therefore, to protect yourself, in the event of the equipment proving inadequate. Your supplier will draw up a contract. Do vet it most carefully, preferably with the help of your solicitor, and do not be afraid to modify the contract to your own particular requirements. Contrary to what the supplier may tell you, there is no such thing as a standard contract, and make sure you have the necessary warranties for continuance of supply. Brick-build the relationship to ensure that you get precisely what you have asked for.

If you are having a software package specially designed for you, then all the safeguards suggested here are doubly important. Your costs will be far greater, and if you are going to the expense and the trouble of having a system designed specifically for you, then it has got to be right, and you must ensure you have the necessary guarantees that it will be.

Finding the right supplier is absolutely vital. Do not be tempted to rush into the decision. It should be stressed that, where possible, you should try to find a supplier who has been personally recommended. In fact, the best reassurance you can have is to see a similar system to the one you will be buying, up and running, in real life. You can then talk to the staff who are actually using the equipment and see how the system works in practice as well as theory. A good supplier should offer you this facility.

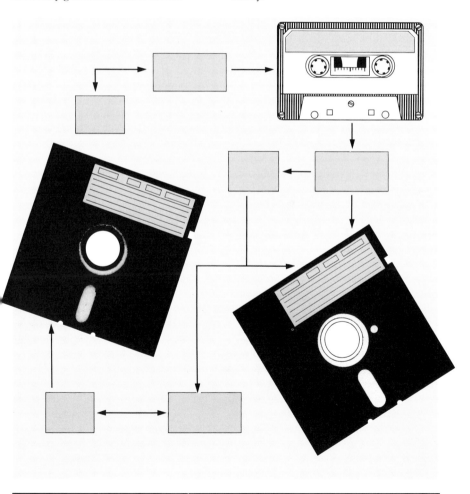

The question you have to ask yourself is whether you (or someone within your business) has sufficient knowledge, experience and time to:

a) Undertake a complete and detailed review of your own operations, administrative routines and requirements.

b) Prepare a sufficiently comprehensive description of your requirements to invite tenders from potential suppliers.

c) Prepare a list of suppliers to approach.

d) Evaluate the response.

The truthful answer most likely is that you do not have the skill and time to do the job properly. Remember that mistakes can be unbelievably costly. If you have any doubts at all as to your ability to cope, call in a consultant.

The key to employing a consultant is to find one who is truly independent. All too many consultants, in all fields of business, have their own vested interests, or are in reality linked to a particular supplier.

Consultants are not cheap. They can cost anything from £150 to £1,000 a day for their services, and it is vital you ensure that the consultant you choose is truly worth the money.

Choosing a consultant

1 Use a consultant whose sole source of income is obtained from the advice and service he gives to his clients. In other words, question the consultant closely, and establish that he does not receive agency fees or commission from any supplier.

2 Ask for business and technical credentials and take up references before hiring a consultant.

3 Carefully assess the consultant's approach to your business during the interview. Is the consultant truly interested in you and your problem, or more concerned with pushing you into a purchase? A good consultant should be

THE MARK IV CONSULTANT IS PRONE TO A LOSS OF DEFINITION

prepared to investigate thoroughly what makes your business tick before recommending the purchase of a computer at all.

4 Insist on a written proposal from any potential consultant, spelling out precisely what tasks he is prepared to undertake and how much money will be charged. This proposal should contain very tangible details of the sort of work that will be done. You need to know how often the consultant will be visiting, what progress reports will be made, for how long and in what form the presentation will be made to you.

It is a fundamental mistake to hold any expert in reverence. Computer consultants have the edge on most of us, since they move in a world which is unfamiliar ground to us and all too often seek refuge in gobbledegook when asked the simplest and most straightforward questions. All of the consultant's findings and recommendations should be questioned, alternatives suggested, benefits queried. Your role is to play the devil's advocate, and you should play it to the hilt. If you do not understand what you are being told, for heaven's sake say so. The reverse of this, of course, is to play fair by your consultant – do not withhold information that is pertinent to the work – there is little point in keeping a dog and barking yourself. Some people, and you may be one of them, are not good at taking advice, and there is little point in hiring a consultant if you are going to ignore what that person has to say. Similarly, ensure that your staff understand why a consultant has been brought in. There may be staff resentment unless you explain the situation carefully. An obvious point which is sometimes overlooked – make sure your consultant has somewhere peaceful to work.

Good consultants, frankly, are worth their weight in gold. Of course, their worth does not finish with the selection of the correct equipment. They can stay on as long as you need them, while the computer is installed and up and running. They can stand between you and the supplier, and have the necessary technical knowledge to make sure you get what you need. Do not be persuaded that a supplier or software house can give you independent advice. They are there to sell their products and services. Many firms of accountants have specialist departments, and you may be tempted to use one of these on a consultancy basis. Be careful, though – many firms do have close links with specific systems houses. Remember, you are looking for completely independent advice. Your local Small Firms Division of the Department of Industry will know several local consultants. Similarly, your branch of the Council of Small Industries in Rural Areas should be able to assist you. Seek help from your bank manager/solicitor/accountant, who again should be able to pass on the name of a recommended consultant.

There is an Association of Professional Computer Consultants. You can contact them at: 109 Baker Street, London W1M 2BH (telephone 01 267 7144). It is worth consulting them, too, for specific recommendations.

Because consultants are not cheap, you may consider that they are one element of cost you can save upon. However, you need to recognize that without a consultant, you may well end up with inappropriate equipment, and this could prove far more costly than a few weeks' consultant's fees. **With an eye on cost, it should be noted that there are government grants available, designed to encourage the use of computers within industry**. These grants can go a long way towards the cost of employing a consultant and, at a later stage, can assist with in-house training costs. Consult the Small Firms Division for further information.

Financing the Purchase

The decision to move from a manual system into computerization, either partially or fully, is a significant one for any business. It is also likely to involve a significant cost. Yes, hardware has become cheaper as a result of volume production and technical innovation, but a computer system appropriate to your particular business continues to be a major capital investment – regardless of the size of your business. Costs tend to be relative. The bigger your business, the bigger your spend will be on computerization. You need to recognize that you may have to spend up to 5 per cent of your turnover on a computer system – however, you should not have to spend more. If you run a secretarial bureau from your home, then the right commercial word processor for you is going to prove an expensive piece of equipment. If your engineering works has a turnover of two million per annum, you are likely to need to spend over £100,000 on putting in the right computerized system.

Within any business, the first decision you will need to make is whether you intend to buy the equipment outright, or on hire purchase or a finance lease, or whether you should rent with maintenance. There are various options, and what you decide to do depends on your business's overall capital expenditure programme. Clearly, if you have just purchased new premises, you may well be renting your computer system. Like any major business decision, the factor which will influence you most will be the financial shape of your business – the resources you have available, your attitude to borrowing, your future cash-flow forecasts and likely profits. In spending money on a computer, however, it is perhaps as relevant to look at the nature of the investment as it is to look at the financial shape of your business. If you are seeking outside finance of any sort, bear in mind that the bank or finance house you approach will be well aware of the special factors which relate to the purchase of a computer system. What are these special factors?

1   *Obsolescence* In three years' time the current version of your Model 4 computer, purchased this year, will be the Model 7. It will be the same price but will do the job twice as fast. However, you probably will not be able to afford to change to a Model 7. Why? Because your present Model 4 will have little or no resale value attached to it. The computer world is moving so fast that there is a natural resistance to purchasing equipment which is anything other than the latest model. This being the case, any finance you seek will need to be linked to a three-year repayment programme, or five-year at the very most. No finance house will give you more.

2   *Short term resale value – hardware* You may find that once your hardware is fully operational, it is not up to the job – or simply wrong. It may take you some months to assess this, but even if you realize the position in a matter of weeks, the resale value of your equipment will be very low indeed. It does not matter that it has been hardly used, that the supplier is reputable, and the system fully maintained – any mistakes on hardware will prove very expensive.

3   *Short-term resale value – software* If your software package has been tailor-made for your business, its resale value can be very simply assessed – **you will get absolutely nothing for it.** However, even with a perfectly standard software package you will be very lucky indeed to find anybody willing to buy it.

Given these circumstances, it is small wonder that finance is not easy to obtain on a long-term basis. To borrow money to make any purchase you have to provide the finance house with security. It is very questionable whether a computer system represents any security at all.

In a typical computer system, two-thirds of the cost is applicable to the hardware and a third to the software. However, increasingly, it is not unusual for that cost to be split on a fifty-fifty basis. Future trends are likely to have the hardware cost continuing to fall while increasingly sophisticated, labour-intensive software development will make software the major investment. So within a few years it is likely that the situation will reverse, and hardware will represent no more than a third of the overall costs.

Example
You might decide that leasing (HP under another name) is the most sensible course for your business. The problem is that most finance houses will not finance software, though some will accept the finance of software provided it is no more than 10 per cent of the total package.

Result – you may well be able to lease over a five-year period if you bargain aggressively, but effectively you will have to pay 40 per cent upfront.

Example
You might decide that short-term rental is best for you, because you can negotiate an option to change the equipment after a year.

Result – this is a very expensive exercise. You could end up by being forced to pay for the entire equipment over a two-year period.

Example
You have convinced yourself that your computerization programme is a viable project but you cannot justify leasing or renting and cannot afford to buy outright. Talk to your bank manager.

Result – you should receive a five-year loan, agreed at normal interest rates, with fixed repayments. If you express your confidence in the scheme by offering to make the repayment programme over four years, your bank manager will be ecstatic and you will still be way ahead of any other form of specialist finance.

The conclusion of these examples is this. Avoid if you can specialist leasing or rental. The finance packages which your supplier will offer you are expensive and very short-term. Far better go to your bank and ask for a straightforward loan.

Caution

One of the mistakes which many people make, in looking at the computerization of their business, is to fondly believe that it will save them money. It will not – if anything, in the short term, it will cost you far more than it will save. It needs to be recognized that whilst, in theory, a computer may reduce staffing levels, in practice your existing staff will be stretched to the hilt, coping with the new system. This being the case, in working out your finance requirements never, never budget for any form of overhead saving by the installation of a computer system. All you can expect your computer to do for you is to make your business more efficient and ultimately enable you to expand, without a significant increase in overhead cost.

Marketing – What's it all About?

Marketing is a two-tier process. First, before the start-up or expansion of any business, you must carefully define the market at which you are aiming. The term used is **market research**, and this has been covered in full in the second section of this book, 'Market Potential'. Suffice to say here that you may think you have a wonderful idea, so may your spouse, your mother and your best friend, but all of you could be wrong. Your idea is not worth a jot unless you have potential customers out there somewhere wanting what you have got to offer. Time spent in thorough market research is time well spent. Repenting at leisure, with shelves full of obsolete stock and a crippling bank overdraft, is no joke.

The second function of marketing, the one which will be dealt with in detail in this section, is to provide a continuing back-up to the selling effort. In other words, not so much **marketing** as **monitoring**. Just because you have found a market for your product or service, it does not mean you have it for all time. Your thinking needs to be constantly updated in all aspects of your field of operation. Indeed, being alert to market trends is an absolutely essential ingredient for running a consistently successful business.

The successful establishment of a place in your chosen market is much like getting married – it is not the end, it is just the beginning. Like marriage, it can be very unpredictable at times and needs working at! Monitoring means keeping a constant watching brief and being always on the lookout for signs of change and development. Can you provide not only what your customer wants today, but what that customer is likely to want tomorrow? What is happening to your market in terms of technology, image and price? What are your competitors doing? Can you keep pace with them? Do you need to? There was a time when the commercial world was a simpler place, but now, subject to the vagaries of inflation, fluctuating money markets and microchips, business is far

from simple. Indeed, you can no longer look at your business in isolation – its development can be, and usually will be, tremendously influenced by outside factors. Here is a checklist of those areas you should watch constantly:

◆ Trade magazines – if you are running your own business, these should be your bedtime reading. Sorry, but it is really necessary.

◆ Competitors – regularly send for all your competitors' sales literature. Where possible, call on your main competitors, or get someone else to, posing as a customer, to see what is being offered. Watch your competitors' prices, watch out for new products, listen to rumours in the trade – one of your competitors getting into financial trouble could be an enormous benefit to you. You can capitalize on your competitor's weaknesses. If their delivery is slow, guarantee an express service; if you learn that a number of their products are being returned as faulty, then stress your quality. Move fast, be one step ahead and it will be YOU who is grabbing the business.

◆ Local affairs – keep abreast of local events and above all, local people. Everyone loves to gossip – talk regularly with your bank manager, solicitor, accountant, local publican . . . anyone and everyone who can keep you informed as to what is going on. It could be useful.

◆ Suppliers and their representatives – your suppliers are not only suppliers of goods, they are also suppliers of information. If they are selling to you, then they are selling to your competitors, and there is an awful lot you can find out about the competition simply by asking. Salesmen, by dint of their outgoing personality, tend to be frightfully indiscreet and are only too happy to gossip about what your competitors are up to. Remember not to be too garrulous yourself, though –

the information should be flowing all one way.

◆ Consumer information – if your product is destined for the consumer market, do keep checking retail outlets for customer reaction. Particularly if you are selling via a wholesaler, it is easy to become alienated from your customers' requirements.

The suggestion that you remain adaptable does not mean that your business should be subject to constant change. If you have found a good niche in the market, which is making you money, hang on to it for grim death – it is very precious. It is worth considering that even if your product or service does not need any radical change, a relatively small alteration or adjustment could make an enormous difference to sales.

Monitoring should also take account of *how* you do things. Let us suppose you make and sell Welsh dressers, employing several craftsmen and selling the dressers via a wholesaler. Because you are selling in this way, your profit margin is small and you may feel that while you keep taking on more and more staff and turning out more and more dressers, the profits barely justify the effort involved. Rather than change the product to a more profitable one, consider the situation. What your wholesaler has done for you, as well as sell your merchandise, is prove that there is a market for what you produce. Surely, if you are wanting to make more profit you should be rethinking your sales operation. Would it be better, perhaps, to have your own shop or sell direct to the retail trade? You know the market is out there now, so if you can reach it yourself you are going to keep a great deal more of the profit.

Never lose sight of the fact that business today is extremely volatile. Your apparently safe market may have doubled, halved or completely disappeared by this time next year. So be prepared – it's called **monitoring.**

Case history – Alan Fowler, accountant and author

A few years ago, I bought a sewing-machine company. The company were specialists and had been trading for more than fifty years. They were profitable, but sales had dropped off in recent years. Immediately the company was mine, I appointed a management team to undertake a programme of market research, and after a few months they came to the conclusion that the sewing machine being produced was exactly right for the requirements of the market at the time – yet it was not selling.

The answer was simple. The machine was being produced in maroon. At the time sewing machines were almost entirely produced in black, and the market was not ready for a product which was so unfamiliar as to be another colour. We went back into production, manufacturing exactly the same product in black. The company became an overnight success and is still running successfully today.

If you are starting your own business, it may be that in the early days, at any rate, you are responsible for your own sales. Even if you are in an existing business, employing your own sales team, it is nonetheless important to understand and appreciate selling techniques. Only by recognizing how things should be done can you guide your salesmen to maximum effect.

Your sales approach

Here are some golden rules which are worthy of consideration when you are presenting your product or service to a potential customer.

◆ *Trial run* If you have a new business or are launching a new product, never make your first sales approach to the company or individual you think most likely to buy your merchandise. You need a few dummy runs and a little experience before making your major approach to the customer that matters. Good buyers ask a lot of questions – questions that never in your wildest dreams would have occurred to you. You need experience of how to handle these before approaching your most potentially valuable customer.

◆ *Initial approach* As a general rule, you should always make a telephone appointment first, before calling on a buyer. This does not mean to say that if you happen to find yourself in an area with time to spare, and spot a likely-looking business, there is any harm in calling to see if the buyer is available – you may strike lucky. However, as a general matter of policy, it is courteous to make an appointment first – and also practical.

A great many buyers simply will not see a sales representative without an appointment, and abortive calls are expensive.

◆ *The telephone call* Do not be trapped into lengthy conversation when making

an appointment. By far the best approach, if you can manage it, is to find someone who has access to the buyer's diary and fix an appointment without even speaking to the buyer. This way you will not have to justify your reason for the appointment. Unless you have been trained in telephone sales, trying to project your product or service over the phone can be very difficult. If you are forced into giving details of what you are offering, try to make the point that the buyer will be missing something important if he does not see you, and that what you have to show is far easier to demonstrate face to face.

◆ *The appointment* Never see a buyer too early in the day, nor too late in the afternoon. Buyers are likely to be most receptive mid-morning, when the post is cleared away from their desk and their minds are still fresh. The later in the day it is, the more likely they are to be jaundiced, sceptical and hard to please.

◆ *Keep cheerful* Do not be depressed if your first visit does not result in an order – frankly, it is very unlikely to do so. What is terribly important at that first interview is to listen and learn. Take an intelligent interest in what your buyer has to say. What product are they using at the moment? How much is it costing them? How often do they want delivery, in what quantities and at what price? Learn as much as you can about their business and learn as much as you can about the buyer's character. There is no need to be pushy but be alert and interested.

◆ *Buyers are busy people* Whilst buyers need the basic information concerning you, your business and your product, they do not need a personal biography. A woolly approach is the kiss of death, and it is surprising how many representatives rabbit on about everything under the sun. Pass the odd remark about the weather, the state of the country, the buyer's children, your children, or whatever may be appropriate, but what is far more important is that you have all the information you require at your fingertips. If possible, you want to avoid having to go back to the office to work out a price – quote the buyer there and then. Have an up-to-date list of production schedules so that you can make an instant commitment as to how long it will take to fulfil any order you may receive. You are far more likely to receive an order if you can be positive on the spot as to what you can and cannot do.

◆ *Closing a sale*   It is very difficult to generalize on this technique. Certainly it does not sound very helpful to say you should rely on instinct until you gain experience, but that is the fact. Knowing the right moment to strike is not easy. If you apply pressure for a decision too soon your buyer may turn you down flat. On the other hand, give them too much time to make up their mind and you may find that someone else beats you to it. Be prepared to compromise – at the point at which you are trying to close your sale and can feel the order slipping away from you, you must quickly undertake a salvage operation. If buyers start saying something along the lines that basically they are happy with their current suppliers and cannot justify moving their business elsewhere, you do have a defence. Suggest to them that you can well understand their reluctance to change suppliers. So how about giving you a piece of the business on a trial basis? If you can just get one order, however small, you have your toe in the door, and once you have formed a supplier relationship with your customer then it is up to you to work hard and gradually increase your share of the business.

◆ *The follow-up technique*   However abortive your sales call may have been, every call you make must be followed up by some literature in the post, to arrive on the buyer's desk no later than thirty-six hours after your visit. With luck, you may have been asked to send samples and a quotation. If it will take a week or so to provide samples, do not allow that time to pass without any communication with your buyer. Even if you have warned the buyer that the samples will take that long, write immediately, thank the buyer for sparing you the time, give the quotation and confirm that samples will be dispatched within ten days or whatever. If you have been thrown out on your ear, still write to the buyers thanking them for their time. Enclose whatever sales literature you have and ask them to bear you in mind should their circumstances change.

◆ *Record keeping*   It is essential that you keep a card on all your potential customers. The moment you come out of a meeting, sit down and write up your card. Obviously there will be important pieces of information – the buyer may have asked you to ring back in three weeks' time or supply samples or quotations. There will also be less obvious pieces of information that could be useful in the future – the name of his wife, the secretary, how many children. Jot down all this information and do not be tempted to rely on memory.

These, then, are the basic rules for making a sales approach to a potential customer. Follow them yourself, and make sure your staff do, too.

Hiring a Salesman

Employing people is always a gamble. As most of us know from our own experience, it is very difficult to relax sufficiently to behave normally in an interview situation. There is, however, one very distinctive advantage in interviewing sales staff, as opposed to any other type of employee. In theory at any rate, you will end up with the best man, since it will be the one who has been most successful in selling himself to you.

Regardless of the type of industry, there are basically really only two kinds of salesmen available to you – the experienced or the inexperienced person. If you're hiring an experienced person, you should expect to pay highly for his skills, but with him should come a number of very valuable contacts. There is no real limit on his age, though one would expect the salesman to be over thirty to have gained the necessary experience. The inexperienced salesman

should be aged anywhere between twenty and thirty, not too wet behind the ears, but young enough to be trained. What type of person you hire depends rather upon yourself. If you have plenty of sales experience, you may prefer to train a youngster to sell your way. If, however, you have not been involved in selling before then, clearly, you need an experienced salesman, otherwise you are going to be in the position of the blind leading the blind.

There are, of course, a number of ways of attracting would-be salesmen, but the best approach is to advertise in your trade magazine or local or national newspaper, and then carefully sift replies. The interview is all-important. The man sitting the other side of the desk from you may be going to represent your company. Here are some pointers worthy of consideration when interviewing a potential salesman.

- Good personal appearance – you need to look for all those sordid details, like dirty fingernails and dandruff on the collar. If you do not like the look of your potential salesman then neither will your customers.
- Education – whilst a reasonable standard of education is important, unless you are selling a highly technical product, it is quite acceptable – or even preferable – for a salesman to have a fairly unspectacular educational record. Top academic qualifications suggest he may be more of a thinker than a doer – it can also have the effect of making the salesman a little patronizing towards less erudite customers.
- Interests – the wider your potential salesman's interests, the better. It shows he has an alert mind, and will make him more interesting to your customers.
- Health – being a salesman is hard work. He needs to be physically fit, and you should ask for details of his health record.
- Temperament – it is always difficult to reach the man behind the interview technique. Particularly today, when jobs are so scarce, people are usually very nervous, and this may cause them to over- or even under-react. While you may be sympathetic and understanding about this problem, remember that the same displays of nervousness are likely to be visited on your customer. Look for all the obvious signs of confidence – a firm handshake, the ability to look you in the eye, clear concise answers, a friendly smile.
- Marital status – it is preferable for a salesman to be married. He is likely to work harder if he has commitments, and less likely to plan his sales calls around current romantic interests.
- Ambition – ask your potential salesman about his career aims. If he is keen and intelligent, he will have a master plan. If he has none, then there is something wrong.
- Is he a listener – is your potential salesman interested in your business? Is he prepared to listen to what you have to say, and has he done any research? Imagine for a moment that, instead of your interviewing the salesman, he is sitting in front of one of your customers. Is he really listening to what you are saying, thirsty for information about your business, reacting to the information you are giving by pointing out various attributes which he has and which are particularly suitable for the job in hand? If so, then this is the way the salesman is going to sell your products for you.
- Honesty – honesty in an employee is important at every level, and the best way to establish honesty at the interview stage is to make a few provocative remarks. Establish his view on a topic and then express the opposite one. If he drops the argument immediately and agrees with you, honesty does not come naturally.
- Do you like the person – perhaps the most important question of all. If the answer is no, do not hire him, however good the qualifications.

Sales are the lifeblood of your business – without them you have no business. However good your product, your administration and your pricing policy, all of it is worthless unless someone is doing a good job selling what you have to offer. More important than any other appointment, take time and trouble selecting your sales force. Nothing but the best will do for you.

Managing a Sales Force

In considering the hiring and managing of a salesman, let us first question the case of salary versus commission. By tradition, fairly clear guidelines are laid down – staff selling consumer products are normally paid largely by commission, while industrial sales people usually receive a full salary and no commission. Most sales people are provided with a company car and out-of-pocket expenses.

The reason for the difference between consumer products and industry is fairly obvious. A salesman, selling a consumer product – say, vacuum cleaners to electrical retailers – can easily have remuneration linked to achievements. He visits a number of outlets during the course of a week and either makes a sale or does not, and is paid accordingly. In this instance, commission is usually calculated on turnover. In the case of the industrial salesman, part of the job may be the servicing of a major house account, which just happens to fall into his particular area. Very often in industry, technical staff play as big a part in the acquisition of an order as the actual salesman, and it could cause ill-feeling if the salesman was paid a commission. Industrial sales often take a long time to finalize and sales people have to live in the meantime. Also, since the orders are often very large, they frequently involve senior management in negotiation.

On balance it is not recommended to employ a commission-only salesman, regardless of the industry. Although it seems a good idea to pay on achievement, without some form of basic salary the salesman has no inbred loyalty towards you or your company. The pressure to achieve is great. The salesman will either panic and fail altogether, or start to use some fairly underhand tricks to obtain orders. The best mix is a good basic salary, with a small bonus scheme linked to target achievements.

Golden rule

Never give price-negotiation authority to a salesman who is on commission. That salesman's primary objective will be to obtain the order, and he may well do so at an uneconomic price rather than lose commission.

How to control your sales staff

In order to run a successful sales force you need to instil a sense of personal discipline into your sales people, since their day-to-day life is fairly free from it. Here are a few pointers which are well worth implementing:

◆ It may sound obvious, but it is worth mentioning – you need to ensure that your sales people have a loose-leaf address book in which they keep every scrap of information that comes their way.

◆ Record cards – your salesmen need to keep a record card on every person they visit, whether they are successful in obtaining an order or not.

◆ Weekly sales report – you must insist on your sales people submitting these on time each week, carefully and neatly written, with full information on every day of their working week. You should suggest to them that these reports are completed on a daily basis, while the visits are still fresh in their minds. You should make it clearly understood that it is a requirement of the job that these reports are properly submitted.

◆ You must insist that your salesmen ring into the office first thing every morning and last thing in the afternoon. They need to do this for a variety of reasons. You need to know their itinerary for the day so that you can contact them if you need to. You may need to give them instructions, or you may have some queries regarding an order. They may need to pass through requests for samples or technical information, and at the end of the day your sales people need to make sure that none of their customers have been trying to contact them. Again, you must insist on this procedure being followed. Of course, from time to time on a particular evening, a salesman may be so involved with a customer that he is unable to ring in, but this should not be a regular occurrence.

◆ Regular sales meetings are vital. You need to strike a balance here. Your sales people are only doing your company any good if they are out in the field selling. Sitting around, talking about it in the office, does not pay their wages. The right balance is a fortnightly meeting. Getting your sales people together every other week is often enough to keep in regular touch, but not too often to disrupt the working week. Regular sales meetings are terribly important as a basis for exchange of views, instruction and advice.

◆ To complement your sales reports, it is also very important that you report to your sales force on any changes or developments within your business. It is vital that you make them feel part of the business, and important to it. Out there on the road all day, it is difficult to give them a sense of belonging. Obviously, they will be advised of major changes of policy, but send them memos on relatively trivial matters, such as minor changes of staff, the new facsimile machine, the change of menu in the staff canteen. Since the very birth of industry, there has always been an element of rivalry and mistrust between sales and production staff. Production staff believe that sales swan around all day, eating expense account lunches. Sales believe that production have no idea of pressure and plod along at half-speed. On a regular basis, aim to get together your sales force and

your production or technical staff. Encourage a frank exchange of views – both parties will learn a lot, and your business will benefit accordingly. Sales people, for example, may receive a persistent complaint about some element of your product or service, but only a meeting with your technical staff will actually jog their memories sufficiently to have the problem aired and dealt with.

There are lazy, indifferent, dishonest and downright hopeless men and women around, who have the audacity to call themselves salesmen. Picking a winner is not easy, but when you have found yourself an averagely good salesman, who is enthusiastic and caring about your business, whether that salesman succeeds or fails will largely depend upon you. There is a lot to be said for the view that sales people are as good as the business they represent.

SELLING AND MARKETING

Agents have a place in all types of industry. Traditionally, perhaps, the term is best known in the context of their representing freelance artists – established actors, writers and musicians almost always have their interests looked after by an agent.

In the fuller sense, however, an agent is a person who, operating entirely separately from the business he represents, goes out to sell its wares.

Selling through an agent

Finding an agent to represent your business is difficult – finding a *good* agent still more so. Open most trade papers, regardless of your type of business, and you most probably will see a great many advertisements placed by various of your competitors, seeking agents. Indeed, in some industries there will be more advertisements seeking agents than the rest of the classified advertising put together. If you are looking for an agent, this comment is not intended to depress you, but to emphasize that once you have found one, you should look after a good agent.

What are the advantages of employing an agent? The main one has to be that you only have to pay for what you actually get. Small businesses, particularly, are terribly at risk if they start employing a sales force. Even if your sales people are employed on a commission-only basis, there is still the question of cars, expenses and, of course, the administration involved in controlling them. Agents, by contrast, work freelance. They meet all their own expenses, operate their own schedule, provide their own transport and only look to you for commission when they have made a sale. Basically, employing an agent as opposed to a salesman means a shift of risk. Instead of *you* taking the risk of investing *your* time and money in a salesman, whose abilities may prove ineffectual, by employing an agent you are asking *him* to risk *his* time and money in the saleability of your products.

An agent's commission is usually around 10 per cent of selling price, excluding VAT, which is not particularly high considering the outgoings an agent is likely to incur on your behalf. Because of this, unless you have a proven product, you may have a problem actually finding an agent to represent you. If agency selling is right for your business, you should reward the really effective agents by a rising commission scale based on sales targets. Since all an agent has to sell is time and skill, it is vital, from the agent's point of view, that both are used to maximum effect. The agent has to be convinced that representing your product is going to be worth while for him, as well as for you.

The most important aspect to consider when employing an agent is his contacts. A good agent will have a range of valuable contacts, and it is these the agent is really selling – in other words, the ability to get you to a customer who otherwise might prove inaccessible. A good agent is really a

selling service. Efficient agents will travel the length and breadth of the country if necessary, to see that samples are delivered on time. They stand sandwiched between buyer and seller, being careful to tread a middle road. In their presentation to potential customers, good agents will convince a buyer that they are working for the buyer as well as the business they represent, and to an extent this is true. No good agent wants to make a sale, however big, to a valued customer if he knows the goods are of questionable quality.

Agents rarely work for one company – normally they represent several within a particular industry. This gives them a unique feel as to what is going on in their particular trade, and to this extent a buyer is likely to listen to what they have to say. There is an obvious disadvantage in an agent representing other companies within your industry, but here again, a reputable agent is not going to abuse the position. In putting forward the case for employing sales people, as opposed to an agent, it is true to say that when a salesman goes to see a potential customer, he is selling your goods and no one else's. When an agent

goes to see a potential customer, he will sell those goods he feels most appropriate, and those may not necessarily be yours. Having said that, an agent's view carries more weight with a buyer, and when the agent does recommend your goods, the agent is probably more likely to make a sale than your own salesman.

If you acquire an agent, or several agents, to help you develop your sales, do help them to help you. Make sure your agent has plenty of samples and point-of-sale material. When the agent rings up asking for a sample order, drop everything and make sure it arrives on time. The day the agent can rely on you to back up his selling effort, that agent will stop representing you, and rightly so. Selling is a tense business, and if your agent is on to a red-hot lead which has to be followed up immediately, you must provide the right back-up. It could be panic samples, or it could be your presence is required in Liverpool in three hours flat. Whatever it is, do as the agent asks. If you do not do so, not only are you wasting his time, but you are wasting your own in hiring the agent's services.

Public Relations (PR) is simply a question of persuading the media to tell the world that your business is wonderful! Actually journalists could do with some PR to polish up their image. On the whole they are an awfully nice bunch of people and surprisingly caring. Most journalists are only too happy to give some coverage to a commercial venture – provided, of course, that the business has something interesting to offer. PR as a business function is generally placed far too low on the priority list. People tend to see it as window dressing rather than making a serious contribution to the development of a business, yet it is far less expensive than advertising, and in the main far more effective. How do you set about it?

Local PR

The best way to make contact with your local newspaper is to go and see them. First telephone the editorial department/sports page/women's page, or whatever is relevant, and try to make an appointment to see the appropriate journalist. What the journalist will be looking for is some sort of angle to your business. For example, suppose you have just opened a local restaurant. The news in itself may not warrant any coverage, but perhaps there is some twist to your story – perhaps the menu consists of dishes from your grandmother's recipe book. You have just opened a small manufacturing unit. There are plenty of small manufacturing units in your town, what is the angle? Perhaps you have landed an export order; perhaps you have made it a business policy to employ unemployed school leavers; perhaps your premises are haunted! You have to tell a story – it is as simple as that.

Try and make friends with your local journalists. Meet in the pub – in that respect their reputation is entirely justified – most of them do enjoy their drink! If you are asked to provide some information for an article, make sure you submit it on time.

If you are anxious that the article should not appear before a certain date, simply write the words EMBARGOED UNTIL 24th AUGUST, or whatever date is appropriate. When submitting photographs, make sure they are black and white prints and make sure they are captioned. Always stress to the journalist the need to state some practical information – their poetic licence tends to lead them away from the basics – your potential customers need to know what you sell, where you sell it and how they get hold of it.

Local media are not restricted to newspapers, of course. You will find local radio tremendously helpful and nearly always willing to interview you if you have something interesting to say. If you happen to have expert knowledge on anything which is of interest to the public, local radio always welcome a 'phone-in'. It is somewhat nerve-wracking having live questions fired at you, but you do receive a tremendous amount of air time. You can also approach regional television. It is not easy to obtain coverage. What is terribly helpful with all the media, but television in particular, is knowing someone, who knows someone, who knows someone on the staff! As with everything really, personal contacts are a tremendous help.

National PR

Obtaining national PR does require professional help. If you have a medium to large company, whose products/services are aimed specifically at the consumer, then you might consider installing your own PR department. However, there is a tendency for in-house PR to be rather sluggish and ineffectual. Certainly your head of PR, cocooned in a secure job, will not be as hungry for publicity as a freelance PR consultant – who knows that lack of performance will mean the loss of your contract.

PR consultants come in all guises – from solo outfits to large publicity agencies. Let us look at them in more detail.

PR consultants

The best way to find a reputable firm of public relations consultants is to contact the Institute of Public Relations, 1 Great James Street, London WC1 (telephone 01 405 5505). They will give you a list of PR consultants in your area, and will be pleased to advise you of the type of business which each firm serves best. As with advertising agents, it is far better to select a firm which already has a working knowledge of your trade. Alternatively, all reputable PR consultants are contained in a directory called the *Hollis Press and Public Relations Annual*, which can be obtained from Contact House, Sunbury on Thames, Middlesex T16 5HG (telephone 09327 84781).

Most public relations firms will ask for a monthly retainer, plus expenses. Compared with the average advertising budget, the sum involved is usually fairly small. However, a word of warning – do not expect immediate results. PR takes time. Time to establish contact with journalists, time before the articles are acutally published and time before a gradual build-up of exposure starts to have any tangible effect on your business. There is very little point in undertaking a PR campaign for less than a year, unless, of course, you are specifically wanting to promote one single event.

Appointing a PR consultant does not mean that you should forget publicity. For best results you need to bear in mind the following points:

1   Do keep your PR consultants fully informed of all your company's activities, the direction in which the business is moving, and any changes you are making. As explained earlier, journalists are always looking for an angle on a story. Some aspect of your business development, which may seem comparatively minor to you, could make a wonderful piece of editorial.

2   Provide your PR consultants with a good service. As with your sales force, make sure they have up-to-date sales literature and samples. Journalists seem to operate in a completely different way from the rest of mankind. When you have heard nothing from a newspaper for weeks, they will suddenly ring and say that they must have photographic samples or a picture of the proprietor within a couple of hours, for that night's edition. It is no good moaning about it and saying it is inconvenient. That is the way journalists work, and if you want PR coverage, you have to react.

3   Be prepared to give your PR consultants personal backing. As proprietor, the best selling aid they have is you, yourself. Many journalists are simply not prepared to talk to a PR consultant – they want to speak to the boss. Talking to a journalist, or being interviewed on radio or television for the first time, is a little daunting, but after a while you will find you become surprisingly professional. Be yourself, be friendly and relaxed, but make sure you get across the practical details.

4   If you are embarking on a national PR campaign, make sure that either you or your PR consultants take out a press-clipping service. There are a number of companies who specialize in this. It is their job, for a comparatively small sum of money, to ensure that they obtain a copy of every single piece of printed matter that is written about you. Similarly, if you are interviewed on radio or television, make sure that someone makes a tape or video. These, together with the press cuttings, can be tremendously helpful when selling your business concept to new customers, or indeed, potential investors. Have your press cuttings nicely mounted in a special book.

The most important aspect of PR is that someone else is telling the world how wonderful you are. It's also free!

The justification for advertising spending in any size of business, should be examined very carefully. Unless you are an enormous organization, purely looking at a brand awareness exercise, advertising should never be undertaken unless you are seeking direct tangible results from the advertisement you place.

Never place an advertisement unless you actually want something quite specific from it. Never look on advertising as part of your major sales drive, and never place an advertisement simply because you feel you should be seen to be advertising in a particular publication. Trade magazines are a particular case in point. Many, many companies spend a fortune on advertising in their own trade paper. Presumably they do it to advise their competitors that they are still around, for precious few customers ever read them.

Advertising is one of those aspects of business life which seems to be shrouded in mystique. Otherwise highly intelligent men and women become mesmerized into spending thousands of pounds of hard-earned profit on an advertising programme, which they are seriously led to believe will revolutionize their business – and it practically never does. It is difficult to lay blame at anyone's feet for the amount of money which is squandered on useless advertising. Perhaps it is due to the fact that advertising agents and their clients have very different aims and tend to talk in parallel. Certainly advertising agents greatly over-estimate the impact most advertising campaigns have on a business. Equally certainly, the average executive, with no particular experience of advertising, is often over-influenced by advertising agents' sales techniques and presentation. Of course, there are products and services which owe their success almost entirely to a brilliant advertising campaign, but basically these are few and far between. **Advertising is not a substitute for any other business function.** You must have a marketable product, proper channels of distribution and a proven selling technique before you even contemplate advertising. The very last thing you should try to do is to advertise a product or service which is not selling. Advertising should only be used as an extra fillip. If you have a successful product then you may be justified in advertising it to capitalize on an already proven success.

So when do you advertise?

Perhaps you have opened new premises, designed a new product or service, perhaps you are having a sale or attending a trade exhibition. Perhaps you are looking for staff or for an agent. Perhaps you want to sell your company van or buy one . . . It is very important to place the emphasis here – you need a *raison d'être* to advertise.

There are four main categories of general advertising:
- Space taken in newspapers and magazines.
- Brochures and sales leaflets.
- Radio and television.
- Posters, point of sale material and display cards.

If you decide you are going to advertise in one of these areas, the first thing you need to ask yourself is whether you are going to employ the services of an advertising agent. If your advertising is likely to be a one-off affair, or certainly applicable to a limited

period only, then you may well be able to handle it yourself. However, if you are dealing with a specialist medium – such as radio or television – and intend spending a great deal of money, then it would be advisable to seek the services of an agency. This would also apply if you see advertising as being an ongoing part of your business promotion.

Guide to advertising agencies

Like everything else, advertising has some good agencies and some bad, but unlike everything else, it is often very difficult to differentiate between the two. The time most businesses discover that they are using an incompetent agency is when their advertising programme has failed and they are already involved in spending a great deal of money. In other words – too late.

As already suggested, if your advertising budget is small, do not use an agency, but once you move beyond the occasional advertisement in your local paper or trade press, it is time to look around. It costs nothing in theory to use an advertising agency to place advertisements for you. They receive a 15 per cent discount from the media when placing an advertisement on your behalf, and this discount they keep. You are then invoiced at the same price as you would have been charged had you placed the advertisement direct. However, in most instances, when using an agency to buy space, you are also committed to using them for layout, artwork, etc., and this will cost considerably more than employing a little typesetter down the road. On the other hand, an agency should produce far better results.

In selecting an agency, it is important to find one which specializes in your particular trade. An agency with experience of your market will know and understand which media are likely to work best for you. They will also know, from the successes and failures of their existing clients, what type of advertisement is likely to work. Do not

be influenced by the location or size of your agency – you simply need one that understands your business. The Creative Handbook Limited have a list of advertising agencies. Their address is 100 St Martin's Lane, London WC2N 4A2 (telephone 01 379 7399). They list agencies regionally, and it is well worthwhile trying your local agency first, for it is a myth that good agencies have to be based in London. Take time over your selection and do not be impressed by endless gin-and-tonics. Before every stage of whatever advertising programme you map out, always insist on a detailed quotation. Advertising costs mount up appallingly unless they are watched.

Golden rule

In all advertising, do make sure the statements and claims you are making about your product or service are true to the best of your knowledge. False statements can leave you wide open for prosecution under the Trade Descriptions Act.

Advertising is vital to some businesses, totally unnecessary for others. Once you have a recognized business established, all sorts of people will contact you with requests to advertise in their publications. Ask yourself the same two questions every time you are approached.
1   What is this advertisement actually going to achieve for my business?
2   How many items do I have to sell in order to pay for this advertisement?
Expressed in these simple terms, most advertising proposals suddenly seem what they generally are – expensive and rarely worth it. Never place an advertisement simply in response to somebody's request that you should. If you believe your business needs advertising then set aside a precise budget, based entirely on how much money you can afford to spend, and then see what the sum of money will buy you. Always be in charge of your own destiny, and do not fall for all that jargon!

The object of a sales promotion is to increase sales in the short term, for a particular reason. There are a variety of reasons why a promotion may be appropriate – let us look at those in detail:

1 Sale of surplus goods

Without doubt the most familiar type of promotion is the sale, or stock clearance, where goods are offered at a substantial discount for a short period. The reason for holding such a sale is because there is a surplus of stock, a stock imbalance or the requirement for a seasonal change of goods. Of course many businesses have to undertake such an exercise from time to time, but what you do have to bear in mind is that this kind of promotion contains some very substantial costs. If, for example, you have a retail outlet and decide to hold a sale, there are three quite specific costs to consider –

◆ The cost of profit margin lost by offering a discount on your normal selling price.
◆ The cost of promoting the sale. There is little point in holding a sale unless enough people know about it, and in order to attract sufficient interest you will have to advertise in the local press, television or radio, or organize a leaflet distribution.
◆ The cost of additional staffing levels. If your sale is a success, you will be inundated with customers. Extra temporary staff will be the only way to handle the additional volume. Also, you may feel it justified to be open longer hours, to tie in with specific selling periods. This in turn will involve overtime.

Against these costs, of course, you have to offset what it is costing you to hold dead stock. You probably have an overdraft, warehousing costs and the increasing awareness that the longer you hold on to the stock, the less valuable it becomes. It is

a balancing act, but in these circumstances an alternative option could be to sell off your stock through the trade. In every industry there are people who are willing to buy surplus stock. Their prices may be very low but the overheads are nil and it is an option worth considering.

2 A special line

You may have bought in a cheap line – it could be raw material or finished goods. You believe the items in question are very saleable but you need to sell them fast in order to turn your money over.

3 Special promotions

Various circumstances may bring about a special promotion. It could be your location or the weather, or some particular type of event. For example, you might promote bikinis because of a heatwave, or electric blankets because of a hard winter. You might promote tennis rackets during Wimbledon Fortnight, or design a T-shirt during the Olympic Games. In other words, you adapt your product to suit a particular set of circumstances.

4 Order value

You may wish to increase your order value. Whether you are selling to industry or to the consumer, something for nothing always has an appeal. Putting across the idea to your customers that, if they order a little extra, they will receive something free, can have a big impact on sales – particularly if geared to a short period of time. However, do be very careful about your costings. This sort of promotion can prove a very expensive exercise.

5 Encouraging visitors

If you have a retail outlet, a restaurant, a hotel, or indeed any type of business which the public can visit, you might wish to run a promotion to encourage callers – a free glass of wine at a restaurant, or a 10 per cent discount for first-time buyers at a new shop, are the types of promotion which can prove very effective.

6 Lotteries

This is most popular amongst mail order companies. You will be familiar with this type of promotion – if you order more than £20 worth of goods (within a certain period, the blurb normally says) your name will be put forward to be drawn in a lottery where enormous prizes are available. This form of promotion has been criticized a great deal recently, and not without cause. In most of these lotteries, the odds against winning are enormous and once the public realizes it, the promotion can actually cause resentment. Promotions are supposed to encourage enthusiasm in your business, not disgruntlement. There are quite specific laws on lotteries. Before attempting to run one yourself you should consult your solicitor.

7 Presentation

This, of course, applies most specifically to the retail trade. One form of promotion is to give a particular product prominence in display.

8 Loss leaders

This term applies when a business sells a particular item at a loss in order to attract buyers to purchase other merchandise at normal profit margins. This type of promotion is all very well for a great chain of stores or supermarkets, but is not to be recommended for small businesses. It is a tortuous costing exercise and very difficult to get right without a great deal of experience. Certainly it is not to be recommended unless you are very sure of the outcome.

9 Stamps and vouchers

The only type of sales promotion that attracts customer loyalty is the rather old-

fashioned cigarette card or gift stamp. These promotions were an excellent idea, but their appeal does seem to have waned of late. People generally appear less inclined to collect things. However, the major petrol companies have recently become heavily involved in this form of promotion to build brand loyalty, and it may be possible for you to experiment on a small scale by offering vouchers, which can be saved and exchanged for goods.

Sales promotions are a good idea from time to time – but do not let them detract from your real business. Your aim should be to sell your wares at the right price, in the normal course of day-to-day trading. We can all sell cheap goods – it is easy – but if you are building a business, your priority must be to sell your products at a price which will make you money – preferably plenty of it.

Exhibiting

If you ask the average person to name an exhibition, they will quote you the Ideal Home Exhibition, the Motor Show, or perhaps the Boat Show. Yet 90 per cent of all exhibitions are in fact trade shows aimed at industry and commerce rather than at the general public. Before even considering whether you should exhibit, you need to recognize that attending the average trade exhibition is of immense value to you as a market research exercise, whether you choose ultimately to exhibit there yourself, or not. Assuming for a moment that you are in an industry which *does* exhibit, not only do you have your competitors grouped together under one roof, but incognito you are free to wander amongst them, asking as many questions as you like – providing, of course, you pose as a customer! If you want to know what your industry is doing and where it is going, what could be better than a trade exhibition?

Now to the question of your exhibiting. There are three aspects to consider – the decision to do it, how to do it and how to handle the follow-up procedure.

Deciding to do it

Exhibitions are of value to you and your business if you have a product, or indeed a service, which needs to be seen and touched by your customers. Exhibitions bring the marketplace to you and they bring the right people. Compare, for a moment, an exhibition with normal retailing. People who wander past your retail outlet are simply the general public at large – a great many of whom have no interest at all in your product or service. A trade show, by contrast, acts as a filter. The people wandering past your stand are there because they are interested in your type of product or service.

Let us look at the costs involved. When taking exhibition space, there are two main elements of cost to be considered – the rental of the actual floor space and the cost of the stand itself. Currently, floor space is

costing £70 to £80 per square metre, and there is nothing you can do to ease this cost since it is a fixed charge decided upon by the organizer. However, there is an enormous variance in stand costs, depending entirely on how much you are prepared to spend. While it is important not to spend too much money, anyway in the early days of exhibiting, it is equally pointless to settle for the trestle table with a sheet over it – you must attract people wandering by to come on to *your* stand. There are three ways in which you can tackle the construction of your stand.

◆ You can instruct contractors to build you a stand either to your own design or to theirs, and quite specific to your requirements. This is expensive and the stand remains the property of the contractor – it is not yours to take away. However, good stands can be very effective, attracting much attention.

◆ More and more exhibition organizers are realizing the value of encouraging small businesses to attend their shows, and at most exhibitions you can rent a booth, in what is called a 'shell scheme'. This involves renting a cubicle which, for a two- or three-day show, costs about £400, and to which you can add your own display panels, lights and shelving.

◆ The third alternative is to purchase a modular display system. This is a kit which remains your own property and which you take from exhibition to exhibition. The kit comes in the form of panels and poles, which clip together in a variety of shapes. The good ones are lightweight and easy to assemble, and once you have made the initial purchase, it can prove very cost-effective.

Doing it

Make a friend of the exhibition organizer. He or she is there to make a profit, but the only way organizers do that is to keep their standholders happy and hope they come back next year. Be particularly aggressive about PR coverage – both for the exhibition and your particular stand. Before the exhibition opens, go and see the organizer and say that your product is particularly interesting and you would like to be interviewed by the press or radio or television, when they are around the exhibition floor. Surprisingly, few exhibitors do this, and it is well worth doing.

All too often, not enough importance is given to the staffing of exhibition stands. At all times there should be a very senior member of staff on the stand, who is authorized to make decisions. It is not unreasonable to suggest that a director should be on hand all the time, for many potential customers do not want to speak to junior representatives – they want someone at high level to give them the answers. If you are going to exhibit on a regular basis then you probably need a member of staff whose specific job it is to attend exhibitions, but do not underestimate the calibre of person required.

Obviously you must have a good supply of sales literature, and also a supply of forms for logging enquiries. On a busy stand

the last thing you want to do is to be writing out laborious details. You want a form with a series of boxes which can be ticked for speed and efficiency.

At all times, keep your stand looking busy. Empty stands, where the staff are hanging around looking desperate, are discouraging for potential customers. Even if there is no one visiting your stand, look busy and involved.

Follow-up procedure

The enquiries you receive from an exhibition will fall into three main categories – those people who would like a specific quotation and/or samples, those people who would like further information in a general sense on what you have to offer, and those people who have said they are not interested in your product at the moment but are willing to give you their name and address in case they might be in the future. Within thirty-six hours of the end of the exhibition, every one of these enquirers must have a piece of paper from you on their desk – whether it is simply a card thanking potential customers for their interest or a note advising when samples will be delivered, or the promise of future literature. The need to communicate is paramount. While the exhibition is still fresh in your potential customers' minds, make sure they remember who you are. There is little point in spending all the money you have unless every possible opportunity is exploited to the hilt.

Without doubt, the exhibition industry has contributed enormously to the growth and prosperity of businesses in this country. It gives them a comparatively inexpensive platform from which to display their wares and helps draw industries together. If you are looking at some form of promotional spend, rather than advertising you might well be advised to look at exhibiting as your best method of sales promotion.

Finding an overseas market used to be something that had to be tackled by experts. Only if you had considerable experience in selling abroad could you hope to handle the export of your own product. Not so nowadays.

There is a wealth of help and information available to the first-time exporter now. It comes in the main from a sub-division of the Department of Industry, called the British Overseas Trade Board. It is a national sport to have a healthy lack of respect for most government departments, but the BOTB should be the exception. They are very helpful, very commercial and absolutely red-hot.

The BOTB headquarters are at 1 Victoria Street, London SW1, or you can contact your local Department of Industry, which has regional offices everywhere, and can be found in your telephone directory.

If you have the time available, the best thing you can do is to travel to London and visit Victoria Street. There is an enormous library there, to which you have access, but most of the information is fairly long-winded and it would take you an age to research your subject in full. However, their great boon is the publication of a series of booklets called 'Hints For Exporters'. These booklets are entirely free and are available for just about every country in the world. The details they give are so sensible. There is information on the customs regulations of the country, exchange controls, trading hours, a synopsis of the economy, law and general legislation, hotels and their tariffs and even the cost of posting a letter. They also list the address of each country's Chamber of Commerce in Great Britain.

When you have carefully read your Hints For Exporters booklet, your next port of call should be the relevant Chamber of Commerce. Again, it is well worth calling in person. The Chamber of Commerce

concerned will be able to give you details of the agents, both in their country and in Great Britain, who handle your type of merchandise, and from there it is a question of going direct to the agent, and employing your very best selling skills.

The BOTB's help does not rest there. They also run what they call the Export Intelligence Service, which at the time of publication costs £52. For this you will receive 150 pieces of information. You are given a questionnaire, and you simply have to tick a series of boxes. The questions asked are the type of intelligence you require, the part of the world in which you are interested and the type of service and product you have available. As a result of filling in this questionnaire, every time the Department of Industry receives an enquiry for your type of product, from the country of your choice, you will be sent the name and address of the enquirer.

If you are pioneering a market – in other words you wish to travel abroad to explore the possibility of exporting – the BOTB will send you a form to complete. Provided they are satisfied that you are carrying out a genuine market research programme, they will pay half your travel and half your accommodation costs.

The Department of Industry also assists with the sponsoring of overseas exhibitions. If there is an overseas exhibition of your particular trade abroad, you can be sponsored to attend, and such costs as the building of a stand at any rate will be partly subsidized.

Then there is also the Market Entry Guarantee Scheme which will provide 50 per cent towards the cost of setting up sales facilities in overseas markets. This contribution is repayable by a levy on sales: if there are no sales, there is no repayment.

'The export market' sounds positively euphoric. Certainly, with the tremendous government help available, plus undeniable opportunities overseas, it is a very attractive proposition. However, for the small – and particularly the new – business, it is recommended that you first thoroughly explore the home market before attempting to sell abroad. Why?

1 Selling overseas is extremely time-consuming. Even if you have an agent based in this country and you do not need to travel abroad often, there are still endless delays, a welter of legislation and form-filling before you get anywhere near making a sale. Your business has got to support you, and possibly a family. You cannot live on fresh air. It is far better to establish a good, solid home market, which will pay the rent, before attempting to sell abroad.

2 Selling overseas is still difficult if you have had no experience. If you are a natural salesman, with the prospect of a very good business opportunity, do not let your inexperience stand in the way. But if you are uncertain of the market, and have had no export experience, it might be wiser not to attempt it – yet, at any rate.

Having said that, if you are going to try 'flying the flag' – well done and good luck!

What is Success?... What is Failure?

Defining the success or failure of your business is not as simple as it might appear. You might disagree – success is running a profitable company, failure is going bankrupt. Yet is it really that simple? Success, taken to extremes, may mean that the little company you used to run so happily, is now running you. Like Doctor Frankenstein, you may have created your own monster. Where once you enjoyed the physical aspects of working in your particular field of business, now you may find you are little more than an administrator – hiring and firing staff, talking to bank managers, pushing pieces of paper around your desk all day, while other people do the jobs you once so much enjoyed doing yourself.

Success is difficult to achieve, more difficult to sustain and even more difficult to enjoy.

From your first day in business to your last, keep firmly in the forefront of your mind the reasons WHY you chose to go into business in the first place – and never lose sight of them. Maybe you are in business because you want to make a lot of money, or because you love the challenge, the thrill of the chase, or because you cannot bear working for other people, or because unemployment in your area is so high you have no alternative but to create your own job. Success in business is getting up in the morning and finding yourself looking forward to the day's work ahead. Failure is a sense of dread or, almost worse, indifference.

Horrific figures are bandied about as to the percentage of business failure in the first five years of operation – over 90 per cent according to some. Certainly it is true that more businesses fail than succeed, but usually this is because there is something fundamentally wrong with the whole project. There is no market, the business is under-capitalized, the founder is not committed . . . There are myriad reasons, but whatever the cause, it has usually been present from the first day of trading.

If, however, you have been successful in establishing your business to the point where it is consistently profitable, the biggest danger you have to face is complacency. Once your business is established, an inflexibility of attitude tends to develop, and this you must watch very carefully. **We have always done things this way, so why change?** is the likely sort of attitude you may find yourself adopting. It is a very understandable reaction. The early days of struggle were so exhausting and unpredictable that now you have found a safe plateau from which to operate, what you want more than anything else in the world is a period of stability. Yet the safe plateau is not all that safe. At no time in your business life can you ever say – **I have made it.** You must always remain alert, aware that out of a clear blue sky a new competitor, embargoes on raw material or a change of government policy could come and sweep your business away from you.

If you are losing money the biggest danger you have to face is putting your head in the sand. For most dedicated, hard-working founders, their business looms quite as large in their emotional life as any child, and this is never more evident than when their business is sick. If your business is in a declining market or is hopelessly in debt, trying to save your baby at all costs may be the worst thing you can do. Getting out as fast as you can and leaving the sinking ship is the only sensible course of action.

Never be afraid to make radical decisions in your pursuit of success. If you know you can save your company by halving your workforce or changing the entire direction of your production, do not prevaricate – do it. All too often businesses could have survived and been successful if the principal had just acted quickly enough. It is very often possible to turn failure into success, and provided that you have good controls and proper management accounts, you will be able to recognize what is happening and

Case history – George and Margaret Jennings of Devon

Ten years ago, George and Margaret bought a dilapidated inn, just outside a small fishing port in South Devon. At the time they were in their late twenties, with two small pre-school children. They have worked wonders since then. They have built the inn into a thriving holiday hotel, with an excellent restaurant and busy local bar trade that takes them through the winter months. They now have three children and their eldest, Matthew, is sixteen. Are they thrilled with their success? No – they are heartily fed up. They hate the business, they are tired of being nice to ill-mannered tourists, having to employ somebody else to put the little children to bed and supervise Matthew's homework, of working every weekend and every evening when all their friends are out having a good time. The children do not complain because they have never known a different life, but George and Margaret know that they are not getting a fair deal. So what have they decided to do? They are selling up, and with the proceeds they will buy a smallholding. Everyone says they are mad – their bank manager, their customers, their parents. It is true that at last they have reached the point where the hotel is running as they want it – all the bedrooms have bathrooms, everywhere is gleaming with new paint, the extended car park is finished . . . now is the moment they can really start cashing in on all their years of work. *Just stick it out for another five years,* everyone says, *and then you will make a mint.* But in five years' time Matthew will be leaving home, the younger two will be teenagers and their family life will be slipping away from them. George and Margaret have just completed their sale. After paying back the mortgage they have enough capital to buy and stock the smallholding they had in mind. They have made the right decision. Always ask yourself – what price success?

have sufficient notice to be able to do something about it. To be faced with failure is a terrible thing. The hours, perhaps years of struggle, all coming to nothing. Is it any wonder that we shy away from it, trying to convince ourselves that next month/next year will be better? You do not have time for such an attitude, and you dare not take the risk. You are in an ever-changing world, you are riding a surfboard, and unless you recognize that, you have no hope of staying in business in the long term. While a business is still a going concern, even if it is not viable enough to sell, there is still property, equipment and stock – all of which will fetch a much better price if you are still trading. Disposal of assets in a careful structured way could well clear your debts. When you are faced with bankruptcy, with all around you knowing it, panic selling will leave you hopelessly in debt. Like success, failure is a relative term. You only fail in business if you lose everything. Recognizing that the business has gone sadly wrong, or that your market is dead or dying, is not failure. Success is staying ahead of the game, failure is either not being aware of what is happening to your business, or choosing to ignore it.

Cash-flow Problems and Overtrading

In order to survive, a business must have adequate cash resources to draw on if things are not going well. One of the primary reasons that businesses fail is because of poor cash management. Cash-flow problems can arise for a number of reasons – because the business has insufficient work and therefore is making a loss, or because the overheads are too high and profits are non-existent. However, probably the most common cause of financial distress is overtrading.

The term overtrading means that the volume of trade which the business is doing is too high for the financial resources of the business. At some time in the life of almost every successful business, there has been a period of overtrading. Controlled overtrading – provided it is not a permanent feature – could perhaps better be described as taking advantage of business opportunities. From time to time it is

obviously sensible to stretch the company's resources, in order to service a new customer or section of the market. Provided that this period of excessive trading can be coped with, there are grounds for saying that controlled overtrading actually makes it easier to put up a case for additional capital. However, what begins as looking like positive growth for the company can end in a state of crisis. This fact in turn highlights the absolute necessity for up-to-the-minute cash-flow forecasts. If additional facilities are required to help your business through a period of overtrading, then provided your bankers are informed in good time about what is going to happen, they are almost certain to back you. However, if you put yourself in a position where you are chronically overdrawn rather than agree to extended facilities, your bank is more than likely to start bouncing cheques.

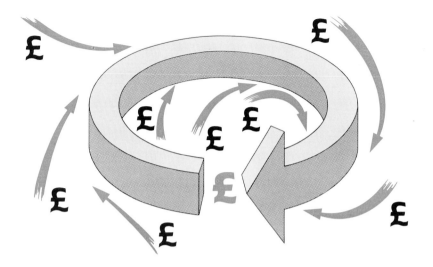

The tragedy is that the businesses which go to the wall because of cash-flow problems are more often than not potentially very profitable. However, once overtrading takes you into a cash-flow spiral, one problem leads to another. It begins with your taking on a big order, bigger than you have ever handled before. You do not make adequate provision for the drain on cash resources. You order large quantities of raw materials, some of which you are requested to pay for immediately because they exceed your credit limit, you take on extra staff and begin paying overtime rates. At the beginning of the new contract, it is money out all the time. Provided your new customer pays promptly, then the crisis point will pass. However, if there is a delay in payment, or you have not done your homework properly and your customer is unable to pay, then you are on the slippery slope to disaster. This is a vital point – overtrading, by definition, suggests new trade and new trade carries with it a high element of risk. This element needs to be fully understood and taken into account. The importance of cash-flow control is absolute. The preparation and careful planning of cash budgets is the single most important business function in these circumstances. It is as simple as this – **an order is not an order until it is paid for.** A good customer is not a good customer unless your invoices are paid on time. It is natural to be hungry for new business, but not to the extent of putting your whole future at risk.

Creative accounting

As a business struggling for your place in the market, it is terribly difficult to turn down an order – any order. The position becomes even worse when that big order fulfils all your dreams. Here is the chance to expand the business in just the way you had always planned. In these circumstances it is terribly tempting to indulge in a little creative accounting – to prepare cash forecasts which show the best possible results, rather than the most realistic. Fooling other people is one thing, fooling yourself is something you must never do. A strain on cash resources which is well anticipated can be coped with and overcome. Unplanned, it is the surest path to bankruptcy.

The reasons for business failure are diverse and complex. Sometimes, failure is unavoidable, but more often it is the combination of bad luck and bad judgement. The five main causes of business failure are:

◆ Underestimating the cash required to run your business.

◆ A lack of sales drive – failure to move with the times and establish and anticipate new markets.

◆ Poor administration, resulting in slow collection of money, high stock levels and generally sloppy running.

◆ Poor costings – the popular misconception that high turnover means high profit. Failing to recognize that gross profit margins have to be maintained to cover overheads.

◆ Bad management. Businesses need a mix of skills – sales, technical, managerial and accounting. Spectacular failures often occur where the principal of the business is dominant in one of these skills, leaving the others unattended – the imbalance is usually disastrous.

Most businesses fail through a combination of the above, in varying degrees, and the problem is that once a business starts heading in a downward spiral, it is amazing how quickly it can collapse.

Bankruptcy

Any individual can sue another individual in bankruptcy. If you owe someone money, cannot pay, and that debt has been incurred in your own name, then you may be sued, made bankrupt and your assets sold in order to raise sufficient money to settle your debts. This raises two points of particular concern with regard to running your own business:

◆ If you are operating as a sole trader or a partnership, and therefore are not protected by a limited company, all your personal assets can be sold to meet your business debts – which

means your house, your furniture, your car – *everything*.

◆ Even if you have the protection of a limited company, be sure that all agreements and contracts into which you enter are made on behalf of your company and not in your personal name. You are only protected by a limited company provided you make it clear that you are operating as one. If you enter into some form of contract in your personal name then you are liable to be sued personally.

The word **bankruptcy** understandably carries considerable stigma. If your debts are enormous and you are declared bankrupt, it may be that ultimately you do not have to pay them in full, as you can apply to the court after a few years to be discharged. Whichever way you look at it, though, you lose a great deal of personal liberty by being declared bankrupt and you must try and avoid it. It should also be noted that going bankrupt is an expensive business. Not only do you have to pay your debt but also your own costs in defending it, and all the legal fees of your creditors. **Do not involve yourself in heavy commitments unless you can be absolutely sure that you can honour them.**

Receivership

If a company gets into trouble, lenders with security normally have powers to appoint a Receiver, whose basic job it is to sell the charged assets in order to recover the loan. In most cases, a Receiver is appointed by a bank, which has a first charge on the assets of the company, against which the loan and overdraft facilities have been advanced. A good Receiver will look at ways of liquidating some of the assets without completely crippling the company and killing it off. Alternatively, the Receiver may find a way of persuading the bank to hold off while helping the management to trade out of their difficulties. You should recognize that you are unlikely to have a Receiver appointed over your head unless you are in serious trouble, but if you can see problems on the horizon, with which you know you cannot cope, it might be better to opt for a voluntary Receivership. If, together with your bank, you decide to appoint a Receiver, you then are in a position to have some choice as to who is selected. Ideally you want a Receiver from a large and reputable firm of accountants to handle your affairs. There are some real sharks about, posing as Receivers, who will sell off the assets of your company for next to nothing, to contacts they have, and leave you destitute. A good Receiver is basically on your side. Contrary to popular belief, the Receiver does not have a bolt through his neck, or a habit of howling at the full moon. Co-operate with the Receiver, if such a situation arises, and together you might well be able to save your business.

Liquidation

If a Receiver is unable to sell some of the company's assets or part of its business, or indeed all of its business, in order to realize sufficient cash to pay the debts, then the only answer is liquidation. Liquidation means that all the company's assets are disposed of and the money received is distributed on a pro rata basis amongst the general creditors, once the secured and preferential creditors have first been satisfied. In effect this means that your bankers, and any financial institutions from which you have borrowed, will be settled first, since they are likely to have a charge on your business. Thereafter, VAT and DHSS debts will need to be settled, since they have preferential rights in the case of liquidation. If there is any money left over, then this is distributed amongst the unsecured creditors, which will most likely be your suppliers. Where there is insufficient money to meet the debts in full, your creditors will be paid so much in the pound.

Bankruptcy and liquidation represent the ultimate management failure on the face of it, yet it is possible to fail successfully. If you recognize there is no hope of saving your business, then face up to that fact and start taking action. The successful way to fail is to fade out slowly, not trade desperately up to the last minute and then go with a bang. Experienced Receivers and liquidators will tell you that more management mistakes are made in the last three months of a business than at any other time. In a desperate attempt to keep your business alive, you will throw good money after bad, take on business you can never fulfil – indeed do anything to avoid the ultimate acceptance of failure. Of course you must try and avoid going out of business, **but not at all costs**. Recognize when the odds against you are just too high.

If you are faced with the unhappy fact of losing your business, do not over-react. Most Receivers would confirm that it takes people at least two years to recover from business failure and be able to cope rationally and sensibly with day-to-day life. It is a very harrowing experience, and obviously, faced with failure, you need to recognize that you cannot be at your best. Do not be tempted to go dashing off at tangents, nor indeed make any major decisions about your future immediately after your business collapse. Do not panic, take time to think out your next move, and even if you have to live on bread and dripping for a while, do so rather than find yourself making the same mistakes again. And remember this – however dreadful the experience, there is a lot of truth in the old adage – **it is better to have tried and failed than to have never tried at all.**

Expansion

There are so many ways in which you can expand a business. What you have to ask yourself first is whether expansion is the right thing to do. Big is not necessarily beautiful, nor even profitable. Doubling your production level can mean bigger premises, higher overheads, and as a result a very marginal increase in profit. And profit potential is just one aspect to consider. Do you personally have the resources, the skill, the stamina and indeed the inclination to run a big organization? The mere fact that you are running your own business at all suggests that you like seeing your own individual effort produce something tangible. Within the confines of a large business, even if you are managing director, or perhaps because you are, it is sometimes very difficult to gauge your own worth.

Let us look at the three main methods of expanding your business.

Expansion of your existing business

Clearly, the simplest way to expand is to do more of what you are already doing, but here it is necessary to consider a few golden rules of marketing. Your market – whatever your business activity – is limited, and however successful your product or service, you can only have a share of that market. It is also true that the first business you obtain is always the easiest. The more greedy you become, the greater the share of the market you require, the harder you have to work to get it, and therefore the more money you have to invest in its promotion. Settling for a modest share of the market is not only sensible, it is practical. It allows for changes and fluctuations – if you lose your major customer, there are others left to go for.

Aside from straightforward expansion, there is the possibility of diversification, but here you have to be very careful. If you are in business in a particular line, then that is clearly what you know about and where your expertise lies. Dashing off in another direction may well be courting disaster, unless you can apply a similar degree of expertise to your new venture. Diversification as an adjunct to your existing business is most likely to succeed. In other words, perhaps you can expand your own manufacturing capacity, and thus do without your sub-contractors or perhaps even your major supplier. If you are a wholesaler, maybe you can develop your own retail outlets. This type of diversification tends to be the most successful, since not only are you operating in a field you know well, but also enhancing the activities of your original business.

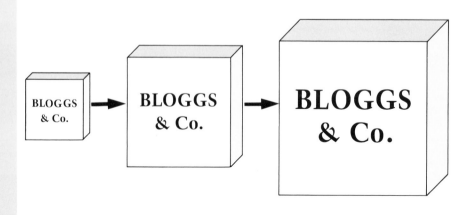

Buying another company

Buying an existing company can be a very good way to expand, particularly if you are interested in expanding in an area where you, yourself do not have expertise. It may be a chance to move into a market sector that at the moment is denied to you, or give you an opportunity to expand your range of products or services. Before looking in any depth at the business in which you are interested, you have to consider first why it is up for sale in the first place. It may be the result of some personal decision on the part of the principals, but it could be because the business has hit financial difficulties, or has anticipated difficulties in its future market. Buying a business has to be approached very carefully indeed and you cannot do it without professional help – an accountant to go through the books and a solicitor to check out the legalities. In the section entitled 'Setting Up Your Business', you will find a detailed account of how to buy an existing business. Suffice to say here that it is an excellent way of expanding, providing you are very thorough.

Merging

Merging your business with another's obviously represents another method of expansion but, particularly for the smaller company, it is fraught with potential problems. This is largely caused by personalities. Merging means just that – two businesses becoming one, two businesses with two bosses and two sets of management. It is bound to lead to internal squabbles. All the same comments concerning the purchase of an existing business apply to merging – the need for caution, the need for professional advice. Above all with a merger there is the need for very clear definition when it comes to who is in charge of what. Merging with another company can best be served if the two businesses are parallel ones, rather than engaged in precisely the same operation.

Business empires are built on the ability to expand, and a degree of expansion is a necessary part of every business's development. Expansion can play so many roles, changing and defining your business for better or for worse. Make sure you know which will be the outcome for you.

Case history

Clive Margot runs a courier business from an office close to Birmingham Airport. Originally he was in freight forwarding, but having been made redundant, he decided to set up on his own. His courier business was aimed at getting packages and letters to places around the world. His service was a very personal one, recognizing the need for trust in a business of his sort, where a great deal can depend on a package being delivered on time. After five years, Clive was doing so well that he decided to expand. He opened an office close to Heathrow, one at Gatwick and another in Manchester. Suddenly the Big Boys saw him as a possible threat and, when it came to tendering for large contracts, they sharpened their pencils. Soon Clive found that he was doing work which was barely profitable. With a dramatic increase in staff, Clive found that the service he was offering was no longer personal. After a particularly unfortunate blunder at Gatwick, he lost his major customer. As he says now, expansion caused other spin-off problems too. His health became poor, he was on sleeping pills and his marriage went through a rocky period.

Clive was sensible. He realized his mistake in time, cut his losses and reduced his business to its original size. He survived and today is back in profit and a far happier man. Clive's experience is a salutary lesson to us all.

Selling Out

Why might you want to sell your business – why cash in the chips? Some people start and build a business with the specific idea of ultimately selling it. Others fondly believe that one day the toddler playing at their feet will take over their business, only to find that their son or daughter has other ideas and wants to be a brain surgeon or a lorry driver. This leaves a business which has to be sold on retirement. Alternatively, bearing in mind that running your own business is unquestionably very hard work, you may be worn out or disillusioned and feel that enough is enough. Whatever your reason for selling your business, here are a few golden rules which are worthy of consideration.

BUSINESS
FOR
SALE

1 To maximize the amount of money you will obtain by the sale of your business, you do need a healthy profit record. Particularly if you are the major shareholder, in recent years you may have been drawing a very hefty salary which, in turn, may have thrown up only a small profit within the company. At the time you will have taken the view that the tax people are going to get you one way or the other, so you might as well pay income tax rather than corporation tax. The fact is, though, that when presenting accounts for approval, although you can explain your extremely high salary, it would be better if you took a dividend payment instead, which would be shown on the accounts as a distribution of profits. If you are not making any profits at all – or even losses – you need to recognize that a loss-making venture, even if it has considerable assets, is of very questionable value. You must build your business into a profit-making machine before selling it.

2 If it is your business and it has been run your way, you probably consider yourself to be fairly indispensable. That position has to be put right before you offer your business for sale. You must build up a strong management team, who can run the business with or without you. Only if you have an entity in its own right have you anything to sell at all.

3 Whatever form your sale takes, it is likely that there will be a requirement for a hand-over period, during which you stay on in some capacity to give advice. Keep this to the minimum. You are going to absolutely loathe the way *your* business is run *their* way. Recognize this fact – however much money you have been paid, however pleased you are with the deal, after a couple of weeks you are going to hate the guts of the people who have bought your business, and you do not want to

leave it with a bitter taste in your mouth.

4   One of the most often used and potentially hazardous methods of buying a business is to make a down payment on hand-over and a further payment, or payments, based on future profits. From the purchasers' point of view, this is a very understandable and desirable deal. They have seen your profit record, but do not know how the company will run without you – and that, after all, is what they are buying. Therefore they make it a condition of sale that part of the proceeds are withheld until they have taken over the company and see it up and running. Avoid this like the plague. Think about the deal for a moment. You are being asked to accept part of your money based on future profits, *over which you have no control*. Supposing the people who have bought your company are fools, sack the wrong people and lose your best customers. And your future payments are going to be based on their idiotic decisions? You have to settle for one thing or the other. Either a cash settlement in full with the new owner having complete control, or, if you are settling for staged payments, then you must maintain a degree of control so that you can safeguard you own position.

5   When referring to the selling of a business here, we have quite deliberately used the word 'company'. If you are selling your business, it is infinitely preferable that you sell a limited company. It is neater and cleaner and everything is so much more clearly defined – the assets, the liabilities, the profits, the losses. Also, from the purchaser's point of view, it means buying an entity in its own right. If you are operating as a sole trader or a partnership, the tendency – even if this is not true – is to consider that you, and/or your partner, are the business

and without you there is no business. If you are shaping up your business for sale you would be well advised to form a limited company (but please consider the tax implications before taking this advice!).

6   One of the reasons you might be selling is because you are in trouble. If this is the case, then you need to be thinking very clearly. If you recognize your business is declining, and you know you cannot recover, then make the decision to sell and sell fast – and do not be too greedy. While you are still in control, if you can realize the value of your assets and get out free of debt, then for heaven's sake do it. Once a Receiver or Liquidator is appointed, the value of your business will plummet overnight. Many of the assets will be completely worthless, and the business, as such, will no longer have any intrinsic value. Then there are the fees of the Receiver and Liquidator to consider, and by the time the sums have been done, you may well find yourself left with a DHSS debt or a commitment against your personal guarantee – not to mention the stigma and unpleasantness of being a part of a business failure.

One fact that you will need to come to terms with is that your prospective purchasers will feel that they can do far better with your business than you have done – if they did not think that, they would not be interested in it. Play on this. Do not resent criticisms of how you are running your business currently and, where possible, agree with schemes for the future. Your business is someone else's dream now, not yours. Curb your resentment, irritation and genuine regret in handing over what you have worked so hard to build. Once you have looked after the future livelihood of your loyal staff and management, the only really relevant factor at the end of the day is the size of the cheque you receive.

Conclusion

There was a time when few people ever considered running their own business – that was left to the wealthy, the innovators, the unhealthily ambitious and the weird. Today, the concept of starting your own business is within everyone's grasp. If you are averagely intelligent, healthy and prepared to work hard, then government and financial institutions alike are falling over backwards to help you.

There was also a time when starting your own business was considered a very risky thing to do, irresponsible even – particularly if you had a spouse and children to consider. Today it is accepted that if you have an established, well-run business in a not too volatile market, you are probably far safer than the employed person in almost any walk of life.

The work ethic means different things to different people. Job satisfaction is not considered important by some. For most people, though, the recognition that one spends more time working than doing anything else brings with it the feeling that to enjoy what you are doing has to be important. The British are a peculiar island race, with enormous regional and cultural differences, but, by and large, we are more fulfilled and better motivated by direct involvement in whatever we do. In a large organization it is so easy to lose your sense of identity and purpose. It is difficult to feel useful and have any awareness of making a contribution. Your own business may be tough, may involve you in harder work than you would have believed possible, but if you are truly committed, you will find hidden resources within yourself you did not even know you had. You *can* make it work because it is YOUR BUSINESS.

Alan and Deborah Fowler